Light

IN THE SHADOW OF

Death

840 Peters Road
New Holland, PA 17557
© Aaron Beiler

First Printing 2008
Second Printing 2009

Carlisle Printing
OF WALNUT CREEK Ltd.

2673 Township Road 421
Sugarcreek, Ohio 44681

Contents

Section Three

Acknowledgments

MY WILL IS to let God be the judge of everything and that praise and the putting down of others does not send us to our end or seal our destiny. At the end of our life we will be judged by our Creator who knows everything we think and do. Also to keep God foremost in our mind and to meet him and be in the glory of his presence. Our God who reaches out with forgiveness if we are willing to repent.

I would like to express my heartfelt thanks to all of the friends, family and others who showed compassion with letters and verses, etc. Also to those of you who understood, knowing the pain and heartache of parting with a loved one.

My way of relieving some of the pain was to write my feelings on paper. Lots of writings, etc. that have been a great lift to me are in this book. My foremost and greatest wish would be that if you can find something in this book to make your load a little bit lighter, you would give our God and Heavenly Father *all* the honor.

—*Aaron F. Beiler*

Praise be to the God and Father of our Lord Jesus Christ, the Father of compassion and the God of all comfort, who comforts us in all our troubles, so that we can comfort those in any trouble with the comfort we ourselves have received from God.

2 Corinthians 1:3-4 (NIV)

#

"GRIEF" IS A word I heard so much, a word that did not really make sense to describe what was happening inside of me. How could a little word like that describe the almost unbearable pain that was pulling me down? The pressure inside of me was giving my heart real pain, not make-believe pain, but real pain, and I could think of nothing else.

I would look at people and see them smile and going on in life and wonder how they could. Couldn't they even "see" this sharp pain and think like I did, that life is over! Surely they couldn't see that endless nothing that was ahead of me as far as I could see. The real pain even made me wonder why I should even go on with the rest of my life—pain that was taking me into a deep dark cave. Yes, sometimes I would try to fight it, but most times I would just let myself be carried further and further down. I even wondered if I was still me, or even if I was still alive.

One day while I was out working in the barn, I began to sing. To my surprise I sang a little song. All of a sudden I thought, *No it can't be. How can I sing without Mervin?* So my guilt drove me back into that deep dark cave again.

As time went on, one day I realized an hour or so after I got up that I had not thought about that big empty hole that morning. That heartache, that empty feeling, was not the first thought on my mind when I woke up. I realized there were more times during the days that I had gone through an hour or so without the pain.

So as time went on, one day I laughed out loud at a funny thing that happened. I really was coming back to life. The pain would go away more and more as time went on and for longer periods of time. When it would come again it was very sharp, but not as intense as before, and not so overwhelming.

I kept living and growing and loving. My life ever so slowly came back to me again. My hopes and feelings came back. I started having more get-up-and-go. I actually felt like a person again.

I have now had some times of real happiness that I was not "let down" with my grief for Mervin. I've had sad and painful times that were not made worse by my grief. Most likely these times were made a little bit easier to bear because of those scars that left a rough spot on my heart.

If I had a wish for you all, it would be that no one would ever have to deal with that kind of loss. But no, I can't give you that gift. One thing I can tell you is that the deep, deep pain you feel at the beginning will be made lighter. The pain you feel now will become bearable, and you will begin to live again if you take one minute, one hour, or one day at a time. Do not try to think too far ahead and you will find the pain becomes bearable.

I'll never forget Mervin. I will never forget how much we loved him and how much he meant to me. I'm really not sorry he was born. I treasure those 23 years I had with him while he was growing up and learning. I am very sorry though that my time with Mervin was way too short, even though I am thankful for the times we had. I treasure those times we spent in the great outdoors, hunting, fishing, and playing catch.

Mervin was our firstborn and he will always live in my heart and I miss him more than words can tell. I keep those memories sealed away safe inside my heart. No one can take them from me, and as time goes on I really *do* want to go on and live again. I'm finding out that the deep dark cave was actually a tunnel; there is a light at the end.

—Dad

In Memory: Mervin Jay Beiler – Born September 30, 1981
Died February 28, 2005 - Age 23 years/5 months

Let Your Grief Have Expression

When the shock of loss is upon you, do not conceal or deny your normal human feelings. Express all the grief you feel. Talk about your loved one. Relive old experiences. Shed tears unashamedly. Remember that at the grave of Lazarus "Jesus wept". To be sure, we are all different in our emotional reactions, and no two persons will respond in the same way to loss. But whatever expression is natural to you should not be suppressed. To suppress grief will do you more harm than to express it. A period of mourning is both natural and necessary.

Face Your Loss and Accept It

You may try to lessen the pain of your loss by pretending everything remains as it was before, perhaps by keeping the loved one's room exactly as it was when he last occupied it, or by saying to yourself, "She is only away, and soon she will return." How much wiser David was at the death of a beloved child. "Now he is dead," he said, "wherefore should I fast? Can I bring him back again? I shall go to him, but he will not return to me" (II Samuel 12:23). Admit the reality of your loss. Don't try to minimize it. Accept it for the tragedy it is, and realize that life will not be the same. Life will still be good, but it will be different.

Remember Where Your Loved One Has Gone

Jesus said, "Today you will be with me in Paradise" (Luke 23:43). Paradise, a Persian word, "means a walled park such as surrounded a royal palace." It suggests beauty and gladness, privilege and blessing. But the greatest thing we can say about the life into which our loved ones enter is that it brings them into immediate fellowship with Christ, their

Savior and Lord. So wonderful is the life beyond that if we knew more about it, we wouldn't want to call back any loved one who has entered it. Great as life is now for the Christian, Paul was sure that "to depart and be with Christ is far better" (Phil. 1:23).

Be Grateful for Fine Memories

Think of your privilege under God of having your loved one as long a time as you did. Nothing can take away the memories—of the grand person he was, of the excellent things she did. These memories are part of you, and you will always be a better person because of them. "I miss Dick," said a young widow. "Of course I miss him. But I haven't room in my heart for anything but thankfulness and gratitude to God. I had a year of Dick's love—a whole year of perfect happiness. If I live to be eighty, I shall not have time to thank God enough. And when I do stop living, Dick and I will begin living together again."

How Can I Go On?

In the first shock of loss, especially sudden loss, we wonder how we are going to live without our loved one. Our lives are bound together in a thousand intimate and endearing ties. To take up life again without the old companionship will not be easy, but God has so constituted the human spirit that one can make adjustment to the most difficult situations. This God-given capacity is within you. It functions most effectively when our trust is in God for daily guidance and strength. Say over and over again, when the going is hard, "I can do all things through Christ which strengthens me" (Phil. 4:13).

How Others Have Gone On

"I didn't know how I could live," said an elderly woman, looking back over eight years to the loss of a devoted husband, to whom she had been happily married for more than forty years. "But I did live," she added quickly, "through the help of faith." Strength to go on is promised, and so many bereaved men and women have found God real and helpful, enabling them to live on courageously, that you, too, can find strength through your faith to do what now seems almost impossible. "I am sure," said Paul, "that neither death nor life… will be able to separate us from the love of God in Christ Jesus, our Lord" (Romans 8:38, 39).

Why Has This Loss Befallen Me?

It has come not because you have done anything to deserve it, but because we all are involved, under the Providence of God, in that total life-process which begins with birth and ends with bodily death. "It is appointed for men to die once," the New Testament reminds us (Heb. 9:27). The exact cause and time of any individual's death are determined by factors too complex for any human mind to comprehend. But if we could see anything as God sees it, we would be content to say, "It is the will of God." Remember what Job said, "The Lord gave, and the Lord hath taken away; blessed be the name of the Lord" (Job 1:21).

Do You Accuse Yourself?

Often, when a loved one has gone, we wish we had done or said something other than what we did do and say. "If only I hadn't made that sharp answer! If only I had been more patient!" The chances are that your quick word or slight impatience was just part of the normal give and take of life. But if you continue to be troubled by feelings of this kind, remember the forgiving love of God. He understands the strain of everyday family relationships, and He is ready to forgive you for any way in which you fell short in your life with your loved one. "If we confess our sins, he is faithful and just, and will forgive us our sins" (1 John 1:9).

Has Your Loss Come Suddenly?

Often we say, "It has come so suddenly. If I had only known, had some warning. Here was my loved one a little while ago, and now I am alone." Sudden loss is exceedingly difficult to accept. But how many people pray that they may be spared long illness. "That is the way I want to go," they say on hearing of someone's sudden death. This was the privilege of your loved one—to have, in place of long, painful illness, a quick transit from earth to heaven. You were mercifully spared the pain of seeing your loved one suffer. How hard that would have been for you.

Has the Loss Come After Long Illness?

"It is a blessed release," we sometimes say. "I wouldn't wish to have the loved one back to continue in the old way." Yes, despite our own sense of relief, our loved one is now released from the handicap of an ailing body and clothed with a new spiritual body. Of this we are assured, "For this perishable nature must put on the imperishable, and this mortal nature must put on immortality" (1 Cor. 15:53), and "God himself will be with them; he will wipe away every tear from their eyes; and death shall be no more, neither shall there be mourning nor crying nor pain anymore" (Rev. 21:4).

Our Loved One Was So Young
"They pass from work to greater work
Who rest before their noon,
Ah, God is very good to them,
They do not die too soon."

An unknown poet here expresses a comforting thought for those who mourn the loss of one who seemed to die too young—because of disease, accident, or war. It suggests that in the eyes of God, length of life is not the important thing. It is enough that a man do his duty as he sees it for whatever time is allowed to him. Beyond time is eternity, and whether one's transition comes at eighteen or eighty, the difference, as God evaluates life and counts time, is slight.

Take Up Normal Tasks Again

"I am going fishing," said Peter after the crucifixion of Jesus and His first appearances. In his distraught mind, unable to adjust himself quickly to all that had happened, this was the wisest thing Peter could have done.

It led him into a new and more wonderful experience of the risen Christ. There will be comfort for you, too, as you return to familiar tasks, resume a regular routine, and keep busy doing something diverting and useful. It may take determination at first, but with the effort will come revived interest and a feeling of stability.

Carrying On a Loved One's Work

There will be interests, activities, and causes that were dear to your loved one. He would be happy to have you carry them forward. She would like you to share her beliefs and standards. By working for ends that were dear to your loved one, you keep his memory green, you honor her in the finest way.

"If I should die and leave you here awhile,
Be not like others, soon undone, who keep
Long vigil by the silent dust, and weep.
For my sake, turn again to life, and smile,
Nerving thy heart and trembling hand to do
Something to comfort weaker hearts than thine.
Complete these dear unfinished tasks of mine,
And I perchance, may therein comfort you."

Thinking of How You Can Help Others

When John Bright lost his beautiful young wife, his friend Richard Cobden came to comfort him in his grief. He told how thousands of British homes were facing hunger because of the Corn Laws. "Come," said Cobden, "let us fight for the women and children of England." Bright accepted the challenge, and in helping to lift the burdens of other people he found solace for himself. Isn't there something you can do—children to care for, shut-in persons to visit, Red Cross work, or some other church or community service? In such effort you will find relief.

Take Time to Make New Plans

If you have lost husband or wife, there may be a question as to whether you should continue in your own home or go to live with a relative. You will receive much earnest counsel from loved ones and friends. You do need companionship—understanding and congenial. But take time to form new arrangements. Canvass all the alternatives. It is generally advisable to remain in your own home—even if you must seek smaller quarters. Visit your children and your friends, but maintain your own residence as long as you can. Many who have too quickly broken up their own homes have come to regret it.

Face Forward… with God

Paul urged early Christians not to "grieve as others do who have no hope" (I Thess. 4:13). It is natural and necessary to grieve for a season, and a great love can never be forgotten. But for our soul's good we must face forward with hope and expectation, For "If God is for us, who is against us? He who did not spare his own Son but gave him up for us all, will he not also give us all things with him?" (Rom. 8:31, 32). Yes, ahead of you, if you walk with God, there will be deepened spiritual comfort and new experiences of which you do not now dream, and beyond time there is eternity with reunion with your loved ones and closer fellowship with God.

Here are some things that I feel are for parents after "losing" a child:

1. I wish you would not be afraid to speak of our child's name now or anytime in the future. Mervin's name makes my heart skip a beat. Mervin lived and was important to me and I need to hear his name. Please leave his remembrances around for me. I don't ever want you to forget Mervin or stop talking about him.

2. If I cry or get emotional it is not because you have hurt me, it is because I have no Mervin. Crying and getting emotional are healing for me. It helps me to release some of that pressure that builds up inside of me.

3. Please do not compare our loss to other losses. Yes, somewhat! But no two deaths are exactly alike. Mervin was "our" child.

4. Being a bereaved parent is not a contagious sickness, so please don't shy away from me. Keep asking me to do things even if I say no sometimes. Your time and attention means a lot to me even if it does not look that way sometimes.

5. Please understand that my "crazy" emotions are very normal grief things. Feelings of depression, anger, frustration, hopelessness, and yes, lots of questions about my belief and my values.

6. Do not put a timetable on my grief. It will not be over in six months. No, it will be something I carry with me through my whole life in different ways and different times. Yes, even though I feel strong and will go on in my life, I will always be a recovering parent.

7. Don't feel like you need to take my grief or pain away or talk me out of being hurt. The best thing you can do for me is tell me you're sorry, or better yet, tell a good story about Mervin. You don't have to think up ways to make me feel better. Just being there means a lot to me.

8. I will go through a wide range of emotions, including numbness, hurt, denial, anger, loneliness, and regret. For a while I may be thinking "what if" or "if only" because my loss is so deep and my mind will do anything to try to change or control it. There are times when I think that it is all a big nightmare and I will wake up. Please stand by me even in those tough times.

9. Birthdays, holidays, anniversaries of his death, vacations, and each "first" we do without Mervin can be terribly painful. It does help if you can remember Mervin on those days and tell us you are thinking about him and us. Even if we are quite withdrawn or sad, don't try to talk us into being cheerful.

10. Please understand that losing a child changes people. In some ways I am not the same person. If you keep wanting me to "get back to my old self" you may be frustrated for a long time. Please respect and understand any changes you notice and please appreciate me for who I am. Remember, there is a hole in my heart and lots missing without Mervin, our son. But with God's help and your prayers we hope to go on and all meet on that beautiful city prepared for us on high.

God bless you,
—Aaron Beiler

Be Careful What You Say

In speaking of another's faults, pray don't forget your own.
Remember those with houses of glass should seldom throw a stone.
If we have nothing else to do than talk of those who sin,
'Tis better to begin at home, and from that point begin.
We have no right to judge a man until he's fairly tried,
Should we not like his company, we know the world is wide.
Some may have faults, and who has not, the old as well as young?
Perhaps we may, for ought we know, have fifty to their one.
I'll tell you of a better plan, and find it works full well,
To try my own defects to cure, ere others faults I tell.
And though I sometimes hope to be no worse than some I know.
My own shortcomings bid me let the faults of others go.
Then let us all, when we begin to slander friends or foe,
Think of the harm one word may do to those we little know.
Remember, curses sometimes, like our chickens, roost at home,
Don't speak of others' faults until we have none of our own.

When Tomorrow Starts Without Me

When tomorrow starts without me, and I'm not here to see.
If the sun should rise and find your eyes all filled with tears for me.
I wish so much you wouldn't cry, the way you did today
While thinking of the many things we didn't get to say.
I know how much you love me, as much as I love you.
And each time you'll think of me, I know you'll miss me, too.
But when tomorrow starts without me, please try to understand
That an angel came and called my name and took me by the hand,
And said my place was ready in Heaven far above
And that I have to leave behind all those I dearly love.
But as I turned to walk away, a tear fell from my eye,
For all my life, I'd always thought, I'd never want to die.
I had so much to live for—and so much yet to do—
It seemed almost impossible that I was leaving you.
I thought of all the yesterdays, the good ones and the bad.
I thought of all the love we shared, and all the fun we had.
If I could relive yesterday, I thought just for awhile,
I'd say good-bye and kiss you, and maybe see you smile.
But then I fully realized that this could never be,
For emptiness and memories would take the place of me.
And when I thought of worldly things that I'd miss, come tomorrow,
I thought of you, and when I did, my heart was filled with sorrow.
But when I walked through Heaven's gate, I felt so much at home
When God looked down and smiled at me from His great golden throne.
He said, "This is eternity, and all I've promised you.
Today your life on earth is past, but it starts anew.
I promise no tomorrows, but today will always last.
And since each day's the same day, there's no longing for the past.
But though I promise no tomorrows on earth to anyone,

So many live each day so sure of seeing one more sun.
But they will never stop to pray and ask forgiveness for their sin.
For many I have turned away, so sad, at Heaven's gate,
For when I called they weren't ready, and it was much too late.
But you have been so faithful, so trusting, and so true,
Tho' there were times you did some things you knew you shouldn't do.
But you have been forgiven and now at last you're free.
So won't you come and take my hand, and share my life with me?
So when tomorrow starts without me, don't think we're far apart,
For every time you think of me, I'm right here in your heart.

Family sorrow... New every morning as I awake to harsh reality. Crushing afresh after each soothing sleep... Is it really true? Why did this happen to us...?? How can I bear this grief...??

Comforts. New every morning. Still no answers to the mysteries of suffering, yet strength for the day. Faith in God and His purpose when all seems hopeless and I am at the end of myself. Trusting God as a child does his father while walking in the dark. Sensing the presence of the person who will never leave me nor forsake me. His love, mercy, and faithfulness are new every morning.

It's just as the Bible says. "The steadfast love of the Lord never ceases, His mercies never come to an end: they are new every morning; great is thy faithfulness..."

My Dear Child,

I'm writing this letter to let you know that I care about you! I see the things you are going through... Many times I know that you feel alone, but I am with you always... You do not need to walk through your life alone... I am just waiting for you to call out to me for help.. You are special to me and I have a plan for your life... There are valleys you will go through, but I promise I will never give you more than you can handle... When those valleys come I beg you to lean on Me... Allow yourself to feel my arms around you and at the same time learn the lessons I have for you... It's through these trials that your character is built and you become more of who I want you to be... As you feel pain and allow me to comfort you, then you will be able to reach out to others and comfort them... When you are feeling down and discouraged I want you to put on the garment of praise... As you praise me I will fill you with peace. When I left this earth I told my disciples that I leave my peace with them. That peace is for you too... Claim it, feel it, let it guide you through each day... And don't forget, weeping may come for a time, but joy comes in the morning! You will be rewarded for your faithfulness to me... Draw nigh to me and I will draw nigh to you. Come, take My yoke upon you. My yoke is easy and My burden is light.. As you walk with me you will never need to walk alone.

I Love You,
Your Heavenly Father

Dead, but Alive

STRETCHING SLEEPILY, JIMMY wondered why he had that strange, empty feeling in his stomach. Then it all came back to him. He glanced over at the other bed. Yes, it was empty. It really was true—his big brother, Jack, was gone. It was almost two weeks since Jack had left for school in the morning and had not come back. Tears rolled down Jimmy's cheeks as he remembered. There had been an accident, and Jack had been killed. Mom said he had gone to heaven.

The door to Jimmy's room opened, and his mother came in. "Good morning! I see you're already awake," she said. Noticing his tears, she sat beside him on the bed. "You're thinking of Jack, aren't you, honey?" she asked. "Daddy and I miss him, too, but we try to remember how happy he is with Jesus."

"But, Mom, how do you know that?" asked Jimmy.

"I know because Jack accepted Jesus as his Savior," Mom answered, "and the Bible says that when those who trust in Jesus leave this life, they go to be with Him."

Jimmy nodded. "Yes, but I still don't understand," he said with a sob. "You always say Jack's in heaven, but he was right there in the casket and then he was put in the ground at the cemetery." Jimmy covered his face with his hands.

"Jack's body is in the grave, but his soul, or his life—the real Jack—is with Jesus," explained Mom.

Jimmy looked at his hands. "But ... my head and my hands and my ears and eyes ... this is me, isn't it?"

Mom shook her head. "Not really," she told him. "Your body is just a house in which the real you—your soul—lives. Your body may die, but not your soul. It lives! Jack's body died and we buried it, but God took Jack's life—his soul—to heaven. So when I think of Jack, I think of him in heaven, not in the cemetery."

Jimmy sighed. "But I still wish I could see Jack every day," he said slowly.

"I know," Mom answered, giving him a hug. "We all do. We can't see him again here on earth, but because we all know Jesus, we can look forward to seeing him in heaven one day. Then we'll all be together forever!"

Bodies Die; Souls Don't

Read:

2 Corinthians 5:1,6-9

Memorize:

2 Corinthians 5:8

We are ... willing rather to be absent from the body, and to be present with the Lord." (KJV)

We ... would prefer to be away from the body and at home with the Lord." (NIV)

How about you?

Do you know that your life, or soul, lives forever—in either heaven or in hell? When a Christian dies, his soul goes to be with Jesus. Be sure you have accepted the Savior. If you've done that, you will live forever in heaven.

Is Your Face Toward Me?

A YOUNG BOY named Ben experienced a great loss in his life. Ben's mother had died. After coming home from the funeral with his dad, both Ben and his dad went to bed as soon as it was dark, because there just didn't seem to be anything else to do. As the little boy lay in his bed in the darkness, he broke the quiet with this question for his dad, "Daddy, where is Mommy?"

The father answered the question as best as he could, but Ben kept asking more questions. After awhile the dad got up, scooped up the boy in his arms, and brought him to his bed. Ben continued to ask his questions. Finally he reached out in the darkness, placed his hand on his dad's face, and asked him, "Daddy, is your face toward me?"

His dad assured him that his face was indeed toward him. Then Ben said, "If your face is toward me, I think I can go to sleep."

A short while later he was quiet and sleeping The dad lay in the bed in the darkness and prayed to his Father in heaven. He prayed something like this, "O God, it is very dark, and right now I don't see how I can make it. But if your face is toward me, somehow I think I can make it."

Ben had taught his dad an important lesson. It made Ben feel peaceful and able to rest to have his dad's face toward him. In the same way, we can find peace and rest when our heavenly Father's face is toward us.

From *Beside the Still Waters*
—by Mervin Byler, Newaygo, MI

The Lord bless thee, and keep thee: The Lord make his face shine upon thee, and be gracious unto thee: The Lord lift up his countenance upon thee: and give thee peace (Numbers 6:24-26).

I'D LIKE TO share with you the best tip I've ever had. This tip was given to us by Robert Hastings.

Tucked away in our subconscious is an idyllic vision. We see ourselves on a long trip that spans the continent. We are traveling by train. Out the windows we drink in the passing scene of cars on highways, of children waving, of smoke from a power plant, of rows of corn and wheat, of mountains and rolling hills, of city skylines and village halls.

But uppermost in our minds is the final destination. On a certain day, at a certain hour, we will pull into the station. Once we get there, so many wonderful dreams will come true and the pieces of our lives will fit together like a completed jigsaw puzzle. How restlessly we pace the aisles—waiting, waiting, waiting for the station.

"When we reach the station that will be it!" we cry. "When I'm eighteen." "When I have paid off the mortgage!" "When I get a promotion." "When I reach the age of retirement." "I shall live happily ever after."

Sooner or later we must realize there is no station. The true joy of life is the trip. The station is only a dream. It constantly outdistances us.

"Relish the moment" is a good motto. It isn't the burdens of today that drive men mad. It is the regrets of yesterday and the fear of tomorrow. Regret and fear are twin thieves who rob us of today.

So stop pacing the aisles and counting the miles; instead climb more mountains, swim more rivers, watch more sunsets, laugh more, cry less. Life must be lived as we go along. The station will come soon enough.

A Love Letter from Jesus

HOW ARE YOU? I just had to send you this letter to tell you how much I love you and care about you. I saw you yesterday as you were walking with your friends. I waited all day, hoping you would walk and talk with me also. As evening drew near, I gave you a sunset to close your day, and a cool breeze to rest you. Then I waited, but you never came. Oh yes, it hurt me, but I still love you because I am your friend.

I saw you fall asleep last night, and I longed to touch your brow. So I spilled moonlight upon your pillow and your face … Again I waited, wanting to rush down so we could talk. I have so many gifts for you.

You awakened late this morning and rushed off for the day. My tears were in the rain. Today you looked so sad, so alone. It makes my heart ache, because I understand. My friends let me down and hurt me many times, but I love you. I try to tell you in the quiet green grass. I whisper it in the leaves and trees, and breathe it in the color of the flowers. I shout it to you in the mountain streams, and give the birds love songs to sing. I clothe you with warm sunshine and perfume the air. My love for you is deeper than the oceans and bigger than the biggest want or need you could ever have.

We will spend eternity together in heaven. I know how hard it is on earth. I really know, because I was there, and I want to help you. My Father wants to help you, too. He's that way, you know. Just call me, ask me, talk to me. It is your decision … I have chosen you, and because of this I will wait … because I love you.

Your Friend,

—Jesus

Why Do We Need Your Prayers?

Almost 1 out of 3 children live in a single-parent home.
70% of long-term prison inmates come from fatherless homes.
4 out of 5 psychiatric admissions are from fatherless homes.

Teenagers watch an average of 5 hours of TV per day.
Teens listen to an average of 40 hours of music per week.
Youths spend approx. 16.5 hrs. a week on the internet or emailing.
Much of the music and video games are violent or sexual.

2 out of 3 teens say the devil, or Satan, is not a living being.
3 out of 5 teens believe you get into Heaven by doing good.
83% of teens say that moral truth depends on circumstances.
Only 6% believe that moral truth is absolute.

50% of teens are sexually active. Only half of 13-15-year-olds
    say sex before marriage is wrong.
Only 32% of 16–17-year-olds say it is wrong.
4 in 10 teenage girls get pregnant before they turn 20.

1 in 4 girls and 1 in 7 boys are molested before age 18.
95% of prostitutes are runaways.
There are 600,000 adolescents involved in prostitution.
A runaway's first act of prostitution occurs around 14 years old.
About 1 billion dollars is spent on prostitution per year in the U.S.

18% of teenagers drink more than once per month.
5.1 million teens say they binge drink (+5 drinks/setting).
19% of the high school boys admit they've been drunk at school.
56% of youth reported marijuana as easy to obtain.
21% of youth reported heroin as easy to obtain.
14% of youth were approached for drugs in the last month.

More than 1 in 3 students say they don't feel safe at school.
More than 1 in 5 h. s. boys took a weapon to school last year.
15% of middle school boys took a weapon to school.
75% of boys said they hit someone in the last year out of anger.

2 out of 3 teenage girls are trying to lose weight.
39% of girls grades 5-8 are on a diet.
11% of young people have anorexia, nervosa, or bulimia.

1 in 8 adolescents struggle with depression.
12% of the college age population harms their own bodies by cutting,
    slashing, scarring, self-tattooing, or burning themselves.
In the U.S. a teenager takes his life every 100 minutes.
Suicide is the third leading cause of death of 15 to 24-year-olds.
Adolescent suicides have nearly tripled over the last 40 years.

I WAS EIGHT years old when the little gift catalogue came in the mail. "This ornamental poppy is the most amazing thing we have yet offered!" it boasted as it described the 10¢ artificial plant whose bud would blossom into a scarlet poppy when dropped into water. What a wonderful gift for my mother, I thought.

When the package came, I was heartbroken. It looked anything but magical. The stem was kinked wire, and no matter how hard I tried, I couldn't imagine the shapeless curl of paper at the end of the wire ever turning into anything resembling a bloom.

Almost tearfully, I wrapped the gift. "I paid a whole dime for it and it's not going to work," I said sadly when I presented the gift.

My mother smiled and said, "We don't know until we try."

We filled a jar with water and dropped in the worthless-looking trinket. The promised miracle happened! The wire stem straightened up and one by one the perfectly shaped, opaque petals opened in a burst of crimson glory, while fragile fernlike leaves unfurled up and down the now-straight stem. The ornamental poppy truly was a thing of beauty. All it needed was the magic of water. And that's all we need too—the living water of Christ that brings out the glory in our drab lives. Only He can serve us "living water."

—June Masters Bacher

The Dash Between the Dates
1981-20??

WHILE WALKING IN a graveyard one day, I noticed that there was a similar marking on nearly every tombstone. Each one had two years cut into its face. These, of course, were different. But the thing that was the same on each was the dash between the dates.

That dash was placed there to represent someone's life span—the time that each person had spent between birth and death. How strange to reduce a whole lifetime to a mere dash. But how important the time which that dash represents!

The Bible says in James 4:14, "What is your life? It is even a vapour, that appeareth for a little time, and then vanisheth away." Maybe it is not so strange after all to compare a lifetime with a dash. The psalmist writes in Psalm 39:5, "Behold, thou hast made my days as an handbreadth; and mine age is as nothing before thee."

God is a God of eternity. He has always existed and always will exist. Psalm 90:2 says, "Before the mountains were brought forth, or ever thou hadst formed the earth and the world, even from everlasting to everlasting, thou art God." By the power of God, life is given, and life is also taken again. It is before Him that every man will someday need to stand and give account of how he used the time represented by that dash on his stone. The Scriptures tell us that "We must all appear before the judgment seat of Christ; that every one may receive the things done in his body, according to that he hath done, whether it be good or bad" (2 Corinthians 5:10).

If you could draw a line long enough to reach around the world, and then take out of that line a section short enough to be the dash on the tombstone, you still would not have a fair comparison of the length of this life as it compares to eternity. In Matthew 25:46, the Lord Himself speaks about the wicked when He says, "And these shall go away into everlasting punishment: but the righteous into life eternal." Everlasting and eternal are translated from the same Greek word. As long as heaven lasts (eternally), that is how long hell will be endured. This makes the dash between the dates extremely important. The thoughts, the words, the deeds of that time determine the eternal destiny of the soul.

Right now, each of us is living in time. Before long, all of us will be in eternity. Our "dash" of time will determine the words we will hear from the Judge of all the earth. Will we hear, "Well done, thou good and faithful servant," or will the words "I never knew you: depart from me" seal our eternal destiny? No chance will be given then to go back and make wrongs right. No cry for mercy will save anyone then. The Scriptures tell us that "now is the accepted time; behold, now is the day of salvation." May each of us use the present time to qualify, for the "gift of God is eternal life through Jesus Christ our Lord" (Romans 6:23). Why work for such a costly damnation when salvation has been made available for all?

—Harry Erb

"Here a Little, and There a Little"

TEACHING CHILDREN IS like filling a glass at the kitchen faucet. If you turn on the water with too much force, the glass never gets full. But if you reduce the pressure and let the water flow gently, the glass is soon filled.

Fathers and mothers need to be firm and wise. But they also need to be gentle and loving. When they give too much advice, too many rules, and too frequent instructions, they are wasting their words. The children cannot absorb them all.

This does not mean that parents should just "let their children go." It means that they teach them faithfully and patiently, a little at a time.

The Bible says, "Precept must be upon precept… line upon line… here a little, and there a little…"

This is the way of effective teaching in the home.

All I really need to know I learned from Noah's Ark

1. Don't miss the boat.
2. Don't forget that we're all in the same boat.
3. Plan ahead. It wasn't raining when Noah built the ark.
4. Stay fit. When you're 600 years old, someone might ask you to do something really big.
5. Don't listen to critics, just get on with what has to be done.
6. Build your future on high ground.
7. For safety's sake travel in pairs.
8. Two heads are better than one.
9. Speed isn't always an advantage; the snails were on board with the cheetahs.
10. When you're stressed, float awhile.
11. Remember that the ark was built by amateurs; the *Titanic* was built by professionals.
12. Remember that woodpeckers inside are a larger threat than the storm outside.
13. No matter the storm, when you're with God there's a rainbow waiting.

The original source of the above words of wisdom is unknown.

THERE IS A story of an Amish home in which two boys, twins, died on the same day. The father was absent from home, on business, at the time. The next day he returned, not knowing of the grief which was awaiting him. His wife met him at the door quietly and calmly, not betraying her sorrow. When he came in she said to him, "I have had a strange visitor since you went away."

"Who was it?" asked the husband, with no thought of her meaning.

"Five years ago," answered the mother, "a friend lent me two beautiful jewels. Yesterday he came and asked me to give them back to him again. What should I do?"

"Were the jewels his?" asked the father.

"Yes, they were his, and were only lent to me," answered the mother.

"Well, if they belong to him, he certainly had a right to reclaim them, if he wishes," replied the father, "and you can not refuse."

Leading the husband to the children's room, the mother drew down the sheet from their bed and there lay the forms, white and beautiful as marble.

"These are my jewels," said the mother. "Five years ago God gave them to me, and yesterday He came and asked for them again. What shall we do?"

The father bowed his head and said with deep emotion, "The will of God be done."

This is the story of sorrow, dear ones. God gave you the beautiful jewel, which has become so priceless to your hearts. Yesterday He came and asked for it again. Be it yours to lay it back in His hands in sweet trust and joy, saying, "The will of the Lord be done."

You Ask Me How I'm Doing

My son went first, he lives with God
And here I must remain.
Now it's up to me to learn
To live with grief and pain.

You ask me how I'm doing.
I don't know what to say.
Sometimes I'm doing pretty good,
It's different every day.

Sometimes I smile. Sometimes I cry.
Sometimes I feel okay.
Sometimes I think I'm going nuts.
It's difficult to say.

Sometimes I hear him call my name
Or see him wave good-bye.
Sometimes I feel him here with me
And then I start to cry.

His gentle hugs are memories now.
His smiles are gone for good.
I'd love to hold his hand again;
Oh, if I only could.

It's lonely here without him,
But the world keeps right on turning.
And the pain I'm feeling in my heart?
That keeps right on burning...

So ask me how I'm doing
And I won't know what to say.
I haven't really, truly known
Since Mervin went away.

Running with the Wrong Crowd

HE IS RUNNING with the wrong crowd. Who hasn't heard this saying from their parents at one time or other in their life? I heard this from my parents.

Sometimes throughout my life, they were talking about me. But the thinking behind this saying comes from good judgment because, like it or not, people act like their friends and turn out like them most of the time. So if one is running with the wrong crowd, there is a good chance that they will end up getting into some trouble.

The people that we surround ourselves with will influence us, whether for good or bad. That is why we as parents are always worried about the friends that our children hang out with.

A lot of times, throughout the teen years and early twenties, there are not many people who are doing the "right thing." Many people, including me, have run wild during those years and it is only by God's grace that I was not hurt or killed. I can recall many times throughout those years when I along with my friends could have ended up in some real trouble. Luckily, for our sakes we never had any truly bad outcomes. But like I said, we were lucky.

Thankfully, as time went on things got better. I was able to get my life back on track and begin a life that is worthwhile and for the betterment of others' lives. This was not easy.

When a person decides to take a stand and say he is not going down the path that many trod, he finds that the going is very lonely at times. But the bleak outlook will not last forever, and if we stick to the course we will see the light at the end of the tunnel.

Continuing down the same path of riotous living will only lead to one's mixed-up life and we will hit bottom. Oh yes, there are some who will go on for a very long time, living a rowdy lifestyle, but sooner or later the ride will come to a screeching halt.

Unfortunately for those people, the happening that causes them to change, or the need to change, could cause damage to him or others beyond repair. It is really sad when a person must learn his lesson and others feel the pain of his bad decision.

For you young people, learn to take advice from others who have been through this experience. Listening to wise words of someone may keep you from experiencing a lot of heartache that is unnecessary.

"He that walketh with wise men shall be wise, but a companion of fools shall be destroyed. Be not deceived: evil communications corrupt good manners" (Proverbs 13:20/1 Corinthians 15:33).

If you are running with the wrong crowd, stop, look, and listen to that still small voice. Now—while there is still time—start walking with Jesus. He wants so much to come into your life if you will only let him.

—Aaron F. Beiler

Your heart is numb with pain and grief.
Just now it seems beyond belief...
That this dear loved one is gone to stay,
That he has really passed away.
That you will see his face no more
Upon this cold and earthly shore.
Just now you cannot understand,
The reason why the Lord has planned
To lead this way. Why does he need
To rend your heart and make it bleed?
Why is there pain, and grief, and woe?
Why must the tears so often flow?

Sad soul, the Lord would have you gain
Through this experience of pain
A deeper faith, a richer life,
For when your sorrows, pain, and strife...
Drive you to Christ, in Him you'll seek

Enduring strength with spirit meek.
He'll draw quite near and you will find
All you require with peace of mind.
Perhaps God needed all these tears
To cleanse your heart of fear.
To magnify your former view,
Your inner vision to renew.

And now that you have loved and lost,
And felt the pain and borne the cost,
You'll have a greater mission here,
For other hearts are needing cheer.
For other hearts will ache and bleed.
Your understanding they will need.
Take heart, for when this life is o'er
You'll meet your loved one on that shore
Where God has wiped away all tears,
And you shall feel no pain nor tears.

my heavenly garden

Come to my heavenly garden
To see a perfect bloom
The flower you loved so dearly
And thought I plucked too soon
Then you will know the reason
Though you know it not today
When in his early manhood
I took your son away …….

Grieving Time, a Time for Love

If a loved one has departed,
And left an empty space,
Seek the inner stillness,
Set a slower pace.

Take time to remember,
Allow yourself to cry,
Acknowledge your emotions,
Let sadness pass on by.

Then center in the oneness,
Remember…God is here,
Death is but a change in form,
Your loved one is still near.

Treat yourself with kindness,
Allow yourself to feel,
God will do the mending,
And time will help you heal.

Perhaps my time seemed all too brief;
Don't lengthen it now with undue grief.
Lift up your heart and share with me
God wanted me now; He set me free.

His Shoes Spoke to Me

His shoes still sit on the closet floor,
Tho' he's been gone a decade and more.

Some days my memories are a bit hazy.
Is it a nightmare or am I going crazy?

I go to the closet and there are his shoes.
It's easy to see they really were used.

The prints of his feet are still inside.
He really did live, but too soon he died.

Reality returns, with his shoes on the floor.
How long will they be there?
'Til I need them no more.

His bronzed baby shoes sit on a shelf.
They help me to meet a need in myself.

These baby shoes speak of a life just beginning.
The work shoes tell about life and its ending.

With the passing of years, some peace I've attained.
But the happiness I once knew cannot be regained.

Yet there's much about life I still want to live.
To my family and others, I still yearn to give.

I've cried many tears, felt the guilt and the pain.
My grief has diminished and I can laugh once again.

—by Ora S. Lewis

"You cannot direct the wind But You Can Adjust the Sails"

I SAW THE above quote on a poster in our church and it occurred to me that "grief work" is just that—adjusting your sails. When a child dies, our lives are changed forever—the wind changes direction. When the direction of our life is so tragically changed, we have two choices. We can deal with our grief and adjust our sails, or we can deny our grief and drift helplessly and hopelessly out to sea.

In the beginning stages of grief we merely "reef our sails" and go with the tide. That is not a bad idea. At that time we are in a state of shock and not capable of sound decisions. We need quite a bit of time to ride out the storm. But when the initial storm of intense pain begins to subside, we need to adjust our sails for our own survival.

You, and only you, can make the decisions regarding the rest of your life. You may find fulfillment in reaching out to help others or becoming more active in your church or temple. Maybe you'll want to take as big a step as getting a job or returning to school. Perhaps you will make only subtle changes in your priorities. But if you have made the decision to have a direction instead of drifting, get started now! You may have several false starts before you are really on course again. That's okay. Don't give up! The healing is in the trying. If you don't give up, eventually you'll once again have "smooth sailing."

—Marge Frankenberg, TCF.
Arlington Heights, Illinois

It's Not Unusual to......

- Feel physically exhausted, but have difficulty sleeping.
- Feel tightness in the throat, heaviness in the chest, or a lump in the stomach.
- Wander aimlessly, forget in the middle of a sentence, neglect to finish tasks. Feel restless, look for activity, but be unable to concentrate.
- Think you're losing your mind.
- Feel the need to take care of others who seem uncomfortable around you.
- Feel you don't want to go on.
- Say to yourself, "If only I had…"
- Keep asking, "Why?"
- Feel that the loss isn't real.
- Sense the loved one's presence by expecting him to walk in the door or phone at the usual time. Hear the voice or see the face.
- Look for him in a crowd or see reminders unexpectedly.
- Need to tell and retell things about your loved one and the death.
- Cry at unexpected times.
- Feel able to cope, but then fall back again.
- Feel depressed.

All of these reactions are natural and normal. Know that you are not alone in having them.

Excerpted from an article by—Ruth Eiseman, Louisville, KY

Somebody Needs You

If you're feeling low and worthless,
There seems nothing you can do,
Just take courage and remember,
There is someone needing you.

You were created for a purpose,
For a part in God's great plan;
Bear ye one another's burdens,
So fulfill Christ's law to man.

Are you father, son, or daughter?
You've a work none else can do.
Are you husband, wife, or mother?
There is someone needing you.

If perhaps in bed you're lying,
You can smile or press the hand
Of the one who tells his story;
He will know you understand.

There are many sad and lonely,
And discouraged, not a few,
Who a little cheer are needing,
And there's someone needing you.

Someone needs your faith and courage,
Someone needs your love and prayer,
Someone needs your inspiration,
Thus to help their cross to bear.

Do not think your work is ended,
There is much that you can do,
And as long as you're on earth,
There is someone needing you.

When Grief Is New

When grief is new, it's hard to pray,
"Thy will be done," is hard to say.
With heart and mind all numb with pain,
We cry, "Beloved, come back again."
But can we really ask that he
Return from God's Eternity;
To suffer and grow old in years?
The selfish cry is drowned in tears.

Death comes to all; one first must go,
If he were left he'd sorrow so.
It's better that I wait awhile,
God grant I do it with a smile.

Softly the leaves of memories fall,
Sadly we stoop to gather them all,
Unseen, unheard, yet always near,
Still loved, still missed....
And very dear!

Neighbors

Neighbors are God's angels,
In many different ways.
They help in death and sickness
And ask no word of praise…

Whenever there is trouble
You always can depend
That someone will come running
Their sympathy to lend…

When life isn't going smoothly
How often will appear,
A plate of fresh-baked cookies,
Along with words of cheer…

They're always standing ready,
To do their share or more,
Neighbors are God's angels,
I know, we've got them everywhere…

"The Absent One"

As we gather at the table
And watch each shining face,
The hearts fill with emotion
To see the vacant place.
We may strive to hide our longing
In the midst of mirth and fun,
But we're thinking, thinking, thinking,
Of the loved, the absent one.

When we gather around in the evening
With merry laugh and zest,
How we wish the absent, dear one,
Was here with all the rest.
Still we join in all the frolic,
But we wish the day was done,
For we're thinking, thinking, thinking,
Of the loved, the absent one.

Yet when the day is over
And they all have gone to rest,
We feel our Heavenly Father
Does all things for the best.
So we cheer our drooping spirits
With the rising of the sun,
But we can't help thinking, thinking,
Of the loved, the absent one.

A Little Talk with Jesus

A little talk with Jesus,
How it smooths the rugged road,
How it cheers and helps me onward
When I faint beneath my load.

When my heart is crushed with sorrow
And my eyes with tears are dim,
There is naught can yield me comfort
Like a little talk with Him.

Though my way is often dreary
And my walk is weak and slow,
A little talk with Jesus
Tells me all I need to know.

And He answers me so gently
In a soft and loving tone,
"I am with you always;
You will never be alone."

He tells me that He loves me,
And paid the ransom for my soul,
Now He is my brother;
His love has made me whole.

I cannot live without Him;
His love is all I know;
A little talk with Jesus
Gives me all I need to grow.

Oh, I often feel impatient
And I mourn His long delay,
For I never can be settled
While He yet remains away.

I think we'd smile
Instead of weep,
If we could see them there,
So free for all eternity,
So free from every care.
I think we'd bear our loneliness
With but one mournful thought,
If we could only realize
The joy home coming brought.

God Knows Best

Our Father knows what's best for us,
So why should we complain—
We always want the sunshine,
But He knows there must be rain...
We love the sound of laughter
And the merriment of cheer,
But our hearts would lose their tenderness
If we never shed a tear...
Our Father tests us often
With suffering and with sorrow,
He tests us, not to punish us,
But to help us meet tomorrow...
For growing trees are strengthened

When they withstand the storm,
And the sharp cut of the chisel
Gives the marble grace and form...
God never hurts us needlessly,
And He never wastes our pain,
For every loss He sends to us
Is followed by high gain...
And when we count the blessings
That God has so freely sent,
We will find no cause for murmuring
And no time to lament...
For our Father loves His children,
And to Him all things are plain,
So He never sends us pleasure
When the soul's deep need is pain...
So whenever we are troubled,
And when everything goes wrong,
It is just God working in us
To make our spirit strong.

The Forgotten Grievers
—by Diane Bojanowski

DIANE BOJANOWSKI'S FATHER, Thomas Bojanowski, died of cancer on March 8, 1982. Mourning his death were his wife, Cheryl, a son, Bryan, age 6, and Diane, age 7. Grieving has no time limit, nor do the thoughts that surround it. At the age of 13, Diane wrote this article.

When a death occurs in a family or to someone close, it is a tragic experience. It is never forgotten, even by a child. Children, however, are often overlooked during times of bereavement. Adults may be so absorbed in their own grief that they simply don't think about the grieving child. Sometimes adults think children don't understand or they will get over it quickly because they are young. These attitudes ignore the grief children experience.

Each child reacts differently to death. A death experience may make some children more mature when they are suddenly forced to accept more responsibility. Another child may become disobedient and hostile.

At times, children will blame themselves for causing the death. Some think that by fighting with a sister or brother or by wishing someone harm, they in fact are responsible when the person dies. Children's superstitions can convince a child it was his fault because of something he did or said. If a child doesn't blame himself, he may blame God. He may hate God, refuse to pray to Him, and wonder why God took the loved one away.

Sometimes after a death, children need and want to talk about it with someone their own age, but sometimes other children aren't willing to listen. They feel uncomfortable talking about death or they don't understand what the bereaved is feeling. As a result, a child who has experienced a loss may sometimes wonder if he is the only one to feel this way. Some children have trouble talking about death with a parent. Many also dislike going to the cemetery because they hate to see parents or loved ones cry.

Many children are angry, confused, and hurt as the result of a death. After awhile, a child's memories of the deceased person are unclear and this is devastating. Holidays are sorrowful because the loved one isn't there to celebrate with the family. Many little things such as a song on the radio may reopen the terrible wound of death.

"In the book *The Secret Garden,* the plot is built around the physical and emotional injury to a child brought on by the unwise attitude of the child's father in mourning for his mother. The child is healed of paralysis and emotional seizures when he is restored to healthy relations with others again and is allowed to face the full fact of what happened to his mother."

Children need to be helped and supported by all. The first thing people can do is to start telling children about death at an early age. Use the child's interest in a dead insect or a dead pet to help them understand that death is forever. People confuse children by using words such as "passed away" or "lost" instead of "dead" to describe a deceased loved one. This gives children the idea that death is temporary. For example, when a child has been told a pet has been "put to sleep," the child might think, "Well, when is it going to wake up?"

When it is time to tell a child that a person has died, he or she should be told in simple terms. A person the child knows well and is close to should tell him or her about the death. They should be encouraged to ask questions and express their feelings and fears.

Never rush anybody's grief. Don't say, "Don't be so depressed," or "Get on with your life" to a bereaved person. Keep the memory of the deceased person alive through pictures or conversations or stories, especially for the child who may have been very young when the loved one died and cannot remember him or her well. All the people in the child's life need to know about the death so they can help the child.

"Grief shared is grief diminished."2 A saying that is so true, yet not many people see it. Support groups are essential for the bereaved. There are many groups, but not many for children. They need to discuss the death they've experienced with children their own age. A support group for children helps them carry on with their lives.

Children are human beings that need support and attention while experiencing the death of a loved one. Never forget the grieving children.

Footnotes—

Edgar N. Jackson, Understanding Grief (Nashville: Arlington Press, 1978), page 203

2W.O.W. & Company Support Group

Home Is Where God Is

There's no place like home
and there's no home like the one
God is preparing for us someday.
We cling to the familiar, not understanding
that a far greater miracle awaits us
when we cross from this life into eternity.
There, Jesus waits to escort His own
into a place of sweet peace and blessed rest.
There, we can finally see with veil removed
the beauty which our souls
have so longed to know.
There, our loved ones wait with eager anticipation
for us to celebrate with them
the joys for which we were ultimately created.
If we were allowed one glimpse of that place,
our real home, we would not hold too tightly
to the ones gone before us.
Instead, we would grieve because we cannot
go with them—because home, after all,
is where God is.

Give Your Flowers Now

I would rather have one little rose from the garden of my friend,
Than to have the choicest flowers when my stay on earth must end.
I would rather have the kindly words which may now be said to me,
than flattered when my heart is still, and this life has ceased to be.
I would rather have a loving smile from friends I know are true.
Than tears shed 'round my casket when this world I've bid adieu.
Bring me all your flowers today. Whether pink, or white, or red;
I'd rather have one blossom now than a truckload when I'm dead.

Give Me My Flowers While I Live

—Gertrude LeFevre Graff

Have you a thought that me would help,
A gentle word to give?
Wait not until my ears are closed,
But tell me while I live.
If any thought or word of mine
Has helped you on your way,
It will encourage me to know
That I have helped today.
Oh, do not wait until I'm dead,
My ears and eyes quite closed—
Give me my flowers while I live,
If but a single rose.
If unkind words you thought to speak,
Hold them until that hour
When unkind words won't hurt my heart,
Their sting deprived of power.
Give me my flowers while I live,
When dead I cannot see
Nor hear the words you meant to say,
Though gentle they may be.
And kind words spoken always bring
A lighter heart—to bear
The heavy burdens—and you too
Lightheartedness will share.
I care not if there are no flowers
When I am laid away—
But give my flowers while I live,
And they will last for aye.

—*Gospel Messenger*

"Hold Us Up, Lord!"

Lord, we know You're always busy,
For You've many things to do.
But when sorrow overcomes us,
Well, we need to talk to You,
For we've lost someone precious.
And they're with You there above,
And it's someone that we needed.
And it's someone that we love…
We are feeling lost and all alone,
And though we do believe,
We need You, Lord, to hold us up,
To help us while we grieve.
Please give us strength and courage, Lord,
To bear what we must bear.
And nudge us when our faith is weak,
To remind us You are there.
Give us hope for our tomorrows,
Tell us life will still go on.
Show us, Lord, that all this darkness
Will be followed by the dawn…
You've led us through so many things,
You've pulled us through before,
Hold us up, Lord, till we're through this
And we are strong once more.

Peace to You in Your Sorrow

When clouds dip low and veil the sun,
The days seem drear and long,
And comfort is a fleeting thing,
Your life has lost its song,
May He who stilled the stormy sea
Speak peace to all your fear,
And bring you comfort with the thought
That He is ever near.

The Broken Chain

We little knew that morning that
God was going to call your name,
In life we loved you dearly,
In death we do the same.
It broke our hearts to lose you,
You did not go alone;
For part of us went with you,
The day God called you home.
You left us peaceful memories,
Your love is still our guide,
And though we cannot see you,
You are always at our side.
Our family chain is broken,
And nothing seems the same;
But God calls us one by one,
The chain will link again.

Oh, What Do You think the Angels Say?

"Oh, what do you think the angels say?"
Said the children up in heaven.
"There's a dear little boy coming home today,
From the earth where we need to live in."
"Let's go and open the gates of joy,
Open them wide for the dear little boy,"
Said the children up in heaven.

"God wanted him here where His little ones meet,"
Said the children up in heaven.
"He shall play with us in the golden street;
He has grown too fair, he had grown too sweet
For the earth where we used to live in.
He needed the sunshine, this dear little boy,
That gilds this side of the gates of joy,"
Said the children up in heaven.

"So the King called down from the angels' dome,"
Said the children up in heaven.
"My dear little darling, arise and come
To the place prepared in my Father's home—
The home my children live in."
"Let's go and watch the gates of joy,
Ready to welcome the new little boy,"
Said the children up in heaven.

"Far down on the earth, do you hear them weep?"
Said the children up in heaven.
"For the dear little boy has gone to sleep,
The shadows fall and the night clouds sweep
Over the earth we need to live in.
But we'll go and open the gates of joy.
Oh, why do they weep for the dear little boy?"
Said the children up in heaven.

"Fly with him gently, Oh angels dear, "
Said the children up in heaven.
See!—he is coming. Look there! Look there!
At the jasper light on his sunny hair
Where the veiling clouds are riven.
Oh, hush, hush, hush, all the swift wings furl,
For the King Himself at the gates of joy
Is taking his hand, dear tired little boy,
And is leading him into heaven.

For One Who Has Loved and Lost

Your heart is numb with pain and grief—
Just now it seems beyond belief
That this dear one is gone to stay,
That he has really passed away,
That you will see his face no more
Upon this cold and earthly shore.
Just now you cannot understand
The reason why the Lord has planned
To lead this way. Why does He need
To rend your heart and make it bleed?
Why is there pain and grief and woe?
Why must the tears so often flow?
Sad soul, the Lord would have you gain
Through this experience of pain
A deeper faith, a richer life;
For when your sorrows, pain, and strife
Drive you to Christ, in Him you'll seek
Enduring strength with spirit meek.
He'll draw quite near and you will find
All you require, with peace of mind.
Perhaps God needed all these tears
To cleanse your heart of foolish fears,
To magnify your former view,
Your inner vision to renew.
For now that you have loved and lost,
And felt the pain and bore the cost,
You'll have a greater mission here:
For other hearts are needing cheer,
For other hearts will ache and bleed,
Your understanding they will need.
Take heart—for when this life is o'er,
You'll meet your loved one on that shore
Where God has wiped away all tears.

One Day at a Time

Oh we were so happy, our hearts were so light
The future looked rosy and golden and bright
In youthful ambition with life at its prime
But now we are taking one day at a time.

Yet a day at a time would be too much to bear
If family and friends would forget us in prayer
For God in His wisdom has dealt us a blow
Oh, may this experience inspire us to grow.

Grow richer and better, not bitter instead
Though something of value has vanished and fled
When darkness surrounds us and life seems unfair
It's a comfort to know that our Savior is there.

If God draws a period, then how do we dare
To hang in our weakness a question mark there
'Twas nothing but love though we scarce understand
As trembling and smitten we hold to His hand.

Though we are afraid of the path we must tread
With knowledge of many rough days still ahead
And though we are struggling till faith is quite dim
We believe there is never an error with Him.

And since we can't change the position we're in
Submission is surely the best way to win
Our God will supply every need as we climb
And we will continue… one day at a time.

"Miss Me, But Let Me Go"

When I come to the end of the road—
   And the sun has set for me…
Gather my friends in solemn rite,
   And think of my soul set free.

Miss me, dear ones, with tender thought,
   Grieve not, with spirits low—
Remember the love that once we shared…
   "Miss me, but let me go."

For this is a journey we all must take,
   And each must go alone!
It's all a part of the Master's plan,
   A step along the way "Home."

When you are lonely and faint of heart—
   Go to the friends you know…
Bury your sorrow in doing and deeds,
   "Miss me, but let me go."

Farther Along

Tempted and tried we're oft made to wonder
Why it should be thus all the day long,
While there are others living about us,
Never molested tho in the wrong.

Chorus
Farther along we'll know all about it,
Farther along we'll understand why;
Cheer up, my brother, live in the sunshine,
We'll understand it all by and by.

When death has come and taken our loved ones,
It leaves our home so lonely and drear;
Then do we wonder why others prosper,
Living so wicked year after year.

Chorus
Farther along we'll know all about it,
Farther along we'll understand why;
Cheer up, my brother, live in the sunshine,
We'll understand it all by and by.

Faithful till death said our loving Master,
A few more days to labor and wait;
Toils of the road will then seem as nothing,
As we sweep thru the beautiful gate.

Chorus
Farther along we'll know all about it,
Farther along we'll understand why;
Cheer up, my brother, live in the sunshine,
We'll understand it all by and by.
When we see Jesus coming in glory,
When He comes from His home in the sky;
Then we shall meet Him in that bright mansion,
We'll understand it all by and by.

Chorus
Farther along we'll know all about it,
Farther along we'll understand why;
Cheer up, my brother, live in the sunshine,
We'll understand it all by and by.

"Thy Will Be Done"

God did not promise "sun without rain,"
"light without darkness" or " joy without pain"—
He only promised us "STRENGTH for the DAY"
when "the darkness" comes and we lose our way,
For only through sorrow do we grow more aware
that God is our refuge in times of despair....
For when we are happy and life's bright and fair,
we often forget to kneel down in prayer,
But God seems much closer and needed much more
when trouble and sorrow stand outside our door,
For then we seek shelter in His wondrous love
and we ask Him to send us help from above....
And that is the reason we know it is true

that bright, shining hours and dark, sad ones, too,
Are part of the plan God made for each one,
and all we can pray is "THY WILL BE DONE!"

—Helen Steiner Rice

The Day You Left

You bid no one a last farewell,
  You never said good-bye
You were gone before we knew it,
  And only God knows why.
A million times we needed you,
  A million times we cried.
If love alone could have saved you,
  You never would have died.
In life we loved you dearly,
  In death we love you still,
In our hearts you hold the place
  No one else can ever fill.
It broke our hearts to lose you
  But you didn't go alone—
For a part of us went with you
  The day God took you Home.
Weep briefly for your loved ones
  As they enter into the Kingdom of God.
For they shall possess a joy and peace
  That is not attained on God's earthly realm.
Rather rejoice in their total and everlasting happiness

Light in the Shadow of Death

For their eyes have seen God.

⌒

"*A lovely flower gathered in its prime, to bloom in God's own crown, in God's own time.*"

Why?

Listen to the One whose eternal answer is not "Because," but "I AM,"... I am with you, I know what I'm doing. I love you with an everlasting love. Trust Me! —Lotz

⌒

We give them back to you, dear Lord,
    Who gavest them to us.
Yet as Thou didst not lose in the giving,
    So we have not lost them by their return.
For what is Thine is ours always, if we are Thine.
    And life is eternal and love is immortal.
And death is only a horizon.
    And a horizon is nothing more
Than the limit of our sight.—Quaker Prayer

⌒

And can it be that...the loss of one...makes a void in my heart,
so wide and deep that nothing but the width and depth of eternity
can fill it up!—C. Dickens

I can face the grief with eternal hope and say,
"It's okay"—because it is well with my soul; it's my
heart that is hurting.—Ziglar

⌒

Death cannot come to him untimely who is fit to die; the less of this cold world, the more of heaven; the briefer life, the earlier immortality.
—Millman

If Jesus Came to Your House

If Jesus came to your house to spend a day or two—
If He came unexpectedly, I wonder what you'd do.
Oh, I know you'd give your nicest room to such an honored Guest,
And all the food you'd serve to Him would be the very best,
And you would keep assuring Him you're glad to have Him there—
That serving Him in your own home is joy beyond compare.

But—when you saw Him coming, would you meet Him at the door
With arms outstretched in welcome to your heavenly Visitor?
Or would you have to change your clothes before you let Him in?
Or hide some magazines and put the Bible where they'd been?
Would you turn off the radio and hope He hadn't heard?
And wish you hadn't uttered that last, loud, hasty word?

Would you hide your worldly music and put some hymnbooks out?
Could you let Jesus walk right in, or would you rush about?
And I wonder—if the Saviour spent a day or two with you,
Would you go right on doing the things you always do?
Would you go right on saying the things you always say?
Would life for you continue as it does from day to day?

Would your family conversation keep up its usual pace?
And would you find it hard each meal to say a table grace?
Would you sing the songs you always sing, and read the
    books you read,
And let Him know the things on which your mind and spirit feed?
Would you take Jesus with you everywhere you'd planned to go?
Or would you maybe change your plans for just a day or so?

Would you be glad to have Him meet your very closest friends?
Or would you hope they'd stay away until His visit ends?
Would you be glad to have Him stay forever on and on?
Or would you sigh with great relief when He at last was gone?
It might be interesting to know the things that you would do
If Jesus Christ in person came to spend some time with you.

—Lois Blanchard Eades

Teach Me to Wait

Oh teach me, dear Father, to patiently wait;
Your timing is never one moment too late.
You know all the questions—each "How?" and each "Why?"
That with their persistence my heart often try.
Not one single part of my life is unplanned;
You hold every thread, precious Lord, in Your hand.

Lord, why does it seem that the areas You touch
Are the ones that are tender and hurt, oh, so much,
Because they're entwined with deep longings so great
And heart-drawing happenings—and then you say "Wait"?
Lord, teach me Thy patience to see as I should
That somehow it all will work out for my good.

And, Lord, if these longings must crucified be
Then keep Thou Thy kind, loving arms around me.
And may I not question; Thy way is the best;
'Tis only in thee that my heart can have rest.
Each trial and test is because of Your love.

That I may grow more like my Father above.
So teach me, dear Father, to patiently wait;
I know that Your timing is never too late.

How Can I Smile?

How can I smile when my heart aches?
  And I am lonely and sad?
Because my Savior has entered my life
  And He can make me glad.

How can I smile when my life seems
  A burden too great to bear?
Because my heavenly Father is here,
  Awaiting my burdens to share.

How can I smile when I am bereft
  Of much that life holds dear?
Because, though earthly friends forsake,
  My heavenly Father is near.

How can I smile when sorrow and pain
  Are a part of my daily life?
Because a loving hand is stretched
  To help me bear the strife.

How can I smile when home and love
  Are taken away from me?
Because my Savior sends His Spirit,
  A comfort and guide to be.

And so I can smile from day to day,
  Though sorrow and loss I bear,
For Jesus, my Savior, knows and loves;
  I am ever in His care.

—Florence B. Hodgdon

CHILDREN ARE LIKE balloons with a message inside. They start out small and we inflate them with something of ourselves. As we pour our lives into them, they spread sunshine, give joy, brighten the days of grandmas and grandpas, and cheer up the sick. They remind us of being young and that life is fragile. They celebrate living! When they are discouraged they are like a balloon that deflates. A simple openness allows us to refill them… with hope for the future, a feeling that they are special and the knowledge that God loves them. Their enthusiasm is like a balloon carried on the wind with never-ending energy. They sway and drift. It's then that they need our prayers and loving guidance, without too much pressure that would cause them to burst. The time comes, sprinkled with tears and joy, when others are able to read the message we have written on their hearts. So we let go and let God have His way with our precious balloons… not the end… but truly the beginning!

Just a Heartbeat

We are living on the border of eternity each day
We are just as close to heaven as the stars so far away
And the only thing between us—whether we are big or small
Is a tender little heartbeat—just a heartbeat, that is all.
Just a heartbeat from the glory, just a heartbeat nothing more.
Just a tender little heartbeat, till we walk the golden shore.
Keep your lamp all trimmed and burning. Let it shine, you'll never fall.
Just a heartbeat from the glory, just a heartbeat, that is all.
In this land of sin and sorrow, whether old or in our prime
We are only just a heartbeat from the glory anytime.
No one has the lease on living, any moment death may call.
It is only by God's mercy—that we live or breathe at all.
There is a place beyond the river, where we'll lay our burdens down.
Where we'll meet our friends and loved ones, and we'll wear a starring crown.
All our troubles will be over and no tears shall ever fall
Just a heartbeat from the glory—just a heartbeat, that is all.

Two Golden Days

—Robert J. Burdette

THERE ARE TWO days of the week upon and about which I never worry...two carefree days kept sacredly free from fear and all its cares and frets. This first day I refuse to worry about is yesterday. All its pains and aches, with all its faults, its mistakes and blunders have passed forever beyond the reach of my recall. I cannot undo an act that I wrought. I cannot unsay a word that I said. All that it holds of my life, of wrongs, regret and sorrow, is in the hands of the Mighty Love that can bring honey out of the rocks and sweet waters out of the bitterest desert. Save for the beautiful memories, sweet and tender, that linger like the perfume of roses in the heart of the day that is gone, I have nothing to do with yesterday. It *was* mine...now it is God's.

And the other day that I do not worry about is tomorrow. Tomorrow, with all its possible adversities, its burdens, its perils, its larger promise and poor performance, its failures and mistakes, is as far beyond the reach of my mastery as its dead sister, yesterday. It is a day of God's. Its sun will rise in roseate splendor, or behind a mask of weeping clouds. But it will rise. Until then, the same love and patience that held yesterday will hold tomorrow, shining with tender promise into the heart of today. I have no possession in that unborn day of grace. All else is in the safekeeping of the Infinite Love that holds for me the treasure of yesterday. The love that is higher than the stars, wider than the skies, deeper than the seas. Tomorrow...it is God's day. It will be mine.

There is left for myself then but one day of the week...today. A man can fight the battles of today. Any woman can carry the burden of just one day. Any man can resist the temptations of today. Oh friend, it is only when to the burdens and cares of today, carefully measured out to us by the Infinite Wisdom and Might that gives them with the promise "as thy day so shall thy strength be," we add the burden of those two awful eternities, yesterday and tomorrow, such burdens as only the Mighty God can sustain, that we break down. It isn't the experience of today that drives men mad. It is remorse for something that happened yesterday or the dread of what tomorrow may disclose. Those are God's days. Leave them with Him.

Therefore, I think, and I do, and I journey but one day at a time. That is the easy day. That is the man's day. Nay, rather, that is our day…God's and mine. And while faithfully and dutifully I run my course, and work my appointed task on that day of ours, God the Almighty and the All-loving takes care of yesterday and tomorrow.

Now the Preacher Is Dead

THIS PREACHER I knew was food to have around. He wasn't such an outstanding man. Nevertheless, people knew he was around. He was often the conversation piece of the community. Sunday dinner seemed to taste better if he was on the burner. And they usually cooked him tender.

But he was handy to have around. When there was a problem in the church, he was a good hanger to hang it on. He was accused when things didn't go smoothly. If the church didn't grow—he was to blame. If the youth didn't turn out as expected—it was the preacher. If anyone slept during the worship service—it was the preacher's fault. If attendance was poor—well, who wants to hear him? If someone backslid and left—he chased them away. When there was a community problem—he was often used to hang the blame on.

So he was handy to have around. Folks with personal problems, church problems, and neighbor problems could use the convenience of hanging him with the blame. No question about it, he was a person, and caused some of the irritations. But it seemed strange that he should be caught with the blame for everyone's problems. But then it is convenient to justify your sin by blaming the preacher and walking away.

The phone rang. I answered. The word—he died. Now the preacher is dead. A large crowd gathered to pay respect. Blaming was turned to tears. People were talking of this wonderful person. He was given a first-class service by the ministers in charge, who gave him top rating. He was classed a man of faith. He was a man of high principles, based on the Word of God. We edged close for the final word at the graveside and a final look of deep respect before his body was covered with six feet of earth.

Well, what a relief. The preacher is now six feet under. The church should move smoothly and grow. Youth problems should be over. Personal problems should be solved.

It has been many moons ago that he died. And how are the people doing? About the same. The problems are still there. He is dead and six feet under, but the problems are above ground and very much alive.

So here we are. We haven't learned what to do with our problems and conflicts. We tried to hang them on the preacher. That served as a pacifier till he died. We can no longer use him—so what do we do?

What lessons can we learn from this? First, if there is a conflict and a problem, chances are the real cause is standing in your tracks. Second, hanging problems on others is a childish way of attempting to solve them. Third, pushing blame is no answer at all. Fourth, blaming others fuels the situation and causes it to spread and soon infect the entire group. Fifth, taking a final look at a friend in his coffin that you've been blaming doesn't feel like a clear conscience and a happy way to face the future. Finally, problems are to be solved, settled, and confessed, but never pushed around and hung on someone else.

Blaming the preacher is an all too familiar game to many Christians. We get involved in this sinful game for a bit of self-justification to haze out our faults. Paul instructs the Christian to "put them in mind...to speak evil of no man" (Titus 3:1, 2). I find it difficult to push the blame of my irritation on someone else without speaking evil of him. But Jesus takes the case even further. If a man uses you absolutely wrong, you are to "love him" (Matt. 5:44).

So who do we blame if we are restless inside? Blame the preacher? Not if you want peace. To discover a peace that "passeth all understanding," put the blame where it is most likely to be—right where you are. You can start changing yourself and your attitudes right now. But you'll have a job on your hands to change the other person to your liking. The Bible has an answer that works for a starter to resolve problems and conflicts. "Confess your faults one to another" (James 5:16). We hear a lot of confessing, but seldom the right one—our own. Imagine what would happen if we confessed a personal fault each time we blamed another person. This is a recipe we would do well to discover. Only with a clean slate are we entitled to blame someone else. And with a clean slate we'll give up doing that.

Who are you blaming for your problems? The person you are blaming may die, then what will you do? Really now, let us be Christians. Confess it to Christ; He is the irritation absorber. Then confess it to the other one involved, as the Bible instructs. Leave it with Christ. Move out of your hang-up. Move on to helping others and the church.

Life is too short to waste it blaming others. Christ's forgiveness offers perfect release from irritations and problems, but we must recognize them and take them to Him. In fact, that is what He died for. So we can put our problems on Him and not hang them on others—who offer no forgiveness anyway.

So who are you going to blame when you have "had it"? That is really up to you, but if you hang it on the preacher, he may die, leaving you stuck with your hang-up.

Are You Blessed?

If you own just one Bible, you are abundantly blessed. One third of all the world does not have access to one.

If you woke up this morning with more health than illness, you are more blessed than the million who will not survive this week.

If you have never experienced the danger of battle, the loneliness of imprisonment, the agony of torture, or the pangs of starvation, you are ahead of 500 million people in the world.

If you can attend a church meeting without fear of harassment, arrest, torture, or death, you are more blessed than three billion people in the world.

If you have food in the refrigerator, clothes on your back, a roof overhead, and a place to sleep, you are richer than 75% of this world.

If you have money in the bank, in your wallet, and spare change someplace, you are among the top 8% of the world's wealthy.

If your parents are still alive and still married, you are very rare, even in the United States.

If you hold up your head with a smile on your face and are truly thankful, you are blessed because the majority can, but most do not.

If you can hold someone's hand, hug them, or even touch them on the shoulder, you are blessed because you can offer God's healing touch.

If you prayed yesterday and today, you are in the minority, because you believe God does hear and answer prayers.

If you can read this message, you are more blessed than over 2 billion people in the world who cannot read at all.

Is Friendliness Next to Godliness?

People don't go to the sanctuary just to be inspired by the sermon or singing; they go first in search of a sincere smile that might warm a cold world.

CHARLOTTE, N.C.—You think faith is a mystery? Try figuring out why some congregations ooze warmth while others are colder than an empty sanctuary with the windows open in January.

I've been to some houses of worship where I could barely get to my car after the closing hymn for all the genuine handshakes and hugs.

Then I've been to others with special parking for visitors, greeters at the door, a smiling preacher on the pulpit, and the passing of the peace during worship. That's a fancy phrase for taking a minute to say hey to the person in the next pew. But even after all that manufactured geniality, I still went home with a lonely feeling in the pit of my soul.

Why does one sanctuary wrap its arms around a stranger and another pushes him away? Is it because some people are basically cold fish when they arrive for a service? Or do they come with outgoing intentions, only to have the good cheer sucked out of them by a distant pastor, snobby congregation...

I have a theory or two.

A new national survey confirms what I've long thought about the connection between faith and friendship. A lot of folks don't go to the sanctuary just to be inspired by the sermon or singing. They go first in search of a sincere smile that might warm a cold world.

The Gallup survey, to be included in a "Friendship First" church guide set for release in June, found that friendships are key to the growth and success of a congregation.

The survey found that among those who describe their church as "very friendly," 98 percent said they are very or somewhat satisfied with their membership. Among those who say their best friend attends their church,

87 percent said they are very satisfied.

The survey tells us much of what we know. We are drawn to a friendly experience. It gives us examples of friendship in action: sharing meals, for example, and making friends through children's church activities. But it doesn't take much of a stab at why this congregation smiles and that one frowns, so I'll offer three observations:

The more diverse the congregation, the friendlier the folks. I get more smiles in sanctuaries that are home to people of more than one color, culture, and economic class. They love welcoming new and different worshipers and aren't afraid to show it. I've walked into a church or two where everyone looks and dresses alike and felt like I've crashed the wrong party.

The more evangelical-minded the congregation, the friendlier the folks. If a believer lives to spread his faith, he's going to start with a smile. I've been to some Pentecostal services where they all but lined up to meet me.

The newer the congregation, the friendlier the folks. There's an enthusiasm there that time hasn't eroded. I've been to some 150-year-old houses of worship with the freshness of seemingly being born yesterday. But I've been to others that appear to have succumbed to time.

One final thought:

Name tags, greeters, and passing the peace are fine. But if you don't mean it—truly mean it—drop the friendly act.

"As Months Go By"

You may think we have forgotten
When you see a smile we wear,
But underneath there is a heartache,
Only God knows it is there.

You may think we are adjusting
To his absence in our home,
Still, there are days we keenly miss him.
And the longing tears will come.

You may think we'd stop to miss him
As the time goes marching on,
But sometimes we still are wondering,
"Is our brother really gone?"

You may think that time is healing,
So it is, but still we weep,
Wishing we could see our brother,
Oh, the longing goes so deep!

You may think our tears are over,
But they're flowing where God can see,
Longing hearts still broken, bleeding,
We're still grieving silently.

You may think we have forgotten
When you see us traveling on.
But we trust and hope to meet him
At the setting of life's sun....

AN AMERICAN BUSINESSMAN was at the pier of a tiny coastal Mexican village when a small boat with just one fisherman came in. Inside the boat were several large yellow-fin tuna. The American complimented the fisherman on the quality of the fish and asked how long it took to catch them.

The fisherman replied that it took just a little while.

The American then asked why he didn't stay out and catch more fish, to which the fisherman replied that he had enough to support the family's needs.

"But what do you do with the rest of your time?" asked the American.

"I sleep late, fish a little, play with my children, take siestas, stroll into the village each evening to relax, and sing with my amigos," answered the fisherman.

The American scoffed. "You should spend more time fishing and with the proceeds buy a bigger boat. Eventually you could buy several boats and end up with a fleet. Instead of selling your catch to the middleman, you could go directly to the processor, and eventually open your own cannery. You could control the product, as well as processing and distribution. You would need to leave this village and move to Mexico City and even on to the States."

"But what then?" asked the fisherman.

The American laughed and said, "That's the best part. When the time is right you would announce an IPO and sell your company stock to the public and become very rich. You would make millions."

"Millions?" the surprised fisherman said. "Then what?"

"Then you could retire, move to a tiny coastal village where you could sleep late, fish a little, play with your grandchildren, take siestas, stroll to the village in the evenings where you could relax, and sing with your amigos!"

Note that he said, "Play with your grandchildren."

The Bravest Thing

Many people envy heroes,
And think them brave and fine.
They say, "I wish adventure
Would walk this path of mine."

But really, you're a hero
If you can only sing
And see a little bit of good
In every living thing.

If you can pray to God above
With faith within your heart,
And if, in simple living,
You can only do your part.

You truly are a hero
If you can laugh and smile,
And make somebody happy
For just a little while.

If you can do a little good
To help this world along,
The bravest thing that you can do
Is smile when things go wrong.

—Author Unknown

Light in the Shadow of Death

'Twas a new-made grave, a mound of earth,
On the hillside…cold and stark;
The sod was rent in a gaping wound,
And the clouds hung low and dark.

Winter came and the snow fell soft,
And covered the earth so bare;
Though hidden under a blanket white,
Still the wound in the earth was there.

But spring came gently, the sun shone warm
And called out each grass and flower,
The broken sod began to respond,
To the touch of nature's power.

The showers of summer caressed the hills,
And the bird song swelled with mirth,
The breeze blew warm and the grass reached out,
To cover the wound in the earth.

Fall came again, some time had passed,
And I knelt there on the ground;
I saw how the broken sod was healed,
For the grass had covered the mound.

Yes, one dark day there we stood,
So filled with grief and pain;
For this dear one was gone, yes, gone.
Our lonely hearts were rent in twain.

We turned away, we tried to smile,
Though the hurt was hard to bear;
Behind each smile, wherever we went,
The wound in our hearts was there.

But the warmth of God's love reached deep within
And helped us again to stand;
And the broken hearts began to respond,
To the touch of the Master's hand.

He binds our wounds with His love and care,
His sympathy eases the pain;
And we must say, "Thy will be done."
And climb to healing again.

As God, through time, lets the grasses grow,
To cover the wounded sod;
So His love brings peace to the wounded heart,
It is healed by the touch of God.

Only Today

Help me to place in Thy hands today...
The thing that my heart most fears,
Tomorrow's anguish and bitter pain—
Tomorrow's sorrow and tears,
The long, long years, and the loneliness,
The silence, the vacant chair,
The grief of today is enough, dear Lord,
But tomorrow's I cannot bear!

Ease thou my burden and lighten my load,
  Until only today is left.......
Still comes His voice in the hush of my soul,
  "Oh, broken heart and bereft,
My grace is sufficient for you TODAY;
  Pillow upon my breast—
Thy weary head, in my circling arms,
  Today thou shalt find rest.

"Today I can meet thine every need,
  Today my love can fill...
The echoing chambers of thy heart,
  Then rest there and be still;
Be still and trust—tomorrow's tears—
  May all be wiped away....
By God Himself. Oh, grieving heart,
  Thy Lord may come today!"

I'm Free

Don't grieve for me, for now I'm free,
I'm following the path God laid for me.
I took His hand when I heard Him call;
I turned my back and left it all.

I could not stay another day
To laugh, to love, to work or play.
Tasks left undone must stay that way.
I found that place at the close of day.

If my parting has left a void
Then fill it with remembered joy.
A friendship shared, a laugh, a kiss;
Ah yes, these things, I too will miss.
Be not burdened with times of sorrow.
I wish you the sunshine of tomorrow,
My life's been full, I savored much.
Good friends, good times, a loved one's touch.

Perhaps my time seemed all too brief;
Don't lengthen it now with undue grief.
Lift up your heart and share with me
God wanted me now, He set me free.

To All Parents

"I'll lend you for a little time a child of Mine," He said,
    "For you to love the while he lives and mourn for when he's dead.
It may be six or seven years, or twenty-two or three,
    But will you, till I call him back, take care of him for Me?
He'll bring his charms to gladden you, and shall his stay be brief,
    You'll have his lovely memories as solace for your grief.

"I cannot promise he will stay, since all from earth return,
    But there are lessons taught down there I want this child to learn.
I've looked the wide world over in my search for teachers true,
    And from the throngs that crowd life's lanes, I have selected you.
Now will you give him all your love, nor think the labor vain,
    Nor hate Me when I come to call to take him back again?"

I fancied that I heard them say, "Dear Lord, Thy will be done!
    For all the joy Thy child shall bring, the risk of grief we'll run.
We'll shelter him with tenderness, we'll love him while we may,
    And for the happiness we've known, forever grateful stay;
But shall the angels call him much sooner than we've planned,
    We'll brave the bitter grief that comes and try to understand."

You Never Know When Your Time's Up

RECENTLY, A FRIEND passed away at the age of 22. He was the third person that I knew who had passed away this year, and all three were young men in their early to mid-twenties. When people as young as these depart from this world, their untimely deaths cause one to reflect upon life and the true meaning thereof.

Money, cars, and luxurious houses mean very little to someone who has either passed away or is on his deathbed. It's rather ironic how some people spend their whole lives trying to attain as much wealth and material possessions as they can, only to be faced with the reality that we come into this world with nothing and that is exactly the way we will leave this world.

Many people squander their time, energy, and efforts upon things that really do not mean anything in the grand scheme of life. When push comes to shove, the only things that really matter in life are people.

We as humans should spend a lot more time and energy in helping others and caring about others rather than pursuing the almighty dollar. Take a look at those who pursue money and material wealth all their lives and compare those individuals with those who attempt to help others.

Those who help others will undoubtedly embody a happiness that is not present with seekers of riches. Likewise, those who seek to lend a hand to others will also leave an indelible mark upon others, an achievement that money-hungry individuals are not able to claim.

Living life to its fullest is another lesson that should be learned from the passing of a young individual. Don't breeze through life merely going through the motions. Live! We never know which day is our last, so we should live each day to the fullest. Even if one lives to be 100 years old, within his life span there will be many things that he has not experienced or seen.

Do something that you have never done before. Hang out or befriend someone who is out of the normal realm of your friends and/or comfort zone. Don't pass on a chance to do something new, for that may be the last time that the opportunity presents itself.

Sometimes the things we fear or shy away from can become our passions if we will jump over the hurdle of fear and truly embrace a new experience.

Along with the fact that one never knows which day is his last here on earth, no one knows when another's last day here on earth will take place. Therefore, we need to forgive one another. Time spent hating or being angry with someone is time that is wasted. And most of the time, the individual that is angry is the only one that is affected by the situation.

Forgiving someone, while very hard to do at times, can lead to a wonderful relationship between two individuals, whether it be friendship or romance. The reason being, if someone is forgiven of something truly "horrible," how much then does the individual that forgave care for the one that committed the act?

When one person forgives another, there is also a sense of gratitude from the one who was forgiven, and so there should be. This gratitude in turn leads to compassion for the forgiver. A wonderful cycle of love, compassion, and forgiveness is thus set into motion; this is far greater than a cycle of anger, hatred, and lashing out.

The passing of these human beings has bought more clarity and insight regarding my concern for others. The love and care that I already have for those individuals in my life that I cherish has been deepened and I am gaining more concern for others that are in my life as well.

If an individual accomplishes nothing more in life than to have people say when he is dead, "That guy really cared about people," then that individual's time here on earth was well spent.

Clay Balls

A MAN WAS exploring caves by the seashore. In one of the caves he found a canvas bag with a bunch of hardened clay balls. It was like someone had rolled clay balls and left them out in the sun to bake.

They didn't look like very much, but they intrigued the man, so he took the bag out of the cave with him. As he strolled along the beach, he would throw clay balls one at a time out into the ocean as far as he could.

He thought little about it until he dropped one of the clay balls and it cracked open on a rock. Inside was a beautiful, precious stone!

Excited, the man started breaking open the remaining clay balls. Each contained a similar treasure. He found thousands of dollars' worth of jewels in the twenty or so clay balls he had left. Then it struck him.

He had been on the beach a long time. He had thrown maybe fifty or sixty of the clay balls with their hidden treasures into the ocean waves. Instead of thousands of dollars in treasure, he could have taken home tens of thousands, but he had just thrown it away!

It's like that with people. We look at someone, maybe even ourselves, and we see the external clay vessel. It doesn't look like much from the outside. It isn't always beautiful or sparkling, so we discount it.

We see that person as less important than someone more beautiful or stylish or well known or wealthy; but we have not taken the time to find the treasure hidden inside that person.

There is a treasure in each and every one of us. If we take the time to get to know that person, and if we ask God to show us that person the way He sees them, then the clay begins to peel away and the brilliant gem begins to shine forth.

May we not come to the end of our lives and find out that we have thrown away a fortune in friendships because the gems were hidden in bits of clay. May we see the people in our world as God sees them.

I am so blessed by the gems of friendship I have with each of you.

Thank you for looking beyond my clay vessel.

—A clay ball

Take Your Time

The one phrase we hear more than any other is, "It'll take time for you to get over your child's death." We know that this is spoken with care and love. But little do we know at the beginning of our grief just what time means—the first time, the daytime, the nighttime, the last time, all of these times. The one thing we can say is "take it." Take all the time you need. Grief is hard work and we need to take the time for all of the aspects we talk so much about and really work through it.

Take the time to feel; it's hard but worth it. We can't just push those feelings aside, because they are part of who we are, how we've managed, and the life we've had. All of our life experiences combine to affect our feelings.

Take the time to talk. Talk to anyone who seems to care about you. Ask friends and family if they will take the time to listen.

Take the time to read. When you read the experiences of others, you will realize that you're not alone. Maybe a special book will help you understand what is happening to you during this time we call bereavement. Take the time to read and reread the paragraphs or chapters that help.

Take the time to physically take care of yourself. If you like to walk, jog, or run, go out and use that time to make you feel better. Get enough rest, take the time to sleep late some days, or go to bed earlier if you need to. Sleeping may be an escape, but if it helps you, take the time for an extra few hours. Take care of yourself by eating better. Try to understand that food gives you some energy and that food helps to satisfy unmet needs. Food is always better for you than drugs or alcohol and a small weight gain or loss is not unusual. Take the time to understand what is happening to your body.

Take the time to be angry or guilty without letting these feelings ruin your life. You may think that your life is ruined anyhow and who cares, but anger and guilt turned inward can destroy your self-esteem faster than anything. Take time to sort through these feelings and acknowledge them, then let them go. Know that when someone says, "It'll take time," we can nod and try to accept that part of our getting through these days, months, and years.

Remember that someday you will take time to help someone else and that time will be the most satisfying time of all.

Old Friends

There are no friends like the old friends
And none so good and true;
We greet them when we meet them
As roses greet the dew.
No other friends are dearer
Though born of kindred mold,
And while we prize the new ones,
We treasure more the old.
There are no friends like old friends,
Wherever we dwell or roam,
In lands beyond the ocean
Or near the bounds of home,
And when they smile to gladden
Or sometimes frown to guide,
We fondly wish those old friends
Were always by our side.
There are no friends like old friends,
To help us with the load

That all must bear who journey
O'er life's uneven road.
And when unconquered sorrows
The weary hours invest,
The kindly words of old friends
Are always found the best.
There are no friends like old friends,
To calm our frequent fears
When shadows fall and deepen
Through life's declining years,
And when our faltering footsteps
Approach the Great Divide,
We'll long to meet the old friends
Who wait on the Other Side.

Thoughts to ponder... Those who see God's hand in everything can best leave everything in God's hand.

Some don't know what happiness is until it's gone.

How a Father Treated His Wayward Son
—*Luke 15:11-32*

When children go astray, parents can either help or aggravate the situation. In Jesus' parable of the prodigal son, we find principles to help us react redemptively when faced with a wayward child.

1. The father in the parable did *not disown* his son. There is no trace of anger and retaliation. The father simply *kept* on *loving* his son.

2. The father did not allow himself to *be overcome* with *despair*. Some parents fall apart when a son or daughter goes astray. But the father in the parable went on with his living. *He didn't allow a wayward son to ruin his life.*

3. The father did not chase his son. Overzealous parents can push their children farther away by hounding them. The father allowed his son the *freedom* to go and *to choose* a different lifestyle.

4. The father did not withhold material goods from his son. When the son asked for his share of the father's wealth, the father freely gave it. This stands in contrast to those fathers who pull back and say, "Well, since you've decided to adopt a different lifestyle than I want for you, you can't have anything of mine." It's tempting to control behavior by material means.

5. The *father never gave up hope*. In verse 20 we see the father *looking for* the *return* of his son. Through it all, he *kept believing* in his son—that he would someday come to his senses and return.

6. There is *no evidence* that the father said anything such as, *"I told you so."* He didn't throw his son's mistakes back in his face. He freely forgave his son and welcomed him back.

7. The father involved others in celebrating the son's return. This suggests to me that he had also shared his concern with them earlier. *Parents need* the *support* of others when suffering the hurts of a wayward child.

In this parable, we see a picture of our Heavenly Father. And, of course, here is where we find our example of how to deal with sons or daughters who disappoint us. *We love them* and accept them (not their deeds) just as our Father loves and accepts us. *(He hates the sin but loves the sinner.)*

Choose Life

"Choose to love the Lord your God and to obey Him and to cling to Him, for He is your life…!" (Deuteronomy 30:20)

ALL OF THE great people in the Bible were possibility thinkers. Oh, they were realists—they knew what it was to be discouraged, depressed, or on the verge of defeat. But they were great because even in the midst of their troubles, they chose to turn their attention to God's beautiful possibilities for their todays.

Even Jeremiah, the weeping prophet, in the depths of great depression finally chose to focus on God's great love. When he did, his depression left him (read Lamentations 3:1-24). He chose to look at God's possibilities rather than pay attention to the negative forces surrounding him.

Are you troubled today? Do you feel that life is closing in on you and there is no way to escape? Don't let your mind dwell on negative thoughts. Choose life! Believe in God's ability to overcome the troubles and give you a great and exciting today and tomorrow. God's message for you is, "I know the plans I have for you… plans for good and not for evil, to give you a future and a hope." (Jeremiah 29:11)

I am choosing life—God's life. Therefore I have nothing to fear.

Passing

—by Sharon Eby

"MY GRANDMOTHER PASSED yesterday," a friend informed me. I was a little startled at her expression, "She passed." She didn't say, "She passed away," just, "She passed." Kathy had told me last week that her elderly grandmother was seriously ill and didn't have much longer to live. I knew she meant her grandmother had died.

I pondered her unusual wording. I remembered my school days. One major concern on the last day of school was, "Did I pass?" And then, my friends asked, "Did you pass?"

I'm used to hearing people say, "She passed away" or "He died." That sounds so final, so end-of-the-road. Death is not final. Death is not the end for the Christian, but really a new beginning. Just the beginning of a whole new life, an eternal life.

Oh, we miss those loved ones who are no longer here. Their life on earth is finished. They have passed from a life of pain and sorrow to a life of unmarred joy and perfect peace. They have passed the tests of life and received an incorruptible crown. Doesn't it ease our grief to think of it this way: "Our loved one has passed?"

Grief...
A Tangled "Ball" of Emotions

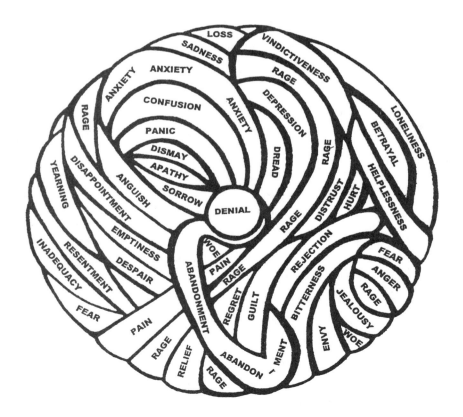

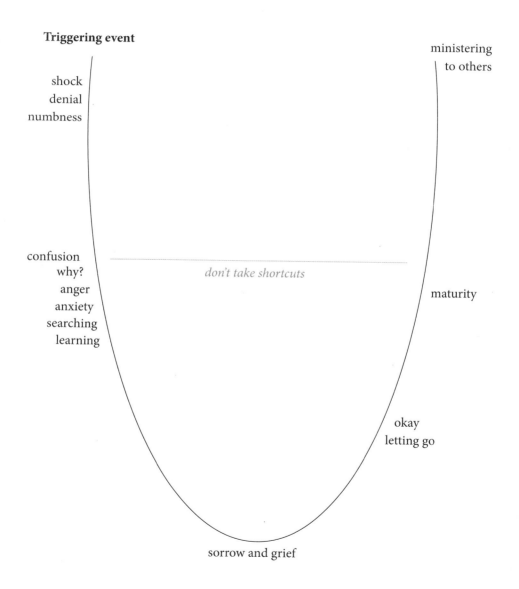

Triggering event

shock
denial
numbness

ministering
to others

confusion
why?
anger
anxiety
searching
learning

don't take shortcuts

maturity

okay
letting go

sorrow and grief

The "Accident" in Wyoming

In memory of Mervin Jay Beiler, age 23 years, five months, died February 28, 2005

SON MERVIN DECIDED to take a three-week vacation to the snow slopes in Utah and Wyoming. Sometimes I think maybe I should have discouraged it, but I knew how much he enjoyed the outdoors. Also, I could always trust and have a good feeling in what he did, so I'll try to write some things that come to mind. No, Mervin was not a perfect child, but left lots of good examples back. I always used to think Father and Mother are supposed to raise their children, but many a time I was listening and learning from Mervin. No, he never said it to hurt me, but he would correct me sometimes in a roundabout way. I thank God we could have him for those very, very short 23 years. Also, thanks to all those who helped in any way (church folks, ministers, etc.) to have Mervin baptized into the church. Mervin came the summer before the accident nine times and these words were said: "My wish is to make peace with God and the church." "Praise the Lord!"

The two boys, Mervin, 23, and Gideon, 20, went on vacation in February 2005, Mervin heading for the West and Gideon going to Florida. Friday night after they were gone, I called both boys from the market to say good-bye. Gideon was in Florida and Mervin was just getting on his trip.

I told them I didn't say good-bye and Mervin said, "Well! You weren't at home!" So we said our good-byes by phone and I said, "Be good and have a good trip."

So the children and my wife called off and on during Mervin's trip. He also left a message saying everything is all right and how nice it is out there; a precious message. Wednesday before he died, he left a message that I was to call as soon as I got the message. I had promised the two boys a western elk hunt, and when he left me the message, they were very close to Afton, WY, where I was planning on taking them. I had been there a couple times years back and remembered so well the hunts with horses way up in the mountains and those are memories I wanted with the boys. But God had other plans!

Anyway, I soon called Mervin back. They were climbing a mountain and reception on the car phone was not very good. I still remember very well we said, "Can you hear me? Are you there?" Then, "Yeah, now I hear you!" etc. Soon they were above the clouds and Mervin made the remark that he would just like to walk right out over those clouds. Well, soon we talked some again and I could follow where they were coming from, south on, I think, route 89 into Afton, WY. I asked him if he sees these cabins on his right just before the town. He said, "Oh yes! There they are!" Then I asked if the horse corral is still there. This was not a first for Mervin in this town. We had gone West about six or seven years ago with the whole family. Oh, those are such precious memories.

Off and on we lost each other on the phone, so we would call again, four times in all. I think the third call I said they are coming up to a good restaurant at the big elk arch over the street in Afton. So I told him to go and get the phone number of the restaurant and let me know the number. I was acting like I wanted to get more information on hunting, but what I wanted to do is then call the restaurant and ask if there are five young boys there at a table. I was going to tell their waitress that when they come to pay, that she should tell them it's all paid. Oh, how I wish I could have done that now, but no, it didn't happen because Mervin never called back with the number, as he had no idea, I'm sure, what I wanted with that number.

Anyway, I sat at the phone for quite a while, maybe a half hour, waiting for his call back. Finally, I decided to call him again, our fourth call, and ask him where they are. In that time, I had talked to a hunting guide and he said, "Tell your son to stop in or call." Well, I told Mervin to stop in, but by then they were a few miles out of town, heading for Jackson Hole, WY. So I gave Mervin the number and we had our last byes. We were talking about the weather and so on. The last words I heard from him went kind of like this on the telephone:

Mervin: "*Dad, there's about two to three feet of snow and it's just real clear, not a cloud in the sky.*"

Dad: "*Wow, I would like to be there.*"

Mervin: "*Yeah, well it's just beautiful out here.*"

Dad: "*OK. Have a good trip.*"

Mervin: "*See ya.*"

Dad: "*See ya.*"

I can now think he might be saying, "Dad, it's just beautiful 'up' here." Oh, how my heart aches as I write this, but I want to say, "Thy will be done." Found out since that he did call that guide in Afton and chatted for a while.

Well, now a little bit about the Sunday before, a day I will never forget. It was a very special Sunday for me, also our church Sunday. Yeah, it was my birthday, number 52, and just an extra good and special day. It seemed all the church people and everybody was so happy. We had preachers from our other district and I remember the one preacher saying if we forget everything else about this day, remember this—it was in Dutch of course but meant, "Evil words bring bad thoughts." Oh, how true! Those words just come to me so often since the accident. Also, thanks to the church people and, oh yeah, neighbors for making that day special. Neighbors were here for a birthday party for me Sunday night. Thanks!

Monday morning came with the forecast calling for snow. About 12:30 p.m., it started snowing. This was the exact time that Mervin had his accident. Oh my, the newspaper said it was an "accident," but no, no, I cannot make myself believe that it was an accident. God makes no mistakes! The words of encouragement and prayer I cannot explain. Someone said we can look at it that just when it started snowing, Mervin died. Yeah, he wasn't perfect, but I think maybe the snow came just to cover the whole thing in pure white, the earth and hopefully his sins, because we all have sins and come short. What a beautiful thought. Also, just at that time, our daughter Esther jumped up and thought of Mervin and heaven. Well this was 10:30 in Wyoming and 12:30 in Pennsylvania. Yeah, it still went five hours until we found out here in Pennsylvania.

Back a little to Sunday night; the boys said it was an extra special night. Mervin made a habit of reading from his Bible or Bible story book every day. They said he was reading at the motel, and how I wonder what he read that last night. They all got ready Monday morning to go snowmobiling for the day. I also wonder sometimes if Mervin might have known. His friends said he slipped on the ice and said, "Whoa! What's going on here?" Then he didn't say anything for a little bit, then said to one of his friends, "What if those would have been my last words?" His friends never gave a thought to how soon after that his last words would be spoken.

Off they went, the five of them, Mervin having the map and heading for a beautiful lookout way out in the wilderness. Well, Mervin was in the lead for about 30 miles, and then they stopped. His hands were getting cold, so someone asked him to look at the map and which way do we go? Mervin, looking at the map with all different trails marked, said, "We want to take Trail A." Those were the last words our precious son spoke here on this earth that anybody could hear. I like to think he and God had a conversation in those next few minutes. So off they go and for the first time, Mervin being on the end.

Also, after going that far, the trails were starting to be too easy, I guess, and they were going off the trails sometimes. Two of his friends got off the trail and came to this little knob, at least it looked little from their side. It had an eight- to ten-foot drop on the other side. The first one across made it, but thought, "I hope no one else takes this." Here came another sled and the front of the sled went into fresh powder, snow sticking almost straight up and the driver flew about 10 or 12 feet past. Two of the boys were there right away. His very good friend, David Smucker, said he thought, "I hope Mervin doesn't take that exact path. I must stop him." Thinking he should quickly go up to the knob and wave him off, here comes Mervin on the exact same trail. He said he was leaning back a little and his landing would have been almost perfect. Flying through the air within inches of the upright sled, he landed in the powdery snow and crash! right onto the bottom of the upright sled and probably broke his neck and had some internal injuries. The boys were there right away and checked for a pulse. It was over. One of his friends said, "Let's pray!" His friends held hands and were praying, "Our Father, which art in Heaven. . . " When about halfway through, Mervin let out a pocket of air and then that was all. He was still sitting on his sled, and the boys decided they didn't want to leave him in that position, so they got him and laid him out real nice on the snow. Pray for his friends!

One of the boys went for help and the others spent about a half hour alone before another group of snowmobiles came. Can we even for a little bit imagine how this was for his friends? Pray for them. One of his friends said he still has such a nice picture in his mind of Mervin, coming over that hill with a big smile on his face. Also, thanks again for all the words of encouragement. Someone said he can just think like this: Mervin never even hit that other sled, but just kept flying through the air and is still flying like an angel. Oh, what a nice thought. "Safe in the arms of Jesus."

After I guess about one-and-a-half hours or so, the first rescue people came, but no, it was finished. Then a helicopter was dispatched, but never came all the way out into the wilderness. After another hour or so, investigators came. After all was done, Mervin was loaded up for the long ride back on a stretcher or a sled.

Now, by Monday evening, February 28, we were eating supper and just finished. Some of the girls were washing dishes, two of the girls were singing at the table, and I was on my old easy chair. The door burst open and, screaming and all, our son-in-law and his wife, our Lydia Jane, tried to tell us what happened. It took a little while, as they were in complete shock. For about a minute, I thought it was little baby Michael that had died. After a while, something about a snowmobile came out, and yes, it's your son, our brother, who was killed in a snowmobile accident. Oh my, we all just cried and cried and I just thought somebody has to come. I got myself together and went to the phone and tried to call Mom. No answer, so I tried to call my oldest brother. Oh yes, he answered, and I said, "Come please, right away. Mervin was killed." His words were, "We will be right there." It seemed very long till someone came. But as the house started filling up with church people, friends, and most of all, Mom, brothers, sisters, and family, it seemed the burden was made a little more easy. Oh, the tears just flow as I write this, but we want to give ourselves up to the Lord. Sometimes I just think, no, this is all a big dream.

My thoughts just kept going to Florida, where our only living son was. He started home within a couple hours with lots of his friends. A long, long ride home, I'm sure. I will never forget how nice it was to see him the next day, I think around 1 p.m.

Now it was, call the funeral home. When can Mervin come home? Well, we were told maybe Wednesday. This was Monday. I remember thinking, "Not that long, please." Oh, it seemed so far away. But, oh my, the next day the funeral director said, "No, you cannot expect Mervin till Thursday around noon." Oh, I just cried and cried. "No, please," I said. "Is there any way that money can buy a plane ticket or something to get him here?" But "No," he said, "there is nothing we can do. I'm so sorry!" I remember thinking that's not tomorrow, but the next day. How am I going to make this?

Again, the prayers from those we love could be felt. Lots of friends were in and out. Words can never thank you all enough. Lots and lots of people, and no, not once did I think, "Go away." I was so glad for you all. And yes, all you young folks will never know what it meant to have you here with us. Thank you! Never did I appreciate "quiet" and stillness as much as over the viewing and funeral. So many times the house was just full of people and so, so quiet. Thank you. Yes, it is not a place to just visit and visit. Many, many people said, "Oh, Aaron, I just don't know what to say." I said to them, "You just said it when you came through that door." Thank you for your support.

Well, Thursday morning finally came, and yes, brother Mervin said, "Your son Mervin is here." Oh my, I could hardly wait to see him and helped bring his casket in. Oh my, never, never did I think how this would be. Mervin leaving so healthy and it seemed like his whole life was ahead of him, and now we are carrying him into the house in a casket. Lord, help me; give me strength to go on. Please! We waited till we were all together, and oh my, so peaceful and beautiful he looked, lying there in front of us. Our once-healthy and so strong son just looked like he could talk, he looked so natural. Well, that was a big page turned for me to actually see him. Yes, Lord, help me, this is true, right? I just could hardly leave the casket. I just wanted every minute I could to be with him, because I thought, "Oh, no! Tomorrow we must take him and put him in the cold, dark earth." Yes, that's tomorrow. Oh my, I could not sleep much that whole week, but did rest some at night. I got up very early Friday morning, the day of the funeral, and went into the room where Mervin was. For over an hour, I was reading and crying, trying to really believe this is true. I will cherish those couple hours that morning forever. Dark, peaceful morning. After a while, I just wanted to talk to someone, so I woke my brother-in-law and we sat with Mervin and just talked. I will remember those hours and cherish them.

Well, all too soon, morning came and people started coming for the funeral. The house was set up for the small funeral and the barn for the big funeral. Never in my life did the words spoken by the ministers sink in and make an impact on my life like this. I truly hope through this I can be a better person, and yes, hopefully can be where Mervin is someday.

After the funeral, the boys carried him out of our barn for the last time. Oh my, Lord, help me to give myself up to this. Out the lane we went, having number one written on the side of our carriage. I thought of so many times when we would wish to be number one, but no, not now. This was one time when I would not have picked to be number one. Up the road to the cemetery, just about one mile from here, we went. There were 57 teams (buggies) and lots of people at the graveyard. Now we had our chance to see Mervin one more time before he would be forever gone in that deep, dark grave. I will probably always hear that first shovelful of dirt being put down, even though it made hardly any noise. Shovelful after shovelful of dirt went down into that hole, and more and more, we knew this was the end. Afterwards, I just kept looking up in the sky and slowly, ever so slowly, a jet stream disappeared. Now when I see jet streams, I can think of Mervin just floating like an angel up there.

Slowly but surely, we must now go. Back home we went, and oh, the feeling I will never be able to explain. Everything was back in place. Thanks to all who helped! This way of doing over funerals, etc., seems so much more important to me now. Let's keep it up.

This is now one week after Mervin was buried and I'm still thinking, "Was this true?" But yes, I want to give myself up to what God has in store for us. I want to put my trust in Jesus and be faithful and true. We know all things work together for good to them that love the Lord. I don't want to doubt, no, not even for a moment, that the Lord didn't have His hands in this. We know there's hope. Yes, hope. "Come unto me all ye that labour and are heavy laden, and I will give you rest." Do we believe that?

So much more could be written, but my hope is that we can meet someday in that beautiful land up there. A big hole was left in our family, but we still have five girls and one son that are very precious to us. Also, a son-in-law and a little grandson. We will cherish them all. Please pray for us that we may stay strong and someday meet Mervin.

Love to you all.

Psalm 147:11: "The Lord taketh pleasure in them that fear him and in those that hope in his mercy."

—Aaron Beiler

Sudden Deaths

AFTER THE FUNERAL and all the clocks still keep ticking. What lies ahead? I will try and write some things that happen, good and bad, I guess. Oh the heartache! Yes, Mervin, I miss you so much. What I write in the following weeks hopefully can help and most certainly I don't want to hurt someone. Yes, people are here every day. Stop-ins and company every evening. That is a big help to me to have people stop in. Thanks to friends and all who help to make the load lighter. Yes, it's true that Mervin is not here with us anymore.

The first Sunday I think we had 32 families visiting. Church was at Emanuel King's and oh how nice that some of Mervin's friends and Gideon's friends came. Thanks for coming. Yes, we expected some visitors on the minister row for sure, but just one came and that was my brother Wilmer. My, I thought it could not be. It was very, very hard for me at church that day. My, how I missed you, Mervin, when the boys came in. Well, after church we came home to lots of visitors. And, oh yes, all those cards in the mail. There were about an average of 25 per day the first two weeks. I remember in the funeral sermon we heard what an awesome God we have. If all the cards would come in one day the mailbox could not handle them all, and if all the company came in one day we could not find room for them. That's how our God works, always right on time. That next week we had lots of stop-ins, and my, I thought, I just can't get started with anything.

Then, "oh," the shock, just when we thought we were healing some, here come Mary Jane and Curvin, our neighbors, early Sunday morning, March 20th. They came to the door, and we were still in bed. I had heard the sirens about an hour before that. I remember thinking, Are the children home? I could still hear, "Aaron, Mary Ann, are you awake?" I was awake but did not go out to the living room. I started to shake. Mary Ann got up and went out. I pulled the covers up over my ears and thought, No, not something else. After a bit I heard Mary Ann come into the bedroom and, oh my, she said Puffly's Jr. was killed. He was 16 years old. Oh, we just started crying and our neighbors asked, "Do you want us to wait and take you over to Puffly's?" "Yes, we will dress right away and go." Oh my, how we were torn open again. Going in the lane, I thought, How can I go into that house? Slowly I got out of the van. Nobody was around! I went to the door, really shaking, and opened it. Oh my, here was their family, just crying. How we just held on to each other, and cried and cried. We said hardly anything. There was nothing to say. We were there for about 10 or 15 minutes alone with them. My, how those were treasured minutes. Soon people started coming. Puffly and I were just sitting on the couch for a long time. We just kept touching each other. Somehow that made us feel good. We stayed until the house was nearly full, then went home to company. I'm not sure of what happened that day. I was really in a daze. The next couple days were all mixed in my mind. We would go to Pufflys as much as we could. Oh, how our hearts ached for them! The day of the funeral it was raining. Our family was in the house for the small funeral. The men held umbrellas for all the people to go from house to shop. It was really raining. The sermon had so much meaning to us; yes, one of Puffly's neighbors had sort of a vision before all this happened. "He saw people at the graveyard, it was raining, and yes, it was someone at Puffly's, a funeral. At first he thought that must be our Mervin's funeral he's seeing, but there was no snow on the ground. So a few days later the news came that Puffly's Jr. was killed. What was God trying to say? How great is our God. So our Mervin was killed February 28, 2005, and Puffly's Jr. was killed March 20, 2005. My, how we could feel for each other. Together we were going through the struggles. So we kept on, company coming and me trying to stop at Puffly's whenever I could.

Now Sunday morning came again and it was our church Sunday. With heavy hearts we went to church. I saw that there were lots of buggies there when we pulled in. Church was at David Kings. My, oh my, people everywhere. It was a very, very touching thing for me. I was standing there as more people came and soon I knew I must go away. I went down to the other barn and cried and cried. I said I never saw such a big pile of "Love" in my life. I did not feel like there were too many people there at all, it was just "overwhelming". We figured approximately 380 people. Mervin's buddies were almost all there too. Thanks! There were 46 boys that were running around that were extra. There were 38 extra "Fremde" families. Also a total of 17 preachers. The sermons were by Enos Petersheim opening and Melvin Beiler main part. What an interesting day. Thank the Lord. Well, home we went to lots of company. Now could life start to be normal again?

The week went by, and Friday night, April 1, 2005, we had some company. Then about 7:00 brother Jr. came in the door. What could he want? He started out saying something happened in our church! What? He said Elam Fisher was killed. What are you saying? Is this a big, bad dream? No, he said he had an accident. He was with a driver and they ran a stop sign. Elam was killed. Oh, I just cried and cried. I said we must go now! I went and left our company. I remember when I was getting my horse ready I was just crying and crying, uncontrolled crying. How my heart was torn open again. Off we went to Elam Fisher. In our church district again, I thought! How can we handle this? When we got there, there were a few people there, so we tied our horse and slowly, ever so slowly, went into the house. How can we go on? Soon the house started to fill up. This was Friday evening and it was pretty late till everybody went home. I really could hardly see how I could go on. I remember I had not had such a good day that day. Oh, I miss you so, Mervin. Someone asked me if I would come outside at Elam's to talk. I said no, what is there to say? Afterward, I felt bad about that. So we had Elam's funeral, a very large funeral, and yes, life goes on.

Now the last two weeks we had Communion services and all. My, I was missing you so much the last two weeks, Mervin. The morning of "ordnung" church I just had to almost force myself to go to church. Mervin only had the chance once since he joined church to be with us. My, how I hurt when you boys came in that are church members. We were singing the first song and my heart just ached. About the last line of the first song something inside me said sing the next song, "the Lob Lied." Oh no, I kept saying to myself. Suppose I don't make it through. Well, that "still small voice" didn't quit. So yes, I'll try, God, if that's what you want. I got through, but barely, I was so choked up.

It seems now that I'm so, so going downhill. I try to stay on top, but I just slide, slide down. Mervin, where are you? Work has no meaning. It's now almost six weeks that you're gone. What's wrong here? I'm really struggling, Lord. Please help me! I can't seem to sleep and can hardly go. Today, April 9, 2005, please help me, God. I feel so alone. The following is what I wrote, thinking maybe putting it on paper like I sometimes do will help. Please, God, help me. I'm feeling so down. Could you just please help me? Yes, this nameless thing, whatever it is, got me. Put it or take it out of my sight. Well now, maybe I could just hand all my heartaches to you. You promised you will help us if we ask. So I'm asking, Lord, please help me. Yes, already I feel you lift me a little higher. Please don't stop. I need you now. When I get knocked down, lift me up, please. Please help me. Oh, how sweet and beautiful heaven must be. Please help me to realize that you are always near me. Lately you seem so far away. Come closer, come closer, and help me to believe that you are taking care of Mervin. Please help me. We loved him so. If he is with you, take good care of him. Please, Lord, help me. Help me to stay humble, help me to stay strong. I really, really need your help now. I have such an empty feeling in my heart. Help me! Thanks in advance. That was written because I need help and I thought maybe if I put it on paper it will help. Yes, I must get ahold of myself, I know, but my mind is just in a turmoil. How can I go any lower, Lord? You could tell me now it's been a year since Mervin was killed, or say it was just last week, and I would probably believe you. I'm so mixed up! It sure lifts me when I go to the phone and listen to the messages sometimes. I just cry and cry in that phone shack. People are trying so hard to lift us up. All those beautiful songs on the voice mail. So many people would sing on the voice mail and then just hang up. Not to be recognized, just to lift me up. Thanks!

Yes, Mervin, today I thought of you doing the evening prayers. You did it so well. I would just like to hear you do it one more time. If only all of us could go down on our knees one more time and you would do the prayer again. Oh, how nice that would be. Are you Okay? Yes, Mervin, you know last week one day I took your things to the bank. I thought, Oh well, I can do this just; be strong. I was standing there at the teller's window and said, "Jan, here are Mervin's bank things, and can you help me?" She said, "Yes, yes, I'm so sorry." Then I just lost it, thinking I was so strong. My, I just cried real loud, uncontrolled. What's going on here? I went into the back room, and they were all so nice about it. I know the bank people well, and they did not at all make me feel bad. "I'm sorry," I said. "I guess I'm rushing things. I will take care of this later." They said, "We are praying for you." So home I go with a heavy heart but feeling better again after a good cry. Lord, help me. I'm feeling so, oh, I don't know, maybe kind of angry. What's wrong with me? We know all things work together for good to them that love the Lord. So what's wrong here? Who am I angry at? At God? Oh no, please help me. And definitely not at Mervin. Oh, Mervin, we miss you so. But why did you have to go over that hill? Why, oh why, did you not stay on the main trail? Why were you at the end this time, when you were the leader before? We miss you so. Maybe I'm angry because I'm tired of crying. I cry so many tears for you! Lord, help me. Please, God, understand me. No, I'm not mad at you, but what's wrong here? Please take my anger away, dear Lord. I read that to deny that we have any anger will surely bring it somehow to a much more destructive level. So please, please understand. Help me, Lord.

Light in the Shadow of Death

"Pilot Me"

NOW HERE I am about eight weeks after you left us, Mervin, and feel so, oh, so down. Lift me up, Lord, "Pilot Me". By now we have about 600 cards and have had many, many visitors, and yes, I thought some evening no one will visit. That evening came, and I knew, yes, other things are happening, like our good friend, Melvin D. Stoltzfus, passed away from cancer. People are thinking about other things now. We must roll our sleeves up a little higher. This was our Mervin and we must carry this load. Lord, help us. Mailman time was such a highlight for me, and then last week one day there was only one card. Oh my, that was kind of scary for me. I knew sometime there would be no cards. But the next day there were, I think, 11 or 12. Thanks, friends! Yes, now the day came. Mailman time, and "no," please not yet—"no mail". Yes, it's true. There are no cards for us today. Those sleeves must be rolled up a little higher. Lord, help us to go on.

One day last week, Mervin, your friend, David Smoker, went along to market. If you could see us, what would you say? I miss you so. Anyway, we went to the eastern shore where you built all those tree stands, and where our good memories were. How about just you and me alone at the shack, just about a month before you were killed. Remember that big hug you gave me. What a big buck that was! You know, I was wishing you had gotten him, but you were so happy for me. Anyway, you got a doe. We were there overnight, just us two. My, I will always treasure that last hunt. I just wish I would have talked more that night, but I was very tired. Yes, Mervin, when I opened the door to the "shack", my, oh my, uncontrolled crying. I went in to the table and just cried and cried. I miss you so. Then I went into the bunk beds where we slept. Your blanket was still there in your bed just as you left it. Oh, how I missed you.

Oh Merv, this last while your friends have been coming a lot. You just wouldn't believe the support they have shown. Sometimes they fill the house. They miss you too. You were a real chum to them, I'm sure. You know Dave, Kicker, Sam, Jonathan, Reuben, and yes, you know all of them. All your girlfriends have been coming too. They miss you so. And yes, your good friend and cousin Sam and his wife do so good in coming. Sam misses you so much; I can see it in him when he comes. And your brother, Gideon, how I know he misses you. He said the other night that he doesn't trust doing anything wrong, because he thinks you would see him. Do you? Where are you? I miss you. Maybe tomorrow I will feel better. I'm in such a daze. Your good friend, Mary, remember her; she comes a lot. So many times I wonder what your future would have been. I really looked forward to seeing you get married and all that. My, I want to give myself up, though, to God's plan. I'm just having a tough time, you know. I'll be okay.

Here I am again about a week later. Hi. I just wish this thing, whatever it is, would get better. I just don't feel like doing anything, or going to market. What's wrong? I'm starting to wonder if it's normal, or am I just being a big baby? God, help me. It seems I just can not give myself up. Please, God, help me. The devil I think has a hold of me; he knows I'm weak. Get away from me! He's trying to steal my joy or something. Will I ever be happy again? The devil is making it look hopeless. If I wouldn't know that more people have lost a teenager I would think this is impossible, but we know others have survived. So help me, God, this sinner. It seems when I'm about as low as I think I can go, God sends someone or a letter right on time. Everything was right on time. So why can't I say you were killed right on time? If God makes no mistakes, why am I not happy that He took you? I miss you so. Just when I'm having a pretty good day this last while, I see one of the children is struggling. Sometimes I long for a good day "all" together. It seems it's such a roller coaster ride. Sometimes we are up and sometimes we are down. I know I just keep sliding further down. I would think I should be at the bottom by now. Help me, God. Thy will be done!

Last week we decided to go with the Simon crew, you know the bunch, to western Maryland to hunt turkey. I just didn't know if I was up to it. I knew your brother Gideon wanted to go. Oh Mervin, if only you could have been along. I really had a struggle there, but yeah, I tried real hard. One morning while going out the road to hunt with Sammy B., real dark, about 4:00, we were listening to your favorite song, "Pilot me". Soon the tears just started rolling. Gideon, your brother, was up front, and I was trying to be strong. Soon I heard Gideon crying, so we just had a real good cry. You would probably say, "Don't cry for me." We can't help it, we miss you, but also we want to let you go. On that day Gideon and I both got a turkey; you were there with us! You know, when I had my turkey there on the trail, I started crying like everything for you. I missed you. Are you okay? Anyway, I thought it's so beautiful and quiet here in the woods, so why not just sit here awhile? After a bit I thought I'm going to try to call a turkey in for you, Mervin. So I gave a few calls and one answered. This was only about 15 minutes after I had shot mine. So I kept calling and he would answer. I went behind a tree and had my gun and turkey lying on the ground beside me. He kept coming, gobbling all the way, to within about 4 or 5 feet from me. I just couldn't believe it was happening. Soon he gave a few putt, putts, and away he flew. I said that was for you, Mervin. Oh Mervin, you should see the beautiful letter your brother Gideon put on my desk after that hunt. He wrote, "This life is hard to understand," but thanked me for taking him on that hunt. He also wrote how he misses you and just thinks at work you should come walking around that corner. We miss you; your little sisters also miss you so much. Help us, Lord, to stay strong.

Here I am again, Mervin. Time goes on. It's now two months or so already. Are you okay? I miss you so. Oh, my mind just keeps reeling. Sometimes I think of you and all of a sudden something comes to mind that we did. You know, Mervin, you were good to Mary Ann and me. How my heart hurt that night at brother-in-law Abner's Sheryl's wedding. Remember, you were not a very good boy. Now I just cry for you. If I could only tell you how much I hurt for you when we went around apologizing to Mose Fishers and Abners. I cried for you when I walked away and left you alone with Mose and Nancy. I pitied you so much, but you know it was something I had to do! I wanted you to grow up and be a good boy and daddy. I thought maybe if I kept on I could make you so much better than me, your dad. I so many times felt like a failure to you. How I wish I could just talk to you one more time. Did I do enough for you? Lord, help me from here on!

This week this verse was in the mail from you, Mervin.

"Perhaps you aren't ready yet to have to say good-bye
Perhaps you have thought of things you wish to say, well so have I
For one thing I would have told you not to worry about me.......
I'm with the Lord in heaven, now you know that's where I'd be
I'm sorry that you're feeling sad, for I'm so happy now
I've asked the Lord to ease the hurt and comfort you somehow
It's hard at the beginning, but I hope you will make it through
I hope it helps to know that I will be waiting here for you
There are no words that I can say
To take your pain and grief away
Nor anything that I can do to bring your loved one back to you
But I can pray that God would give the daily strength you need to live
God keep you close within His touch and hold you while you hurt so much
Until someday His love reveal the beauty in the pain you feel."

Oh, Mervin, yes, we still go to market, but I have not been there a whole week since you were killed. I just have a hard time around all those people. Your sisters are doing so well in keeping on going. I know sometimes it's been real hard for them. We miss you!

Here I am again, Mervin. How are you? I think of you all the time. Oh yeah, we had our yearly brothers' day. Remember? All of us brothers go to Potter Co. for turkey. Spring gobbler! We were all there except brother Elmer. How we missed you. Yeah, you never got the chance to go with your friends then, did you? How the memories flowed when I walked in that door. I cried myself to sleep that night, missing you. Remember that big buck you got last year? I still see your big smile. Well, we went hunting and your brother Gideon got a gobbler. You surely would have been real proud of him. I could see he was having a hard time. We missed you so.... It even snowed some; yeah, it was kind of cold. Bro. Jr. and Bowser each got one. Oh Mervin, there were so many memories that just flowed through my mind. Remember that buck you shot with your gun resting on my shoulder? Wow, what a shot you made. You were so happy. We miss you!

Well, here I am again, Mervin. The Lord has been so good to us. We're still getting lots of visitors, all right on time. Your friends keep coming, Mervin, to sing and visit. They miss you so. "God grant me the serenity to accept the things I cannot change, courage to change the things I can, and the wisdom to know the difference." Living one day at a time; yes, that was told to us, I don't know how many times. As old as it gets it's still so very, very true. We surely don't know what tomorrow will be like, and, you know, I don't really want to know, living one day at a time, enjoying one moment at a time, accepting hardships as the pathway to peace. Taking as Jesus did this sinful world as it is, not as I would have it, trusting that He will make all things right if I surrender to His will. I'm trying so hard. But, Mervin, I miss you. I just want to say, "Thy will be done." I wish I wouldn't doubt so. I know that God's way is the right way. Help me, Lord. I have learned a lot of things through this. Some things stick out though and one is this: I have always enjoyed giving and making someone's day. That can be a blessing and make us feel so good. Now I am on the other side and I am having a hard time being a "cheerful receiver", if you know what I mean. I'm saying if we know how good it feels to give, then we must let them give and accept it cheerfully. Lord, help me. I feel so unworthy. I truly hope I did not make anyone feel bad by not accepting what you wanted to do. I just wish I could pass all your kindness on. "Thank you, everyone."

The Hunt at Three Months

HELLO, MERVIN, HERE I am again. I miss you so. I called your name the other day. Did you hear me? I just wanted so much to talk to you. It's now going on three months that I have seen you. Oh, how I miss you. Last week I just had this feeling that I wanted to be alone. I was wishing to go to Huntington County to my brother. I thought if only I could go there somehow. Oh Mervin, I was really missing you. Humps Amos's Amie was going, so I asked if they would just drop me off along the turnpike as they were going on further out. I got off along the turnpike and was about ½ hour early. Down over the stones I went and waited for my brother Omar to pick me up. I was alone and that's just what I wanted, being under the bright stars. I lay there at 3:30 in the morning, looking up, Mervin, and wondering where you are. It was such a real clear morning and I was missing you so. All too soon, Omar came to pick me up. We went to his house to drink coffee, and then I went out to the woods all alone, not caring if the turkeys gobble or not. It was such a still and peaceful morning. I kept looking for you, Mervin, in the sky. That "still small voice" was talking. The night was dark and the stars were so bright. Where are you, Mervin? I miss you so. Well, after the break of dawn I did some calling. Sure enough, I got an answer. Gobble, gobble. I worked on that turkey for about two hours. Finally, here they come, and yes, I got him, a 9½-inch beard. Oh Mervin, I just sat there and cried my heart out, thinking of you then. What a still morning it was. Well, I kept thinking of you and thought I'm going to try and call another one in for you. Lo and behold, I got an answer. This was about ½ hour later. He kept coming. Here I was all finished, had my gobbler and had laid it with my gun. I kept calling and he kept coming. There he was, just coming toward me. He got to about 20 yards and just could not find the hen. Finally he just slowly walked off. Mervin, another one for you! We loved you so! Miss you!

Hello, Mervin. Here I am again. It will soon be 11 weeks. Oh, I miss you so. I can see that the children and Gideon miss you very much. Where are you? I can hardly stand the thought of you never coming home from the western trip. I'm in such a turmoil. I just don't understand why I can't, or maybe I should say "won't", give myself up. I miss you so. Yesterday I was working outside, and I don't even know how to explain it, but I could have just screamed for you. I didn't know where to go, so I went up to your room, as close as I could get to you, I guess, and just spilled over with tears. Where are you? We miss you! Dear Lord, please calm me down. Help me to accept this as real. Mervin is gone, am I right? We will never see him again. Oh, I hope to meet him again. How will it be, Lord? Help me to understand. I have so many questions. Will I ever give myself up and say, "Thy will be done," and really mean it? Sometimes I think now I'm going to give it all to you and then. . . I thought, you know, I can go to a church friend or anybody, if I wronged them and ask to be forgiven. If they accept it, we can walk free, never to remember or bring whatever it was back again. What a feeling! But Lord, this is different. I keep bringing this all to you, and then it just comes right back to me, then I must come to you again, again, and again, so many times in one day. Is something wrong with me? Help me, Lord. I remember well at first, soon after you were killed, I said, "Lord, I'm not looking for a sign. Thy will be done!" What was I thinking? I'm now looking everywhere for a sign. Show me, Lord. I think of you so often, Lord, and keep looking and watching the sky. Show me a sign, please.

Just give me a nice dream about Mervin. Do something, please. Oh yes, maybe it's that purple martin that's flying around out here. I have been talking to him. You know, I have been trying to get purple martins for 17 years. The last couple weeks there is one here, yes, only one. I call him Mervin. Oh Merv, did you send him? I told him to go get Puffly Jr. to send another one down here. Could there be something to it? Lord, show me! Also, the other day, oh my, what would you say, yes, we got your gravestone. Mervin, it's true; I guess you're gone. We all walked over to the graveyard and had your gravestone on the express wagon. Is this true? That was on Memorial Day 2005. It had rained some early, but was real nice afterward. Our son-in-law, Daniel, and Gideon were digging the hole to put the gravestone in and heard something hit. I did not realize that the coffin was not further down. Yes, we hit your coffin, Mervin, with the digging iron. Mixed feelings we had. We kept going as well as we could with tears flowing. Afterward we sowed grass seed on your grave, Mervin, and set your gravestone. We were all standing there and soon there was a nice rainbow in the sky. Was God talking to us? I said maybe, just maybe, God is telling me to accept, and yes, give myself up. It was a beautiful, peaceful feeling, standing there looking at the rainbow. It seemed so unreal because it had not rained for quite a while before that. What was God trying to say? So I guess that's about the last thing we can do for you, Mervin, set your gravestone. You know, Mervin, Sauders Nursery; Elam gave a tree to plant in your memory. So we, Puffly and I, went to plant them at the graveyard one night, one for Mervin and one for Puffly Jr. We took turns to water the trees last night. Precious memories, how we miss you. "Let not your heart be troubled: ye believe in God, believe also in me. In my Father's house are many mansions: if it were not so, I would have told you. I go to prepare a place for you. And if I go and prepare a place for you, I will come again and receive you unto myself; that where I am, there ye may be also" (John 14:1-3).

Here I am again, Mervin. Now it's June already, with warm days. Yes, time goes on. I still think of you almost all the time, Mervin. You have been gone so long. I miss you so. Your friends were here again. What would you say? Sunday in church I just thought you have to be with the boys, but no, you're gone, right? The other night Rosanna was singing the song, "Oh, how I long to see you again". Oh yeah, Mervin, your cousins were here to sing the other night, the Esh side. Singing has been ringing through the barn since you're gone. They were singing that precious song, "O gentle one, we miss thee here, sweet form we loved so well; but in our Father's better care, we know the child is well". You remember that one, right? Remember how the young folks sang that song when Sammy J.'s girls were killed. How you missed those girls! Are they with you now? What are you doing? Yeah, your cousins were singing that, then it had been raining and the most beautiful, perfect rainbow was in the sky. I got kind of weak in the knees. Remember the rainbow when we were setting your gravestone? What an awesome God we have! Those rainbows will have a great meaning to us now!

I remember where your bookmark was in your story of the Bible. What did you think when you read about where the sun and the moon stand still? My, oh my, Mervin, sometimes I think that's kind of the way it is now. Time is kind of all mixed up, and yes, sometimes it seems like it stands still. I'm really trying hard to accept God's plan here, you know. Lord, help me to go on and stay strong for the rest of the family. Oh yes, your martin, you know the one you sent, that purple martin just keeps hanging around here. I call him Mervin. He's still here. Sunday morning when I went out to get my horse ready to go to church, here was that martin, just singing away. I said, "Good morning, Mervin. Nice to see you!" Oh Mervin, I just found out that you shot a purple martin by mistake one time a long time ago. I forgive you. You must have felt real bad. I mean real bad, knowing how much I wanted purple martins. It's Okay that you didn't tell me. You probably thought I would get upset. Well, thanks for sending this martin now! Yeah, we are planning on going to Indiana this weekend to the "sudden death reunion". I have such mixed feelings about going, you know. Yes, we are now with that crowd, I guess, but my, oh my, are we?

Sudden Death Reunion

chapter 5

HERE I AM again, Mervin; your dad, you know. It's now June 14, 2005, 3½ months since you left us. I wonder what's going to come out of my mind to put on paper this time. It's so full in there, you know. Did we enjoy our trip? we are asked. Well, yes and no, I guess. I would *not* encourage anyone to go to the "sudden death reunion" so soon after a death in the family. Not at all putting the people down in Nappanee, Indiana. They did a good job, but my, oh my, we were not ready for that. You know, I guess I'm trying so hard, Mervin, to lead a life that's a little like before. Am I rushing into things maybe a little too much? Oh, how I long for. . . My, I'm not sure what I long for. Sometimes I am so mixed up, I hardly know what's up. You know, Mervin, I guess I need to say that life has changed and just let come what may. God, help me to give myself up to what you have in store. Not my will, but thine! Yes, it was not all bad, the trip, you know. We met and stayed with Vernon and Darlene Miller of Middlebury, Indiana. Oh Mervin, that was one of the greatest reunions I was ever in. You know their son Joas; is he with you? I wish sometimes I could tell you all these things that are going on. Joas was killed while snowboarding, you know. He also loved the snow. I just wish I could have met him sometime. Are you playing in the snow with him now? Joas was killed the same week that you were, so what a bond we have to share. No, not one that we would choose, but "Thy will be done, O Lord." I could tell Joas's mom and dad miss him so. Oh Mervin, how I long for you sometimes. I don't know, sometimes the last couple days I have this thing again, whatever it is, in my chest. Oh yes, maybe I think it's partly missing you, Mervin. Also, how I long for a more normal family life. It seems my wife Mary Ann is having such a hard time lately. Please help us, Lord, to stay strong! Yes, I want to be here for her and try to stay strong. It seems lately I have been letting the family and everybody down. I'm so mixed up. Last night there were a lot of people here singing again. Is it time to get more normal again? Oh no, not that I don't wish for all your support, but. . .Oh, what am I trying to say? I just wish I could see more clearly what I need. Show me, Lord, or give me what I need. "Thy will be done."

Please do not feel like the "sudden death reunion" was not for me. I think someday I could really enjoy, oh no, not enjoy, well, what's the word for it? I really don't know. I think you know what I mean. Just not so soon! Even though I did meet some very interesting people and just wanted to talk some more to them. One was Eli Weaver of Dundee, Ohio. They also lost, or is that the word for it, a child. Did we really lose them? Hopefully they are not lost, but safe in the arms of Jesus. We must leave it in the Lord's hands, and say, "They are well taken care of." Eli put a very good, interesting book together titled *My Grace Is Sufficient for Thee.* It is full of accounts of people who have bid farewell to loved ones.

Oh Mervin, last week I was riding one of our scooters down the road to our son-in-law Dan and Jane. Out of all those scooters in the barn, I just grabbed one, and as I was riding down the road I looked down and here was the one that had your name etched in the metal. Tears flowed as I thought of your school days, riding down the road on your scooter. I remember when I marked your scooter and you were so proud to call this your scooter. I miss you so! Lord, show me the way. Is this real? Your teachers have such good words for you, Mervin. You were a good student, you know. Sometimes I think, well, what did all that schooling help? Why didn't we just keep you at home with us if we could only have you for 23 years anyway. Why do I think such things? I don't know sometimes why I am writing all these things on paper. Maybe it can be of help to someone someday. I'm surely hoping from the bottom of my heart it will not hurt anyone. Just maybe we can learn something. People talk and I am very much that way! I never realized how important it is to "be careful what we say". Small things can really, really sting. Some people will say, oh, you wait till six months, or how it was at a year. You know, I really don't want to know how it will be a year from now. Please let me take one minute, one hour, or one day at a time. Also, sometimes I think maybe it's me, big baby me. Help me, Lord, to be strong. I saw the other day, firsthand, how words that sound good to some of us can really, really hurt another. We were told that maybe 20 is the age to be responsible for joining the church. Because the children of Israel 20 and younger could get into the Promised Land. Remember, there are people who lost children that are over 20 years old and not members. They need our support. It is in God's hands! All written to just give a little warning, I guess. You know, we must think good things if you are in our shoes. I found out how low we can go, and yes, I feel like I'm gaining ground. Thank the Lord! My thoughts were not good, and I'm telling you, we *must* keep our mind on better things, or we will lose it. That's our mind and we must partly control it. I'm trying very hard lately to "let God". We know death is so final and there is nothing we can do to change it now. I am totally convinced that every death is for those that are left behind, to do better and to learn that God is in control. We must do the best we can to live for the Lord Jesus who died for our sins, and we must live on "hope" that His grace is sufficient for us.

Oh Mervin, you know that purple martin is still here. My heart skips a beat when I hear him, still flying outside our house. This morning when I went out to the barn, I was thinking of you and then there you were. All of a sudden that martin was there. Is there something to it? Yes, I really think that martin was sent to comfort me, from you. The Lord works in ways that we don't know! Why would this martin be here for the last six weeks or so? Thank you, Lord!

Hey, Mervin, here I am again. I called your name this morning. I'm just so, oh, I don't know how to say, something is coming back, that big empty feeling or what is it? The sun is so bright and it's such a beautiful day, so what's wrong here? Your brother left last night for a ten-day hunting trip to Canada. Maybe that's what's wrong. Will he come back? Oh, the thought just makes me weak. I just need to talk to you, Mervin, and tell you what's going on. Last night we were at Yoder's Restaurant with all your friends. When I see your friends I just get this numb or weak feeling. Then I wonder why. The devil is just not quitting; he's trying me out so much. Last night was so touching how the precious words did flow. "Pilot Me" and "Thank You, Mama". Your friends are so respectful; did you realize? Oh yes, I think you did. You chose so many good friends. I just know that you made a difference in their lives. Yes, I just keep thinking of Gideon, your brother, this morning. I need to put my trust in the Lord more. What's wrong here? I went down to the lily pond shack this morning to pray, and oh, how I cried. Mervin, I miss you so. I talked to you. Did you hear me? Your sister Esther had a birthday yesterday. You would have helped to sing "Happy Birthday" when we were around the table. I missed your voice! How is this going to be without you? I mean, when I think about it, I almost get weak. This is final, you're gone. Oh Mervin, we miss you. I know John 14:1-6 by heart for a long time already, so why don't I just say it again and again. "Let not your heart be troubled, Jesus said! Ye believe in God, believe also in me. In my Father's house are many mansions: if it were not so, I would have told you. I go to prepare a place for you. And if I go and prepare a place for you, I will come again, and receive you unto myself; that where I am, there ye may be also. And where I go ye know, and the way ye know." So how can we know the way? "Jesus said! I am the way, the truth, and the life: no man comes to the Father but by me."

Oh Mervin, I read that heaven is so big, and there's room for us all. I have so many questions. Revelation 21 says, "Heaven is 1,500 miles wide, 1,500 miles long and 1,500 miles high." This would be from New York to Denver and from Florida to Canada. This would be by far the largest city man would ever know. Are you there, Mervin? We read that the city is surrounded by a jasper wall that is 216 feet high, and it's 6,000 miles around the city! Oh Mervin, I have so many questions. Will we know each other in heaven? "But then shall I know even as also I am known" (1

Corinthians 13:12). Oh Mervin, I just found this nice Father's Day card in my desk. Gideon wrote, "Happy Father's Day", and said he's sorry he won't be here for Father's Day. Why don't I just "Let go and let God"? We loved you, Mervin.

Hello, Mervin, here I am again. What a beautiful morning. The bobwhites are whistling and other birds are singing. Today is June 21, 2005. Oh my, it will soon be four months since you're gone. Yes, the cousin bus trip is today and, you know, we just really did not feel like going. There are things that we really don't feel like doing yet. I guess people would say, "What's wrong with you?" But when I'm with a group of people I feel so, oh, I don't know how to explain it, alone I guess, and think that I'm just taking the fun out of their trip. It seems like they would just watch me and see that faraway look, and then not be open and have their fun like we used to do. I didn't go because I sure didn't want to spoil anybody's trip. I know that might sound dumb, but that's how I feel.

Oh Mervin, yesterday I spent about four hours at the graveyard. I made it look real nice. I was mowing and weed-eating. My, how my mind did flow. Yes, the grass is growing on top of your grave. Are you okay? You and Puffly's Jr. are there right in a row. That is real nice to think about when I am at the graveyard, you and Puffly Jr. together. Oh yeah, Father's Day came and went and no card from you. Sunday was Father's Day, and at church I just couldn't quit thinking about you. We heard such an interesting sermon. Lots of comfort for me, but still have that, oh, I don't know what it's called, a big empty thing, a feeling I can not describe. I miss you so! You should have seen us the other night, Mervin. I got some helium balloons and little Rosanna wanted to send you a message. So she wrote on the paper, "I miss you, Mervin" and "I love you". So we taped the note on the balloon and let it go. It was very touching to see it float up, up into the sky, on and on till we could not see it anymore. Where did it go? She said if you cannot read it, Mervin, God could read it to you. She misses you too, you know!

Yes, Mervin, I keep thinking you're okay. I don't know why I have so many questions. I was thinking, you know, to follow Jesus was your choice. It was your choice to become a member and be baptized into the church. Thank you, thank you! I just have to think maybe a lesson for us all was left behind. Yes, so we all will do better. Last night some of your friends were here, and yes, I think you made a big difference in their lives. Hopefully, through you leaving us here to mourn, they will want to also follow in your footsteps and join the church. Yes, my heart just goes out to them. I know they want to do what's right and they are trying so hard. They seem so near and dear to us now. Your friends are very, very special to us, Mervin. When they come they most always ask if they can go up to your room. That's one place yet where memories just flow. I really believe what the Bible says. To seek first the kingdom of God, then all other things will be added unto you. Yes, how many of us try to take our own way? Seek *first* the kingdom, it says. It was that way for you, Mervin. I could see it in your life, something got a hold of you! I know what it's like to be with the young folks. It's not always easy, and hard to understand sometimes. I have always really enjoyed being with the young folks and hope and pray that your friends can find that peace that you had found.

Oh yes, Mervin, remember the words in that card I gave you when you were joining the church. My, how I wish I could tell you that one more time. That card says it all, when I think about you. This is what it read: "I'm so proud of you, son. There have been moments when all I wanted to do was hold you in my arms and tell you everything would be all right. But as a parent, sometimes my job was more than just giving a reassuring hug. I had to let you find out things for yourself, even when the outcome was painful. It wasn't always easy, but I believe it was necessary.... If I allowed you to think that any problem you ever had would go away just by wishful thinking, I wouldn't have been filling my role as a parent. You had to learn and grow through your own trials and experiences, slowly but surely, building self-confidence and courage with every step you took. I encouraged you to be yourself, feel comfortable with who you are, and not let any obstacle in front of you frighten you away. I tried to teach you courage and positive thinking to guide you over uncertain waters. I did the best I could with whatever tools I had. I wasn't a 'perfect' parent, but I tried. And through all of the tears and the worrying, you turned out just fine. I'm so proud of you, son, and the accomplishments you've made in your life. You're successful and intelligent, and there is no limit to where you can go or what you can do. But more than just your accomplishments got you where you are today. Good morals, a sense of humor and a loving heart contribute to the wonderful man you are. I love you, and I want you to know how proud I am of you. Love, from Dad. I wish you the best." This was a card I had given to Mervin while he was joining the church. How I wish I could give it to him now again. Mervin, "Rest in Peace".

It's Your Choice

YES, FRIENDS, BUDDIES and everyone else who wants to make a choice, you know it's your choice to become a member and be baptized. Choice—the word has a pleasing sound, a ring of freedom. Everyone likes the feeling of independence and the sense of control that go along with freedom to choose. Choice allows you to see your own identity and decide your own affairs without interference from anyone else.

Who would dare to oppose such an idea? Indeed, the very thought is disgusting. Why would you bow to the wishes of another? Why should you not live and do as you please? It's your choice, isn't it?

But wait, maybe you have overlooked something. Freedom also brings responsibility. Every choice has its consequences. You may choose to ignore God and go your own way of life. You may choose drugs, you may choose abortion, you may choose the "gay" life and so on. But what about the consequences that follow, just as surely as day follows night? Have you thought about them?

If your choices lead to drinking or drug abuse, that destroys your home and your future. What then? If you choose drugs and become addicted, or drinking, how will you reverse your choice? If you choose a lifestyle that leads to terminal disease, will you blame God? It was your choice.

God is a great God, but He will not force you to make the right choices. He does make it quite clear what the results will be of taking your own way. The Bible says, "Be not deceived, God is not mocked, for whatsoever a man or a woman soweth, that shall he also reap." Remember, the choices you make have consequences. They can be forever, never to be changed. Even more scary is the fact that they are eternal, you will live with them "forever". Wouldn't it be better to choose God's way now? "Repent ye therefore and be converted, that your sins may be blotted out" (Acts 3:19). Surrender your life to the Lord and live for Him. God still offers you that choice, but one of these days your choosing will be finished, just like it was with Mervin. In the blink of an eye "it was finished". "Today if you will hear his voice, harden not your hearts" (Hebrews 3:15). It's your choice.

Hello, Mervin, again. Here it is four months since you're gone. Oh, how can it be? People ask, "Does it seem long?" I really don't know sometimes. Yes, it seems real long since we have seen you, Mervin. You know, things are looking up and I'm feeling better. Oh yes, I think never, you know never, here on this earth will we see you again. My, oh my, when I think about that I just, well I don't know what that feeling is or how to describe it. . . If only I could tell you what has been happening around here. Yes, there were so many people here singing already. Last night some of the uncles were here to sing and Grandfather Sammy and Mommy Esh. My heart just went out to them. They have seen so much in their lifetime. They are getting up in age, you know, Mervin, but what special daddy-in-laws they are. Yes, Mervin, church is planned for here on July 17th, and my, oh my, I'm so looking forward to it. It is the main thing on my mind right now. Your friends want to come, Mervin, and hopefully lots of other folks. Oh yeah, your friends were here and said that we are not supposed to get the food ready for church. They are supplying it all. I didn't know better than to try so hard to be a "cheerful" receiver again. Will I ever get used to it? I hope to just pass it on!

I was at the graveyard again yesterday to water your trees. My mind just wanders when I am there. It's pretty dry right now, so I watered the new grass seed on your grave. I just can not explain how that seems, to

try and make the grass grow on your grave. There are so
going on in my mind. I still need to ask God to help me give .
His will. You know, I would still want you here with us, but yes
God's will, so I must, yes, must give myself up. That word mus. is pretty
powerful; you know, I really have no choice. You really are gone. Darkness
upon darkness, sorrow upon sorrow, anguish upon anguish, that's death.
Death is a fearful visitor, snatching away people who are precious to us
and leaving us behind to mourn, grieve and wonder. It blocks the light
that before shined so freely and easily on our lives. Whether we are facing
the prospect of dying or dealing with the death of a loved one, death can
be devastating. It can zap our energy, change our plans, overwhelm our
soul, change our outlook, test our faith, steal our joy and challenge our
meaning of life's purpose.

When we walk through the deep valley, we feel swallowed up by the
shadow and come face to face with fear. The loss and emptiness threatens
the comfort that we had from our trust in God, and so we grow afraid—
afraid of our future, afraid to enjoy life again.

Yes, in that valley, under that shadow, we can say to the Lord, "I will fear
no evil, for you are with me" (Psalm 23:4). His loving arms never let us
go. He is always with us.

Slowly at first, but surely, He provides comfort and release from the
darkness. He gives light. He leads us out. Finally we escape the valley of
the shadow. Death separates us for a time. Christ will reunite us forever.
Are you burdened by worries about what might happen tomorrow? Do
the days ahead seem dark and full of difficulties? Remember that grace
and guidance are given to us like manna in the wilderness (Exodus 16:4),
one day at a time!

Hello, Mervin. How are you? It is July 4, 2005. It is now over four
months since you were killed. Oh, how can it be? Oh yeah, Mervin, I
finally had a pretty good day in church. Why was that so hard for me? I
guess the main reason was when the boys come in, you know, you were
their leader. Well, last night we went to your friends' singing. Oh my,
there is a first for everything since you're gone. I had such mixed feelings,
but yes, life goes on. They sang so nice, but no, you were nowhere to be

seen. I still so much wonder where you are. I should just get it in my head that you're gone and give myself up to what the Lord has planned. Oh yeah, Mervin, I read that it's possible to keep our wound or whatever it is open too long or get stuck in our grief and let it drain energy and the life out of us. You know, I'm trying so hard to "let God". I just can't help it, I miss you so. According to grieving there are stages to go through (I think whether I want to or not)—denial, anger, bargaining, sorrow and acceptance. One thing that I have found out so far, is that these stages will come whether we want them to or not. Yes, we will pass through these stages sometime during our grieving.

Yes, yesterday we had lots of company again and I feel like we have had so much support. It seems like. . . Well, I'm not sure how to explain it. Most people are back to their everyday cares, and no, I'm sure they have not forgotten. But, well, then what am I trying to say? Only those who have gone through this may know that we really are heading into the storm, or whatever you want to call it, rather than coming out of it. Does that make sense? Yes, I don't want to forget that Christ said, "I will never leave you!" He will walk with us through this storm. He says, "Be thankful in all things." I even read in a book where it said, "This too shall pass." My, how can it? I just can't see into that right now! Yes, sometimes I think maybe the Bible verses and so forth have lost their power, or whatever. What's wrong with me? Surely that has power and, yes, comfort for me, so what am I trying to say? Lord, teach me your ways!

The New Normal

YES, I READ of all these things that we feel in the process of grieving—sadness, helplessness, hopelessness, fear, emptiness, irritability, anger, guilt, restlessness and isolation. And all of these feelings fall within the range of "normal"! Maybe I'm normal after all. Yes, one day at a time, Lord. Teach me to take one day at a time. Yes, I'm trying so much to be normal, but I thought, "What's normal?" I really think I must find a new "normal". Oh yeah, things are going better and I know that healing is taking place, but sometimes I wonder, what's going on here? I wonder sometimes how long we can keep on crying and how many tears do we have? Someday, we are promised that there will be no more tears if we trust in the Lord. What a thought! I can not imagine not to be sad and always happy. Also, I want to let the tears flow if they come. Mervin, I miss you so. You would maybe say, "Don't cry for me," but I can't help it. I miss you! I really believe that there is no quick way to get through this thing or whatever it is. So I guess I will just keep on going through it. Oh yeah, maybe some of you would think, "Get over it," or move on with my life. I'm trying so hard, but sometimes I feel like nobody understands. Sometimes in a crowd or at church I just need to cry, so please don't worry about me. I'll be okay, but let me cry! I just can't help it; there is a big part missing in our lives. Yes, I will be okay, just give me time to heal this thing. You know, our lives have been changed forever, and when I think of that I just have to cry, "Lord, thy will be done." Help me please to find my new "normal". There are times when it looks so, oh so dim, just to get through a day or even an hour. So many things, yes, very little things, just get me and it feels like a stab or something got me. Yes, Mervin, your reminders are everywhere I go. Yes, we know Christ will never leave us. He promised to always be there for us (Hebrews 13:5).

Sometimes I think the thing or whatever it is has maybe passed and I can get to my new "normal". Then maybe the next day it will seem like that good day never happened and all that pain just comes shooting right back. I guess that grieving thing has ahold of me rather than me having ahold of it. I don't know. Maybe I should just accept it now and move on. Lord, "strengthen my faith". Yes, I did not only lose you, Mervin, but I also lost my dreams I had for you. Lord, help me to say, "Thy will be done." We have the hope that God will wipe away every tear because He says so (Revelation 21:4). Yes, we also know that Christ came to give us eternal life so that the power of death has no hold over us (Revelation 1:18). Then we must wait until the trumpet will sound and hopefully we will meet our loved ones in the air along with Christ Himself (1 Thessalonians 4:17).

Yes, I'm so afraid that I am just, well, kind of thinking this thing is me and just me. I'm so afraid I am forgetting the other children, but you know I don't really know how. Lord, help me to go to their level. I really wish I could get on their level and do everything I can to help them through this thing. Yes, you know lots of times I just call it this thing. I think you all know what I mean. There really are no words for it, so I just call it a thing. Lord, show me your ways and "strengthen my faith". Sometimes I think, well, why should I know how to do this stuff; I didn't have anybody to teach me how to go through something like this. I'm so dependent on you, Lord, to teach me how. You are the only one I can go to right now, so please help me!

Hello, Mervin, I just have to talk to you. Yes, I know I just wrote to you on Monday and this is only Wednesday. My, I just don't know what's going on. It seems like we are all just falling into this thing more and more. Well, yes, we are still getting some mail and it is very, very precious. Today there were three new cards again. Thanks, folks. The verse written in the one was like this, "He who gives and He who takes. He who never makes mistakes. He who hears us when we cry and will answer by and by. Let us trust Him, He will lead and supply our every need. Let us keep our spirits high, even tho we wonder why. Let us ever keep near the cross. If we never know the cause why our loved one left us here to mourn and our hearts feel broken and torn. Somewhere far beyond the blue, we hope to see that heavenly view. Just hope we are all pardoned from wrong, and all can join that heavenly song." Thanks! Also in the card it read, "May the Lord draw very close to you and make His presence very real as you travel through this sad time." Yes, I guess that is what we are doing, traveling through this time. What a journey it is, Mervin. I miss you so much today. I just thought maybe I am slipping again. Trust, yes, why don't I just give it over to you, Lord, you know this thing. Please, please take some of the weight off of my shoulder. It seems like everybody in the family is now at the same level like I was thinking, but no, not the level I was hoping for. Seems everybody is so, oh, what's the word? Snappy, I guess. Lord, help us through this thing, please. Am I not saying enough? Thy will be done! Please help me to put my trust in you, Lord, and pray that we can all find that peace you promised. Oh Mervin, I guess you would want us to be happy, but we miss you so. I usually have a good cry at least once a day for you. Maybe I should try harder to move on. Today I broke down and just cried three different times. What's going on here? I miss you so! Help me. I saw tonight at the supper table that your brother, Gideon, was missing you so. How can I help him? And your sisters, Mervin, oh, what can I do to make it more, aw, I don't know, better I guess. Your sister Lydia Jane misses you so much, Mervin. Oh, you should see your one and only nephew, Michael. He is growing, and yes, he will never be able to say he knew you, Mervin. When I think of some of the things, I just get such a numb feeling and that nameless thing gets ahold of me. "Strengthen my faith". Your married sister said today she just wishes she could talk about you more. Show her you care, Lord, and help her to go on. Yes, I know, Lord, I feel like Lydia Jane said today. Will life ever be happy again? Will it ever be normal? Oh yes, we must find that new normal. I think sometimes there has got to be a better way than this. But you know, I think we all feel like there should be a big rainbow or a big happy-ever-after here on earth. I am convinced that life, here on earth, can be good. But I am also convinced that it will never be a big bed of roses, if you know what I mean. It is not an easy road, but if we trust in the Lord and believe in Him, we can have a good life here on earth. I guess! Why do I say I guess? Please, Lord, help me to give myself up. Oh yes, Mervin, that purple martin was here again today, right on time. I was thinking about you, and then out of nowhere there was that purple martin. I stop right there and talk to you still. Thank you so much for sending that purple martin, Mervin. He has made my load a little bit easier. Yes, Mervin, I am planning on going to market the next three days. Help me, Lord! Yes, work is there waiting for me. But why don't I feel more like working? Maybe I am not trying hard enough. But you know, I am still meeting customers that I did not see since, and yes, they mean it well and want to talk about you, Mervin. You know there are so many people there and it just makes me want to go somewhere all alone. Last week I was talking to a customer about you, Mervin, and it felt real good. But you know, when I was finished talking to them and wanted to get back to work, there was, about five minutes later, another one that I had not talked to. You know, that person did not realize that I just finished talking to someone else about you. Well, so goes the market life. They sure all really mean it well. Maybe if I would just be myself once again.

Hello, Mervin, here I am again. It's Sunday morning, July 10, 2005. You know, it's now over four months that you are gone. Life goes on without you. I just don't know how to explain my feeling sometimes. I think about you so much. But I know that I must move on and try to take anything that life is going to put at me. I am trying so hard to go on and get a little more normal, you know. It is such a beautiful Sunday morning and the birds are singing, so why do I feel so alone? I still miss you so much. Your brother Gideon was at the market this week. It was the first time for him; you know he still misses you too. I was at market three days in a row for the first time. Hopefully sometime I will enjoy my work again. Sometimes

I think I just have to talk to someone about you. Sometimes that feeling almost takes over. I just don't know how to explain it, but I sure do not want to bring others down with me. I just want to talk. Lots of times I feel like I am just wearing a fake face or something. Lord, help me to be myself. Sometimes I ask to be forgiven for not being a better father to you, Mervin. But then I think, well, what would I do different? I loved you so much. We are all human, I guess, and have regrets. Life has its ups and downs. And its painful times. When I think about you, Mervin, I think, no way, I can't take it over and get it "right" the next time. You really are gone! Lord, help me to be a good father to the rest of the children. I care for and love them all so much. Sometimes I get the feeling it's just not fair. I just think, I can not live with this big hole in my heart, but, Lord, I know it was your plan. So please, I ask you to forgive me for my bad thoughts, and yes, I really want to give myself up to your plan. I am so thankful for your patience with me. Lord, I need you to guide me. Just take me as I am and lead me on this trip or whatever you call it.

I used to think after this time, four months or so, people would not want anybody to talk about their loss. How wrong! Please mention Mervin to me. My heart skips a beat when I hear his name. I must talk about my hurt. Also, let me cry. I just have to cry sometimes. I know talking does change things and crying does help. It surely does not make it worse like I used to think it would. Talking about Mervin and sorrow does *not* make my sorrow worse. So talk to me, please. I am trying so much to just give this "thing" over to the Lord, but I still need my friends' listening ears. Sometimes I just feel like I must find someone to talk to *now*, I mean right away. "The sting of death is sin, and the power of sin is the law. But thanks to God! He gives us the victory through our Lord Jesus Christ. Therefore, my dear brothers, stand firm. Let nothing move you. Always give yourselves fully to the work of the Lord, because you know that your labor in the Lord is not in vain" (1 Corinthians 15:56-58). "Forget the former things; do not dwell on the past" (Isaiah 43:18). Yes, we have so much we can read in the Bible for encouragement. So help me, Lord, to believe your Word and always take what you have in store for me. "Strengthen my faith." I really think for me to heal, I may not dwell on the past and move on from here and try and do the best I can. It is what we do from here, this very day, that matters. While we are still living, let us try and do better always. Yes, everything I did until now is done and *nothing* can be changed. Oh Mervin, you have left me with lots of good memories. Thank you for being who you were. Also, I thank a few select friends for sticking with me and hearing me out, even though it might just make you feel bad. Thank you! Also, I can take comfort in the fact that the Lord will never leave me or forsake me.

Yes, Mervin, I am still not there, where I can say I wouldn't wish you back. I know those thoughts do not help me. But yes, I miss you very much and surely would like to have you here with us. I have to think of Lazarus in the Bible sometimes. Then I think, yes, he came back to life, but we know he had to die later. So Mervin, yes, healing is taking place in my heart and I would not want to go through this again with you. So, Mervin, rest in peace. Lord, help me! I keep thinking if I refuse to let go of the past I am going against God's will. Help me to accept the things I cannot change, Lord. I don't want you, Lord, to think that I'm thinking your timing was wrong. I really want to give myself up! I get a great comfort in sitting at my desk writing about you, Mervin. So here I am again. Are you okay? Yes, Mervin, we are thinking of dividing your things to your nieces and nephews. Is that the right thing to do? Yes, about two months ago your friends were here and I gave them each one of your shirts. Was that okay with you? I think they really appreciated that. I feel like you would want your nephews to have some of your things, right? Maybe we should wait. I just don't know sometimes. Oh no, we are not getting rid of all your things. Lots of your things are here yet, to give me good memories. I'm not trying to block your memories out. I still miss you so much. There are lots of things that you had that I can never let go. "Precious memories." The little things around the house are what hurt the most when someone goes beyond the sky to join the heavenly host. His pillow, his Bible, his shoes or cap—we did not think that such little things would mean so much. Not yonder moving the stones of granite is his tomb. It is within this very house, within this room. There stands the bed in which he slept. The chair where he would sit. His pants, his shirt, God, how the heart leaps at the sight of it. Then let us put the suits away. He will not need them anymore. He has a fairer garb to wear upon a fairer shore. Still in his room we'll dwell and use his bed and chair, but always when we look therein we'll see the memories there. Then time will make us glad we have things he used, to know each will bring a tender thought of him of long ago. When someone far beyond the years is with the heavenly host, the little things around the house are what will count the most.

Hello, Mervin. Here I am again. How are you? It is now July 16, 2005, and my, I just can not believe sometimes that it's going on five months since you're gone. We are having church here at our house tomorrow, and my, you won't be here to help put the horses away tomorrow morning. Your friends are all planning on coming. I guess I am so looking forward to having church here, that I kind of, well, I did have a good last couple of days. Yes, thank the Lord I can say I feel myself healing from that sharp pain I had. I sure hope after all the excitement of having church here is gone, I will not drop back into that, oh you know, that thing or feeling. Thanks so much to your friends for what they are doing, supplying all this food for church. You know, you guys and girls are very precious to us.

Yes, Mervin, sometimes I get such a longing to see you, but no, it's not to be at this time. Right! I'm not sure how to explain this, but I really do not think I have that fear of dying like I had before. Is it because I feel like I have something to die for? Oh, that might not make any sense. What am I trying to say? Well, I have such a longing sometimes to see you that I just can't explain it. I read on a church sign: "Quiet hours with God build up resources for future emergencies." Oh, how true. Today is the day to have those quiet hours with God. Tomorrow may be too late! You know, Mervin, that purple martin was here again today, but it does not come as often anymore. I wonder, does it know that I'm getting better with this thing. So many times that martin came just when I really needed it. Did it just happen? I don't think so! Well, maybe I will have lots to write to you after we have church here tomorrow. How I wish you could be here. Sometimes life seems hard to bear, full of sorrow, trouble and woe. It's then I have to remember that it's in the valley that I grow. If I always stayed on the mountaintop, and never experienced pain, I would never appreciate God's love, and would be living in vain. I have so much to learn and my growth is very slow. Sometimes I need the mountaintops, but it's in the valleys that I grow. I do not always understand why things happen as they do. I am very sure of one thing; my Lord will see me through. My little valleys are nothing when I picture Christ on the cross. He went through the valley of death. His victory was Satan's loss. Forgive me, Lord, for complaining when I am feeling so very low. Just give me a gentle reminder that it's in the valleys that I grow. Continue to strengthen me, Lord, and use my life each day to share your love with others and help them find the way. Thank you for the valleys, Lord. For this one thing I know, the mountaintops are glorious, but it's in the valleys that I grow.

Hello, hello, Mervin, I just have to talk to you. This is Sunday evening and church was here today. I have such mixed feelings tonight. I looked forward to have church here at our house so much, and now, Lord, please lift me up. Everybody went home and here I am sitting out on the deck writing to you, Mervin. We heard such interesting sermons, so what's wrong here? My feelings are doing, well, I'm not sure where they are going. Oh, your friends, Mervin, you just would not believe the support they showed today. Also, all the families that came to show their support. My, oh my, there were 44 of your good guy friends and lots of your girlfriends too. I just could not believe my eyes, so many young people. Thank you all so much. I went to bring them in and I got this big lump in my throat. Now come on, Dad, calm down, you do not want to cry standing here in front of all these people! When your friends were all seated I had to get away, right away, and how I cried. Yes, I was so touched by their support. I could not hold back the tears any longer. All alone, I went into the house to my office and just cried and cried. When I see your friends, Mervin, something inside me just goes, oh my, I don't know how to explain it. It brings back so much homesickness for you. You know, Mervin, how I hated when sometimes you would go play ball Sunday mornings. Yes, I feel very strong about that still. That is no time to go play ball, and what was God saying this morning? Yes, lots of your friends had a tournament and were going to play ball. But God sent rain and the ball field was too wet. So, yes, God works in ways we don't understand. Instead of playing ball, lots and lots of your friends were here in church. Thanks so much, guys. No, I'm not against playing ball, but Sunday mornings, my, oh my, that's the Lord's Day. You know, I think I told you once, Mervin, that if you go to church every time we have church, you are only going about 70 hours a year. Why, that is not much more than the hours in one week's work. Please, friends, if you have church go when you can.

Well, I wish I could remember more of today's sermon. I remember the one preacher saying how Peter cried daily and had homesickness for Jesus after He went to heaven. That helps to know such things, for me, because sometimes I think I just cry too much. Yes, I do cry daily for you, Mervin. Surely you understand. We miss you so much. I really missed you this morning when the people started coming to church and we started to unhitch the horses. Yes, Gideon, your brother, was right there helping me, but my, where were you, Mervin? How long can this go on? Oh yes, Bowser, you remember him. He really pitched in and helped with the horses, but still, where were you? I need the Lord to help me go on again and again. Yes, tonight I have that thing, you know that thing in my, well, where is it, a big hole, missing you again. I had to think of your favorite song, "He will Pilot Me". "Altho' I cannot see the way, o'er life's tempestuous sea, dark sea, I know that Jesus is my Friend and that He'll pilot me. By His hand He'll pilot me, over life's tempestuous sea, when my blinded eyes can't see, cannot see the way; Come what may, let come what may on life's dark and stormy sea, my dear Lord, blessed Lord, He will pilot me. Dark clouds may gather in the sky and rough the sea may be; His love shall ever be my song, I know He'll pilot me. Dear Lord, whate'er the storm may be, I'll simply trust in Thee, relying on Thy love so true to safely pilot me." Yes, Mervin, if I would just trust the Lord more, and let Him pilot me. I am trying, but I must try harder, I guess, or what? "It is appointed unto men once to die, but after this the judgment" (Hebrews 9:27). I so much wonder where you are, Mervin. Are you okay? What are you doing? Why do I have so many questions? Jesus said the hour is coming in which all that are in the graves shall hear His voice and shall come forth. They that have done good, unto the resurrection of life; and they that have done evil, unto the resurrection of damnation (John 5:28 and 29). So then, what's going on here? What are you doing now? Also, Jesus said if ye believe not that I am He, ye shall die in your sins. Whither I go ye cannot come (John 8:21 and 24). Then I often have to think that the man at the cross was a sinner. He asked Jesus to remember him. What an answer he got. Today, yes, He said "today", shalt thou be with Me in paradise (Luke 23:42 and 43). Absent from the body, and present with the Lord (2 Corinthians 5:8). So if today means just that, "today", does that mean that when we die we go right away? Where do we go? Oh my, why do I have so many questions? Maybe I am wondering too much. It's all in the Bible, right? So maybe I should read more. I read in Psalm 107:9, "For he satisfieth the longing soul with goodness." Lord, help me to be satisfied. I'm not sure if my writing tonight makes sense. Lord, help me to understand. As months go by you may think we have forgotten when you see a smile we wear. But underneath there is a heartache. Only God knows it is there. You may think we are adjusting to his absence in our home. Still, there are days we keenly miss him and the longing tears will come. You may think we would stop to miss him as the time goes marching on. But sometimes we still are wondering whether our brother, son is really gone. You may think at times that time is healing. So it is, but still we weep, wishing we could see our brother. Oh, the longing goes so deep. You may think our tears are over, but they are flowing where God can see. Longing hearts still broken and bleeding. We're still grieving silently. You may think we may have forgotten when you see us traveling on. But we trust and hope to meet him at the setting of life's sun. Good night, Mervin.

Hello, Mervin, here I am again so soon. It seems I just have to talk to you more often this last while. I was at your grave today and also yesterday. A new grave was dug in the graveyard yesterday. Neighbor and friend Mike Fisher (Dutch) died. My first thought when I went there was, oh no, not another grave here. But yes, life goes on and people are going down the valley. I was weed-eating at the graveyard to make it look real nice for the funeral today. Yes, I have so much to be thankful for since you are gone, Mervin. Lots and lots of things and experiences I would not have had if it were not for your death. So why don't I give myself up better? Yes, that homesickness just will not go away at this time. I am going to try to make it my goal to make a difference in other people's lives. Lord, help me. If I can just help some people and make their life just a little easier and better. Then "Praise the Lord". Yes, the question of dying and living again must have been with people for many, many years. We know according to the Bible that a man will live again. We can read about Lazarus and the rich man. "And it came to pass that the beggar died, and was carried into Abraham's bosom. The rich man also died, and was buried, and being in torments, he seeth Abraham afar off and Lazarus in his bosom. And he cried and said, Father Abraham, have mercy on me, and send Lazarus that he may dip the tip of his finger in water, and cool my tongue, for I am tormented in this flame. But Abraham said, Son, remember that thou in thy lifetime receivedst thy good things, and likewise Lazarus evil things. But now he is comforted, and thou art tormented. And beside all this, between us and you there is a great gulf fixed, so that they which would pass from here to you cannot, neither can they pass to us that would come from there. Then he said, I pray thee therefore, father, that thou wouldest send him to my father's house, for I have five brethren, that he may testify unto them, lest they also come into this place of torment. Abraham said unto him, They have Moses and the prophets; let them hear them. And he said, Nay, father Abraham, but if one went unto them from the dead, they will repent. And he said unto him, If they hear not Moses and the prophets, neither will they be persuaded though one rose from the dead" (Luke 16:22-31). Yes, we can see the rich man woke up in a world where things were fixed. No more did his money or his influence accomplish a single thing. Yes, he woke up after death in a world where what was done was done, no more time to change things. He remembered his fine clothes and life's pleasures. Then only one minute after death, a whole lifetime had turned into bitterness. Now he believed in God, believed in prayer, believed in heaven, but too late. Friend, do not wait until it's too late! Everlasting thirst for a drop of water would be an awful experience for a man who had everything and knew no wants. Friends, let Jesus Christ into your hearts now. Do not shut the door because if you do, it will be forever, like a circle with no end—forever. As you fall, so will you lie. Will you hear the awful words, son? Remember! Remember the sins, the wasted life, the way you mocked your faithful ministers and parents. The time you fought against that "still small voice" inside you. Will you be awakened too late? Will you see your own end too late? Son, remember "the wages of sin is death; but the gift of God is eternal life through Jesus Christ our Lord" (Romans 6:23). Yes, we found out that in the blink of an eye it's all over. Death to me never seemed as real as it does right now. I just hope and pray through this death of you, Mervin, that some souls can be won. I guess you know if just one soul can be won, your death was not in vain. Can I thank God and really mean it someday? You know, it's still so hard to thank God for putting us through this. Lord, help me to understand. One day at a time! Help me to give myself up. Often I think now I gave myself up, then boom, here comes that feeling again, you know, that thing! Yes, I still do not have a real name for that "thing." I read this today and how true it is: "I am standing on the seashore. A ship spreads her white sails in the morning breeze and starts for the ocean. She is an object of beauty and I stand watching her until at last she fades on the horizon and someone at my side says, 'She is gone.' Gone where? Gone from sight; that is all. The loss of sight is in me, not in her. And just at the moment when someone says, 'She is gone', there are others who are watching her coming. Other voices take up the glad shout 'there she comes', and that is dying."

Change of Attitude

YES, I AM so trying to adjust to this grief that came upon me on February 28th. How long? What could I do to make it a little easier on me? Ask God for help more? Why don't I ask, and yes, really mean it? Maybe change my attitude and say thy will be done. "Strengthen my faith." I guess a lot can be said of the kind of attitude I have after all this pain and heartache. Yes, Mervin, I want to keep a good attitude, no matter what life throws at me. We can count on it; we're all going to experience a certain amount of pain and a certain amount of pleasure as we journey through life. Sometimes we feel like we own the world; at other times we feel like giving up. Lord, help me to keep a happy medium. Probably one of the most important things I can do right now is keep a good attitude. If I let my attitude down, I'm sure it will only bring unhappiness to myself and those around me. Yes, it is easy to keep a good attitude when everything goes right. But when bad things happen, what then? I sure need to work on keeping a good attitude about life and say, "Thy will be done." Did you ever meet a happy person with a bad attitude? I don't think so! Is it possible to keep a cheerful attitude when bad things happen? Sure, I think so! Paul said in Philippians 2:5-7, "Let this mind (or attitude) be in you, which was in Jesus Christ. Who, being in the form of God, made himself of no reputation and took upon himself the form of a servant and was made in the likeness of men." Paul is saying to keep the kind of attitude that Christ would if He would be in our shoes—in joy and in sorrow, in failure or success. One thing about your attitude for sure is, yes, it is not set in concrete. It can be changed. Just because someone mistreated us is no reason to let it poison our spirit. Through the power of Christ, you can return love for hate, blessing for cursing, and forgiveness for injury. The attitude we have is always a matter of "choice". We are free to respond to the blessing and hardships of life in whatever way we please.

Two soldiers were stationed in London during the 2nd World War. Both were directing airplanes in and out of the airfield on their bombing missions. The weather was damp and cold, and the airport was ankle deep in mud. One soldier whistled as he worked. The other grumbled and complained. The situation was the same for both; the attitude is what made the difference.

When the disgruntled soldier asked his friend how he could be so cheerful in this mess, he replied, "I decided long ago, when I found myself in a situation that I did not like but could not change, that I would adjust my attitude to fit the situation." And he did!

What a lesson for me! Yes, this death, this parting, is something I surely cannot change. I need to change my attitude toward death and life for my own good, for the good of my family, and for the good of my friends. Lord, help me! Did you ever see someone with a bad attitude accomplish much? What it does is increase our unhappiness. Why then would I want to keep a bad attitude rather than a good one? I need to quit feeling sorry for myself. Is that what it is? Lord, help me to be thankful in all things, even the death of Mervin. Oh my, I just don't know, I just can't, nor do I just think I can't, be thankful for your death. I know I have experienced so many things I would not have if you had not died. Thank You, Lord, for Your blessings on me! If I would start praising God for all the good things in my life it would take days, my health, my family, my friends and on and on. I really do want to start from here on to guard my attitude very carefully, to be quick to forgive and by all means count the many, many blessings we have. Mervin, rest in peace! We loved you! You came to us a bundle of innocence, making us marvel at the miracle of birth.

We asked God for wisdom to care for you and to teach you. You made our home brighter, busier and noisier, our pocketbooks lighter, and our lives fuller, richer and better. We loved you so much! You caught on fast. We remember the squeeze of your little arms around our necks, the beautiful bouquets of weeds you brought us. We remember the childish hurts and tears, as well as our irritations at times. But love was there and love remains. As you grew, you were alert and curious, learning from everything and everyone about you. Your first attempts at talking and deciding on your own were thrilling, then frightening. While we were your teachers, you were ours. Your questions made us take a fresh look at our beliefs. Later your answers made us review ours. You taught us more about the meaning of forgiveness than all the books and sermons in the world. You deepened us, sometimes painfully in prayer, in faith, and in love toward all young people. Your less and less dependence on us helped us to see that you belong not to us but to the Lord, not to our generation but to yours, and not to the past but to the future. You came to us, but now you go out from us. We had you for only a short while. My, those 23 years seem, oh, so short. I have such a deep longing to see you again. Sometimes I just think you're going to come again, Mervin, from around that corner or home from work. Are you okay? Help me, Lord, to give myself up to this. "Strengthen my faith." I am trying so hard to find that happy medium attitude. It seems like sometimes I am so high or whatever, and then I go so low. What's going on here? Help me, Lord, to find a level in the middle. "One day at a time." It seems like everywhere I go and meet new people, or whatever, when I tell them my name, they say, "Oh, you're Aaron, the one who buried a child!" Yes, Mervin, you made an impact far and wide, I think. It seems like lots and lots of people know about your "accident". I also think of our friends from Indiana, who lost their son Joas. Sometimes I picture you and Joas in heaven with each other. My mind just goes and goes, on and on, thinking and thinking. Yet I want to say, "Thy will be done." Sometimes I pray and just don't know what to pray, but we know the Lord knows our heart, and yes, He hears the faintest cry. Yes, He will answer by and by. He knows me, surely hears me, when I say, "Lord, I just don't understand, but yes, I know what you do is right." There are times when I am working, and then unexpectedly a surge of sorrow comes. I try to just let it come and enjoy the presence of Christ, and be glad that God has a way such as that to draw me closer. Yes, thank You, Lord, for Your blessings on me. The message came one Monday.

It said, My brother; your son has passed away.
Oh, what a shock, could it be real?
What grief and pain our hearts did feel.
Yes, Mervin, you left with no farewell.
The grief it brought no words can tell.
And yet amidst the pain we know,
God's way is best; He planned it so.
You left behind Dad and Mom.
A brother and sisters he too did have.
Although we miss him we can say,
We hope to meet some glorious day.
His friends to him meant very much.
He loved to hunt and keep in touch.
He gave a smile to all he met.
His cheerfulness we won't forget.
We did not know that it would be
That he would leave so suddenly.
And as we gather around that place,
We bow our heads and plead for grace.
Time will heal is what we say,
But as for us and for today,
I choose to pray and comfort seek,
While thus I bow my head and weep.
For memory will serve us now.
While beneath the sod that tender brow
Was laid to rest, so calm and still.
We trust full well it was God's will,
It matters not what we may do.
From time to time the whole day through,
That memories come floating in
Of how it was... or might have been.
And yet we often think above
Where all is peace and all is love.
We wonder what he's doing there
In that bright land, so pure and fair.

The Letter

chapter 9

HELLO, MERVIN, HERE I am again. Can I even write how I feel? Yes, it's now 5 months that you are gone—5 months! We took a vacation; you know, the one, Mervin, to Raystown Lake. My, oh my, I could have just seen you everywhere up there. Sometimes I think if only I knew that you are going away, or where you are. Yes, what more would we have done last year if we had known! Memories were there everywhere; I almost didn't know which way to turn. Oh yes, the family, I think, all really did enjoy the change. But you know, Mervin, there is no quick-fix. I feel so empty this morning and that thing is in me again. Sometimes I just don't know which way to turn. I just wish I could explain it to myself. Then maybe it would get better. Why don't I give myself up better, Lord? You know I'm trying real hard, but maybe You would say, "Try harder." That empty feeling, what is it? Mervin, I miss you so much! Yes, Mervin, we came home last night, and I could have just screamed, or what did I feel like doing when we drove in the lane? We did have a good trip, I guess. But when we got home, you know, it's still true, you are gone. People are still doing so good in letting us know they are thinking of us, but what's wrong? There were baskets and cards lying on the table when we got home. Oh, those reminders. Yes, it's still true; people are actually bringing things to us and dropping them off because we buried our son. Oh, how can this be? Help us, Lord! Yes, I know there are many more people that buried their children too, but why do I feel so all alone in this thing then? I just have to share with you this one card that was on our table when we got home. It reads:

Hello Aaron,

"I hope this finds you in good health and your family as well. My name is Rick. (I only met this man one time.) I never had the pleasure of meeting your son Mervin, but I would like to say that you and your family have my sympathy. Since I met you, I think about what you are going through every day. I'd be a liar if I were to tell you that I know what you are going through, but I do know something about losing someone. I know how it is to be in control of most situations in life and in a split second death takes someone away, and along with them it takes away all our hopes and dreams and plans for the future and we have to start over. I know about the sleepless nights, which turn into endless days and what it's like to finally sleep, but not feel rested. I guess I could go on and on, but there wouldn't be enough paper or words to describe the emptiness that you feel right now. It's been just over five years since my wife was killed, and I would like to be able to tell you it gets easier to accept the fact that she's gone, but for me it doesn't. I still wake up each morning and turn to hold her, but she's not there. I could tell you of a lot of things that we go through, as a family, but it wouldn't bring you any comfort other than knowing that you are not alone. I will tell you where Mervin is though. Remove all the doubts in your mind and know that he is in heaven and that you will see him again. Not because of things he has done or has not done, but because of what our Lord Jesus Christ has done. Mervin is in heaven because of that. I'll tell you the same thing I had to tell my children when the question, "Why? Why now?" came over and over again. God took my wife when she was as close to Him as she was ever going to get. You see, we buried her father two days before she was killed, and I know her thoughts were with God and eternity and she knew that there is no way we can get to heaven on our own. We only get there because God made it possible through His Son. I know you already know these things, but if you are anything like me, you just might need a bit of a reminder now and then. I heard that Mervin had left a message telling you about how beautiful it looks in those mountains above the clouds. I have never seen it, but how can a man see these things that God has made and not rejoice and think about God? Mervin saw it and felt it, and you and me and others may never know what his last thoughts were. But if I am the only man on earth that has no doubt about where my wife is, it doesn't matter to me. I'll go on believing it. She's in heaven. There are only two forces in this world, one is God and the other is Satan, one is good and the other is evil, and in times like this that you and me and others go through, we feel both of their presence. God has made us many promises only He can keep, and Satan will come to us, the dirty dog that he is, to try and confuse us and cause us to doubt every promise that was given to us. I'm sure you know the story of when Jesus walked on the water and how one of the disciples went to meet Him. Anyway, what happened? Yeah! When he lost sight of Jesus he began to sink, didn't he? He didn't sink because he was a bad person or didn't believe what he was supposed to believe. When he looked at Jesus, he was able to get back up and walk on the water again. Don't allow yourself to doubt that Mervin is in heaven. It may take more time than you would like for you to be able to deal with Mervin's death. You may be like me. You may never learn to deal with it, and that's okay. Just don't forget that Mervin is in heaven. Anyway, I've got to get going. You might want to know that my life has been lived pretty foolishly and can be pretty unstable most of the time. But if someone like me can find a way to go on with life, then anyone can. May God bless you and your family."

This was a letter sent from Ohio, and yes, I only met this person one time. My tears just flow right now, but you know, I can never explain how all this mail and everything came right on time. Here is a non-Amish, yes, but what does that have to do with it, we all have sinned and come short. Do we sometimes judge too much? We must be very careful not to judge anyone. I wrote before how we "must" think good things about Mervin and try hard as it is to go on in life. Here I sit trying to write and my crying does not want to stop. Mervin, so many people tried to help us through this thing. How can we ever thank them all? You know, we have between 900 and 1,000 cards and some of them will never be forgotten. I truly believe some people are helped by God to write their letters to us. Just the right words at just the right time. How else could all this be? God is in control. If I could just give myself up to His plan! "Strengthen my faith." Yes, this "thing" does get somewhat better, but it's always there, just going around and around in my mind. Maybe if I keep on writing I will come up with a name for that thing. You're in a better place. I've heard it a thousand times. And at least a thousand times I've rejoiced for you. But the reason why I'm broken, the reason why I cry, is how long must I wait to be with you? I close my eyes and I see your face. If home is where my heart is, then I'm out of place. Lord, won't You give me the strength to make it through somehow! I've never been more homesick than now. Help me, Lord, because I don't understand Your ways. The reason why, I wonder if I'll ever know, but even if You show me the hurt would be the same. Because I'm still so far away from home. In Christ there are no good-byes. In Christ there are no ends. So I'll hold unto Jesus with all that I have, to see you again. Sometimes I write and have no idea what will come next. I really wonder sometimes how many first times there are yet. There are so many times that memories of you just come rushing back when I do something or when I am somewhere. How long will this go on? Oh Mervin, you might think I'm trying to forget you. No, no, no, your memory lives on. It's just that sometimes I wonder how long will it hurt so? Dear brother, son, Mervin, the moment that you died, my heart was split in two. The one side filled with memory. The other died with you. I often lay awake at night, when all the world is fast asleep. I'll take a walk down memory lane with tears upon my cheeks. Remembering you is easy; I do it every day. But missing you is a heartache that never fades away. I hold on tightly within my heart and there you will remain. Life will go on without you but will never be the same. I remember so well you always enjoyed looking at the beautiful rainbows and sunsets. You always told us to come up to your room, on the porch; we could see them better up there. But I'm sure they can't compare to the beauty and joy you share up there. People tell us to keep looking up. Someday we hope to see you again. Every time I think of rainbows and how you would tell us to quickly come and look, I have to think of that rainbow when we were setting your gravestone. My, it was so nice to see that. You really did make a difference in our lives, and helped us to see the beauty sometimes when we were too busy to look. You stopped to look! Your memories live on! Sometimes I can hardly wait till Jesus comes, then all the heartaches will be gone. So come! I guess the most important question we can ask ourselves is if we would die in the next five minutes, are we ready? Jesus died and rose from the dead to make it possible for us to go to heaven. Yes, He wants us there. He wants to take us someday where He is. He has prepared a place for us. Are we ready? We will never grow old in heaven or be sick. Yes, we will never know the sorrow or heartache of losing a loved one up there. How beautiful heaven must be. Sweet home of the happy and free. Yes, I want to make peace with God and make ready for heaven. Jesus paid it all. We are promised that God will wipe away all our tears (Rev. 21:4). All our suffering will be gone; sorrow and sighing will flee away (Isaiah 35:10). Every aching heart will be healed. What a beautiful thought! "Neither shall there be any more mourning, nor crying, nor pain, for the former things are passed away" (Rev. 21:4). "To him that overcometh will I grant to sit with me in my throne, even as I also overcame, and am set down with my Father in his throne" (Rev. 3:21). But yes, we all know until then there is quite a battle to fight, an enemy to defeat. Satan will try us to the end. We know God wants no one to miss it. I have so often wondered where you are, Mervin. I guess it really does not make any difference where we go as long as we are together. Where God is, there is heaven. We look for a city which hath foundations, whose builder and maker is God (Heb. 11:8-10). Soon the journey will be over. Each step and each day brings us closer. I hope and pray we can hear the voice saying, "Well done, thou good and faithful servant, enter into the joy of the Lord." Yes, the trumpets shall sound and life here as we know it will be no more. Are we ready? Never ever in my life did death seem so real. Yes, Mervin, one minute you were so full of fun and healthy, and the next minute you were gone. Gone where? I really did not expect to write so much today, but I'm so full of that thing and I just have to let it out. I really do not think I could really talk to someone today without just crying and crying, so I just do it here on paper. Let the tears roll. I will feel somewhat better after I have a good cry. "Strengthen my faith." I will end my writing today like this. "I'll lend you for a little while a child of mine, He said. For you to love while he lives and mourn when he is dead. It may be six or seven years or twenty-two or three. But will you, till I call him back, take care of him for me? He'll bring his charms to gladden you, and shall his stay be brief, you'll have his lovely memories as solace for your grief. I cannot promise he will stay, since all from earth return. But there are lessons taught down there I want this child to learn. I've looked the wide world over in my search for teachers true, and from the throngs that crowd life's lanes, I have selected you. Now will you give him all your love, nor think the labor vain? Nor hate me when I come to call, to take him back again? I fancied that I heard them say, Dear Lord, Thy will be done. For all the joy thy child shall bring, the risk of grief we'll run. We'll shelter him with tenderness; we'll love him while we may. And for the happiness we've known will ever grateful stay. But shall the angels call for him much sooner than we planned, we'll brave the bitter grief that comes and try to understand." Yes, according to this, Mervin, you were not really ours; you were just here for us for a little while. God had other plans. God gave you to us for a while and then He wanted you back. If I can only get that into my head, that you were not really ours, just put here for us to take care of, not knowing or being promised how long.

We miss you so! We know life is a struggle and is not an easy road. Yesterday I was working outside and after a bit I caught myself singing. It almost scared me, because I do not think I sang out loud once since you died. It really felt kind of good. Thank you, Lord! I have to think back over our vacation last week, and think, yes, it did help some to step in the right direction. At least it looked like the children forgot for awhile and really had fun. I guess life must go on. I so much want the children to enjoy life again and be more normal. "Thy will be done."

Hello, Mervin. Here I am again. It's your dad, you know. I am sitting at the graveyard writing to you. My mind just goes and goes. Yes, I thought I must come over here tonight. I don't know why, but I am missing you so much right now. It has now been 5 months, you know. I'm sitting here on top of this hill and what a view I have from here. Yes, Mervin, you are in a beautiful graveyard. Last night your friends called from Wyoming. Yes, Bowser and some others are out there. They went to the spot where you were killed. When Bowser told me they were there, the chills just went up and down my spine. He said they found some debris from the wreck. Then it's true, I guess, all this we have been hearing about your death. Can't it just be a big, bad dream? He said there were 20 boys standing around that hill yesterday, August of 2005. This was the first time your friends, or anybody from PA, was there. After I hung up last night, I just didn't know which way to go. I went out into the cornfield and just cried and cried. What's wrong with me? Here I am at the graveyard writing and I can hardly see for tears running down my cheeks. Lord, help me to go on! Every time I'm here at the graveyard, I can picture you so well. Your face shone so bright in that casket when we had it open here before we buried you. I can just picture that like it was yesterday. Are you okay? I have such a longing to see where you were killed. I don't know, but I just might jump on the train and go. Yes, people said when we were here at the graveyard to set your gravestone that that's about the last thing we can do for you. I just do not feel like I will be finished until I see the exact spot where you were killed. Oh, how I wonder, did you see Jesus there on that mountain in Wyoming? Where are you? "Lord, strengthen my faith." All I can think of all day long is that spot on the mountain. I laid all your things out today upstairs in the barn. We want to divide them out soon, your clothes that you had on and all your other things. My, oh my, I just have such a hard time today. Will this thing get a little lighter soon? Right now it seems that's about all I can think of, you and how short a time we had together. You know, we had a funeral today, Sam Kinsinger's son, and we didn't go. Why not? I don't know, I'm so torn on which way I'm going. Lord, help me and guide me. "Not my will, but thine." I'm in such a turmoil, not really knowing what I want or where to go. Well, I am going to jump on the scooter and go home.

Light in the Shadow of Death

chapter 10

Another First

HERE I AM again. Time goes on and does not stop for anyone. I'm trying so hard to go on and quite often I stumble and fall. We had a chance to go to a neighboring church district last Sunday with John and Ruth Yoder of Topeka, Indiana. I was very glad we went, as it was another first. You know they are everywhere, those firsts. It was preached of this sign on a church poster board which read, "Preach the Gospel and if necessary use words." Isn't that how it is? Are we letting our light shine? Am I letting my light shine? I was told that grieving and self-pity are first cousins. My, oh my, where is that fine line? I'm so mixed up! Lord, help me to know the difference. I keep thinking, yes, Mervin, you are gone and you are only one of our children, but my, oh my, that number 1 is a real big number. We are getting cards again. How nice that the young people are sending some every day. You young folks will never know how much you have helped to lift us up. Some of the young folks were away at the time of Mervin's death. The card we got from one of them this week was very precious. She wrote, "So many people talked about how the funeral was so touching. Broke many hearts and changed many lives. I wish I could have been there." Some people just know how to lift us up. Thank you very much! If this death could be of help to anyone, then I must "thank God". Mervin, your friends are so precious to us. On Sunday after church we went home and I got this urge to be with you young folks. We all went to supper and singing that night. I just was not in the mood for company. What's going on here? I do like company, but I guess like the Bible says, there is a time for everything. I hope no one thinks we do not want company. It's just that, oh, I don't know how to explain it. I'm having such a hard time knowing that all these boys were at the exact spot where you were killed. It just floods my soul. On another card we got it read, "We know you're going through a difficult time right now, and you can be sure that God knows it too. We wish we could do something to make everything all right for you, but since we can't we just want you to know that we are praying for you. Sometimes we wonder why things like this happen. We don't have the answers, but we do know this much, God won't let you go through this by yourself. He'll be with you all the way. He's always there when you need Him and He wants so much to comfort you. He'll give you the courage to carry on and the strength to handle whatever comes. If there's something we can do for you, we want to help in any way we can. So please remember that you are not alone, for God cares and so do we." That beautiful writing can lift us up. The load of yesterday, today and tomorrow is too heavy to carry all at once. It is a triple burden. The conflicts of yesterday and the fears of tomorrow rob our hearts and homes of peace today.

We can remember yesterday without harboring its hurts. We can plan tomorrow without fear and worry. The Bible tells us that Jesus said we should never be troubled about tomorrow. Tomorrow will take care of itself. "The day's own trouble is enough for the day," said He. This one day, today, has enough demand of its own. If we face it with God, He will give us strength for each "today" as it comes. By His redeeming Son, He will cleanse our hearts from the guilt of yesterday and give us courage for tomorrow. Here in heaven is real peace today, no matter what else happens.

I said, "God, it hurts."
And God said, "I know."
I said, "God, I cry a lot."
And God said, "That's why I gave you tears."
I said, "God, I am so depressed."
And God said, "That's why I gave you sunshine."
I said, "God, life is hard."
And God said, "That is why I gave you loved ones."
I said, "God, my loved one died."
And God said, "So did Mine."
I said, "God, it is such a loss."
And God said, "I saw Mine nailed to a cross."
I said, "God, but Your loved one lives."
And God said, "So does yours."
I said, "God, where are they now?"
And God said, "Mine is on My right side
    and yours is in the light."
I said, "God, it hurts."
And God said, "I know."

Hello, Mervin, it's the middle of August already, yes, five and a half months that you're gone. I get such a longing to see you sometimes. I just can hardly stand it. Sometimes if it would help I would just scream. The company is getting less, and yes, life does go on. I had such a good visit this week with Sam Kinsinger. Yes, how my heart aches for them. Their eighteen-year-old son died last week. What a great testimony he had. This boy, Sam Jr., wrote and said some very touching things. How great is our God. He died in the hospital, and yes, I guess something did go wrong with the operation. But the way he wrote we cannot blame the doctors or anyone else. If I do not live do not put me on life support, just say it was God's will that I die. You know, we like to put the blame on someone or something else whenever we can, don't we? Yes, the doctors do make mistakes, but who doesn't? We think they are perfect or something! No, they are not, but they are trying to do the best they can. I think and I feel like we should not be so quick to blame when something goes wrong. God is in control, and yes, only He can give us life or death. It's all in His hands. But yes, my heart just aches when I think of the Kinsingers and their rough road ahead. Sometimes it seems like it is not even a road at all. We should think often on the four last things:

On death, of which there is nothing more certain.

On the judgment day, of which there is nothing more terrible.

On hell, for there is nothing more unbearable.

And on heaven, for there is nothing more joyful.

He who often thinks on these things will stay away from lots of sins and be and stay more in godliness. My, Mervin, I don't know, but my mind is so busy thinking about you. I often wonder, what was I thinking and what was in my mind before you were killed? It's so full of you and memories now that there is hardly room for anything else. I really do want to give it over to you, Lord. Help me to stay strong. "Precious memories". I talked to some of your friends that were out on the hill where you were killed. How I long to go there! They told me they sang right there on the hill. Did you see Jesus there? They sang, and my, how I cried to know that. How touching. They said they sang, "Precious memories, unseen angels, sent from somewhere to my soul. How they linger ever near me, and the sacred past unfold. Precious memories, how they linger, how they ever flood my soul. In the stillness of the midnight, precious, sacred scenes unfold. Precious father, loving mother, fly across the lonely years, and old home scenes of my childhood in fond memory appears. In the stillness of the midnight echoes from the past I hear; old time singing, gladness bringing, from that lovely land somewhere. As I travel on life's pathway, know not what the years may hold; as I ponder, hope grows fonder, precious memories flood my soul." Did you hear them singing? I keep thinking how that would sound out there on top of that mountain. I just have this, what is it, a longing to see you or what? They took some things out there in the wilderness, verses and so on. One wrote that God our Father came down from heaven and picked a precious flower. He was our dearest friend, now he's gone to bloom above where peace and love never end. The last words spoken are now so precious to me. We hope to meet you there, where we will everlasting be. Yes, how I long to see you again. We should beware of discontentment, or a spirit that's never satisfied. Is that what you call this thing? Please, Lord, help me to be satisfied. Yes, it is the grace of God that allows us to have suffering and troubles. God gives us different blessings so that we do not despair in want, but then He also puts on a portion of trouble and pain lest we become proud and get too great a joy. We know that no matter what comes or how bad things get for us, we must remember that because of our sins we deserve far worse. We all have sinned and come short, so maybe, Mervin, you were killed so that God can show us that He is still in control. Do we forget sometimes and just take our own way? We all need to try a little bit harder and not fall by the way. Help me, Lord!

Stretching sleepily, the boy wondered why he had that strange empty feeling in his stomach. Then it all came back to him. He glanced over at the other bed. Yes, it was empty. It really was true that his big brother, Jimmy was gone. It was almost 6 months since Jimmy had gone out West to Wyoming and had not come back. Tears rolled down the boy's face as he remembered. There had been an accident and Jimmy had been killed. Mom said he had gone to heaven.

The door to the boy's room opened and his mother came in. "Good morning. I see you're already awake," she said. Noticing his tears she sat beside him on the bed. "You're thinking of Jimmy, aren't you?" she asked. "Daddy and I miss him too, but we try to remember how happy he is with Jesus."

"But Mom, how do you know that?" asked the boy.

"I know because Jimmy accepted Jesus as his Savior," Mom answered, "and the Bible says that when those who trust in Jesus leave this life, they go to be with Him."

The boy nodded. "Yes, but I still don't understand," he said with a sob. "You always say Jimmy is in heaven, but he was right there in the casket and then he was put in the ground at the cemetery." The boy covered his face with his hands.

"Jimmy's body is in the grave, but his soul, or his life, the real Jimmy is with Jesus," explained Mom.

The boy looked at his hands. "But my head and my hands and my ears and eyes, this is me, isn't it?"

Mom shook her head. "Not really," she said. "Your body is just a house in which the real you, your soul, lives. Your body may die, but not your soul. It lives. Jimmy's body died, and we buried it, but God took Jimmy's life, his soul, to heaven, not to the cemetery."

The boy sighed. "But I still wish I could see Jimmy every day."

"I know," Mom answered, giving him a hug. "We all do. We can't see him again here on earth, but because we know Jesus, we can look forward to seeing him in heaven one day. Then we'll all be together forever."

Yes, my thoughts are everywhere this last while, so strengthen my faith. People are still trying so hard to cheer us up. Last night we were invited to supper at Ernie's. What a treat that was. It was so nice to be away and be a little more normal. Remember, that new normal I'm looking for! Also, we are still getting mail. Yesterday the card read, "Throughout this time of sorrow, may your faith in God above surround you with the comfort found within His lasting love." Yes, life has so many changes for us and some are sad and touching, and yet how wonderful. The way the Lord planned for us to be on this earth for a season and then He calls us home. No, I can't come to the bottom of it all; it is so deep. We must trust and surrender ourselves and our loved ones in His tender care and be ready when He calls. Sometimes I think death also has a very special and peaceful side to it, if we can look beyond the pain and vision what you, Mervin, at this very minute could be enjoying. We miss you so much. Love brings pain. Does that make sense? We loved you so much and now that love is very painful. "It is better to have loved and lost than to not have loved at all." "Whosoever will come after me, let him deny himself, and take up his cross and follow me. For whosoever will save his life shall lose it, but whosoever shall lose his life for my sake and the gospel's, the same shall save it. For what shall it profit a man if he shall gain the whole world and lose his own soul" (Mark 8:34-36)? You know, it's still so nice when people ask about you, Mervin. My heart skips a beat every time I hear your name. Go ahead and mention my child, the one who died, you know. Don't worry about hurting me further. The depth of my pain doesn't show. Don't worry about making me cry. I'm already crying inside. Help me heal by releasing the tears that I try to hide. I'm hurt when you just keep silent, pretending it doesn't exist. I'd rather you would mention my child, knowing that he has been missed. You ask me how I am doing. I say "pretty good or fine," but healing is something ongoing. I feel it will take a lifetime.

August 14th. Good morning, Mervin. This is Sunday morning before church and I just thought I had to talk to you this morning. I still can really not believe sometimes that this is true and I am so looking for comfort. I was just reading our Scriptures for today in church (Luke 18 & 19). I see that it reads that it is easier for a camel to go through a needle's eye than for a rich man to enter the kingdom of God. What does it mean? A needle's eye in those days was, I think, a small door going into a city. I picture it, as a camel must have had to go way down on his knees to get in. No wonder the people ask, "Who then can be saved?" I have that question so many times. Who then can be saved? Jesus said in Luke 18:27, 29) "God can do things that are not possible for people to do." So it is not possible on our own to earn the kingdom of God. We need God's help! So help us, God. I'm so wondering how the preachers today will explain it. Yes, Mervin, I have so many questions still and I know I should put my trust more in God. I ask God so many times, not really expecting an answer. Why you, Mervin? Then sometimes I catch myself thinking, why not you? Oh no, why not you? But yes, you had accepted Christ as your Savior. I remember you saying, "I believe that Jesus Christ is God's Son." I also read how Jesus explained to the apostles what was going to happen to Him. They just could not understand sometimes. It seems it was told to them pretty clearly what will happen to Jesus, but they just did not understand. Lord, help me to understand Your ways! Okay, now I feel better and it's time to go to church. I miss you so, Mervin!

Hello again. Oh my, here I am again all torn. Church was very interesting, but, you know, Mervin, Sunday afternoon we found out your good friend, Jonathan King Jr., drowned. How can it be? He was not a good swimmer and went underwater and did not come up. Is he with you now? Did you see him when he died? Are you together in heaven now? My heart just aches as we spend time with Jonathan's parents. Hopefully I can be a help to them by just being there. You know, there is so little to say, except, "Thy will be done." Oh Lord, give them strength to hold on to Your ways. The road ahead seems almost impossible, but with Your help, Lord, they will go on. Please help Jonathan's parents, Lord. The funeral is tomorrow and we are going today just to be with them. How our hearts are torn open. Remember, Mervin, Jonathan was here a lot when you were running around. Your friends were all there last night, and some of them just cried and cried. Help them, Lord, so they can stay strong and trust in You. Guide them on a good path. Keep them in Your loving care. You know, Lord, death, well, it does bring us all together. Is that what You want? I don't know why, Lord, but I have such a fear of another one of our children dying, or what's wrong with me? Why do I think stuff like that? I guess because I know it can happen to us. You know, before it was always someone else. Help me, Lord, to trust. Yes, trust and say, "Thy will be done." "The Lord can take away. Blessed be the name of the Lord." Some day hopefully we will know why things like this happen. Help me to be like Job in the Bible. Satan, stay away. We know Satan can work through people that are dear to us, like Job's friends were doing and saying. Can we even imagine having ten children taken in one day? What a lesson we can get out of the book of Job in the Bible. We know in times like this, we must not ask "how" can I get out of this. We should say "what" can I get out of this. When life is difficult it's very easy to give up, but I'm sure giving up would be the worst thing we could do. Yes, I think the best way to help people that are hurting is just to be with them, saying very little or maybe even nothing, just letting them know you care. Don't try to explain everything; explaining will never heal a broken heart. I was at Jonathan's last night, and yes, my mind is so full, but that was not the place or the time to let it all out. Just be there, that's enough. I really do not think there is anything wrong with asking why this or why that, as long as we do not get the idea that God "owes" us an answer. Remember even Jesus said, "Why hast thou forsaken me" (Matthew 27:46)? We must remember that to heal a broken heart it takes lots of love. We can read in Eph. 4:15, "You must speak the truth, but be sure to speak the truth in love." The right words spoken at the right time gave me a boost that I cannot explain. So we must be careful what we say. The wrong words spoken when someone has a broken heart, oh my, I'm saying again, "Be careful what you say." Those words slice like a knife right through our bodies. Even though sometimes those words might be true, yes, people, I think it's better to just say nothing and just be there. Please give grieving parents, brothers, sisters or whoever a chance to come out of that thing, whatever it's called. Yes, I still do not have a name for it. We say and do things that later we wish we would not have, but don't we all, I guess. "Rejoice with those that rejoice, and weep with them that weep" (Romans 12:15). This is very good to follow if we can. We must be careful that we do not ask God to tell other people what they need to know, unless we are willing for Him to show us what we need to know. So help me, Lord. This grief can be shared by many people and they mean well, but it can only be shared for real by those who know what it's like to be so far down in this pit. Yes, and we feel sometimes like God has gone off somewhere taking care of other people. Strengthen my faith! How do we keep a good level of faith in times like these, when severe pain and that big hole is there? Help us, Lord! I feel so much like I am not coming up to, oh, what am I trying to say, I just go so far up and then so far down. Bring us to a "new normal" level, please. Why does it seem that you went so early in life, Mervin? I don't know, I just can't explain my feelings. I guess all I can say is death must be right on time, like a flower. A good prayer to pray each morning for me would be, "Lord, please help me today not to add to anybody's burden; much more, just help someone along the way." If you want to be an encouragement to hurting people, try to see things through their eyes. Be humble enough to admit that there might be other points of view. I read that when God puts His own people into the furnace, He keeps His eye on the clock and His hand on the thermostat. He knows how long and how much. We question why He does it to begin with or why doesn't He turn down the heat or even turn it off. Job 23:10: "But He knows the way that I take; when He has tested me, I shall come forth as gold." Is that how it is? Are we being tested? Gold does not fear the fire; the furnace can only make the gold purer and brighter. I really did not think I would write so much this morning, but the pen just kept on going. Think about this. It's good to enjoy the things money can buy, if you don't lose the things that money can not buy.

The Sermon

I'M BACK, MERVIN. I have just got to talk to you! Today we put your good friend, Jonathan King Jr., in his grave. Oh, how my heart hurt for your friends. I hope they can stay strong. I just can hardly see my way through sometimes. We heard such a good, uplifting sermon. I felt like the preacher was preaching directly to me. Mervin, I have so many questions. I really feel like some of them were answered today. Give God the glory. My tears just flowed and flowed today and these last couple days. My, Mervin, what would you say? Your friends looked so sad. Lord, lift them up, please. We heard about self-pity from the preacher today and I feel an answer to my prayer. I sure do not want to get to the place where self-pity takes over. The preacher said today he thinks if we can have a good cry and then feel better it's not self-pity. My, if that is true, I can really relate to that. I still do feel so much better after a good cry. Thank You, Lord! I even caught myself thanking the Lord for that feeling after I heard your good friend was gone. I thank the Lord that I can have a part of this death thing and can partly feel for Jonathan's parents. Notice that I say partly. Yes, I really think death is death, but different, for us all. So death is different but still the same. Each one in his own way that no one can take away or add to. Mervin, you were special. Oh my, when

I went into the room with your good friend Jonathan lying there in his coffin, uncontrolled crying just came. Lift me up, Lord, and help me in this journey. Also, we heard today from the preacher how homesickness can get our minds all mixed up. My, how true! Sometimes I just can't think straight and surely can not be myself, no matter how hard I try. No, we do not want to say the Lord's timing is wrong. We know all things are right on time. It seems like one step forward and then two steps back. What's wrong here? Am I not trying hard enough or what? You know it will soon be six months that you're gone. Some of you might say, "Get over it. What's wrong with you?" But, you know, I will just let you talk. I need more time, please. Sometimes I just need to be alone and, you know, even Jesus took time to get away and renew Himself in prayer. I just need to get away from the hustle and bustle of life sometimes. I need some time alone. I wonder sometimes, will I be able to say good-bye to you, Mervin, and really mean it? Am I just making it harder by not saying good-bye? The story has ended, I guess, and no matter how much I cry and hope for something different, you're gone. Sometimes it seems like the load is so heavy; for sure when you see one of the children is having a hard day. Sometimes it seems like a double load to carry. My heart so aches for them sometimes. I try so hard to make them feel good, by acting like I'm okay. What would this look like if a hurt could be seen. Yes, we can somewhat hide our hurt so we do not take everybody else down with us. Yes, help me to accept that Mervin is gone. Maybe I can accept that you are gone, but I will never forget you. I guess I will get to the end of this road, but only with God's time. Not when I think, but thy will be done. How long is long enough? I guess as long as it takes! Right! When I heard about your friend Jonathan, I felt like, oh, I don't know, we must go and do something for his parents. Is that what this thing is all about, helping others who are troubled and down and hit rock bottom? Lord, lift them up, please. I think it's in the plan for us to start healing. No, Lord, I do not want to stay in this deep pit or whatever you call it. You, Lord, are the only one who has the power to heal our hurt. Thank you, Lord, that we need not grieve as those who have no hope. We have sorrow but not despair, we have loneliness but we are not alone. No, I can't say now that's over.

I'm done with my grief. No, no, when will it end? I will try to take one day at a time and not try to worry so about tomorrow. Sometimes I reread what I wrote and feel like, yes, Lord, I have come a long way. Help me the rest of the way. When I look back I wonder, did I really hurt that much? We know the journey is not nearly over, but we also know nothing can separate us from the love of God. He will walk with us through that valley and over that mountain. It wasn't you. I thought I saw you today standing there in the checkout line, just out of reach. I started to call your name, but I stopped. My mind said it wasn't you. It couldn't be you. My heart said otherwise. I am embarrassed by the tears that came unbidden to wash away my disappointment. I wrestled like Jacob with the angel until I had conquered. Once more my grief, the struggle, left me. Feeling out of joint, the world slipped away as I left the store. There was only me and my grief, not you. Never again a "you". Finally I grabbed my grief by the neck, shouting and screaming. Oh yeah, we also heard in the sermon today that sometimes when we fall down on our knees to pray, nothing but moaning and groaning comes out. But we were told that God understands that language too. It's okay. The road is rough. I said, "Dear Lord, the many stones hurt me so." He said, "Dear child, I understand. I too walked there for a time, my child." "My burden," I said, "is too great. Oh, how can I bear it so?" "My child, I remember its weight. I carried my cross, you know. I wish there were friends with me, who would make my way their own. Yes," He said, "Gethsemane was so hard to face alone." So now I climb the stony path, content at last to know that where my Master has not gone neither would I want to go. And strangely now I find new friends and life's burdens grow less sore as I remember how long ago He too went this way. We also heard in the sermon about how Adam and Eve were talked into taking of the fruit in the Garden of Eden. How Satan tries to bring us over to his side, but oh, how dark his side can be. "Sin came into the world through one man, Adam, and death through sin, and so death spread to all men because all sinned" (Romans 5:18). Sin wants to have its own way every day, all the time. "Whoever does not believe is condemned already, because he has not believed in the name of the only begotten Son of God" (John 3:18). Jesus stood in for all of us when He died on the cross, taking on Himself all our sins if we ask Him. Don't delay; ask today! Let God into your life today. Jesus offers forgiveness, eternal life and a place in God's family. Yes, Mervin, sometimes I'm so mixed up and just think life is so hard to understand, but there is hope. I have always felt at times like these there is so little anyone can say, for there are no words that have ever been invented to fit the loss of a loved one. Jesus said, "Whosoever liveth and believeth in me shall never die." Death is not the end; it is really the beginning of life. "Eye hath not seen, nor ear heard, neither have entered into the heart of man, the things which God hath prepared for them that love him" (1 Corinthians 2:9). We know sorrow and disappointments come, more to some people than to others, but some comes to us all. But out of sorrow can come good things. Lord, help me to become better and not bitter. Life goes on.

The Half Year Mark

AUGUST 25, 2005, again a sunny hello to you, Mervin. My, oh my, time just keeps on going. I don't know why, but the 28th of August is coming and that will be a half year since you've been gone. Why do I feel so like it just can't be a half year already? So much has been happening. Last night lots of your friends were at our place and they brought pizza and ice cream. I really did enjoy seeing them again, but where were you, Mervin? Things are starting to go pretty good for me again. You know, that feeling is still very strong, but I can have a good laugh now and then. I feel like I'm doing okay. But there are so many things that come up, like the mailman brings so much mail addressed to you. Junk mail, you know, but your name is on the front. My heart skips a beat still when I see your name. I think of you so much and sometimes can hardly wait to see you again. I said I will not be looking for golden streets and crystal clear streams, or what am I saying, but yes, I will be looking for you. I miss you so. People are still sending cards and saying things to make us feel better. We are so looking forward to having our friends come from Indiana, Joas's mom and dad and his brothers and sisters. We have only met them one time but feel like we have known them for a long, long time.

A number of years ago, on the quiet waters of the Niagara River, a young man anchored his boat along a bank. He lay down in his boat to take a nap. While he lay sleeping, the anchor let loose and the boat started out toward Niagara Falls. The people along the bank saw what was happening and called to the young man, screaming and trying to wake him. At last he heard their cries and saw what was going on. The boat caught for a few moments against some rocks, long enough for the young man to be rescued. Would it not have been better for the crowd to have remained quiet and allowed the young man to rest? The scare must have been terrible. You will say that such an attitude would have been almost criminal. But listen, isn't this the attitude so many people are taking about their soul and the soon approaching end. There is a big danger ahead for all of us, a much greater danger than going over a waterfall. It is the danger of an eternity without God. An eternity of terrible torment and anguish. Through love Christ is calling you to flee for refuge from this eternal danger. Escape is yet possible. There is one who can save us from going over the falls. Consider the course you are taking. Are you drifting with the tide toward the falls or have you been rescued? Christ is longing to rescue you! So come.

Good morning, Mervin. Oh my, I'm here at the shack in Maryland where we had our last hunt together. I slept here last night, or tried off and on and would fall asleep. I thought of you so much. Your bed covers are still just like you left them that last night we spent here together. My mind is just going around and around and I hardly know what to do. Last night I was standing on the shack porch at about 3:00 wondering where you are. I looked up in the sky but did not see you. It was such a beautiful night. The moon had a big ring around it. I just stood there with tears rolling down my face. This morning I can hardly stand the thought of you not coming here to hunt with us. I took a walk last night in the woods to look at your tree stand. Is it really true that you are never going to hunt with us again? I'm sitting here at the table in the shack and can hardly see to write. The tears and crying are almost taking over. What's going on here? My, I miss you so much. I could just see you that last night here. You waved as you walked out over the field and we said, "Good luck." I could still see you wave. Please, Lord, I need you now to keep me all in one piece. What's going on here? I just keep looking into your bed and knowing that those covers were left just like that by you, Mervin. Did you know? Really, I don't even want to fix that bed. Precious memories. So many times I think, if I had only known you were going. My, I just want to talk to you again. Last night I talked to you out loud a lot. Did you hear me? I guess just to talk a one-sided conversation is as close as I can get. We loved you so. I just wish I would have showed it more. You know, I'm not that good at voicing my feelings, but you children mean so much to me. Sometimes I just want to hold you and tell you all this stuff. At daybreak this morning when the sun started to come up it was such a beautiful sunrise. I looked for you in those clouds. The sky is full of jet streams as I sit here at the shack writing to you. I keep looking up, thinking maybe I'm missing something up there. Yes, Mervin, your brother was here and put your memory cards on these walls. You live on with us in our minds. I don't want the good memories we have to go away. Good examples you left back for us. Lord, help me to remember. You were never a greedy hunter, always saying good luck and really meaning it. I can not believe how I feel about going out in the woods here. Everywhere I go you were there. That overwhelming feeling gets me any old time it wants. If everybody would hunt like you did, there would be lots of good hunters around. Remember how I asked you to go to the tree stand that I was going to because of that nice big buck? You said, "No way. That's your stand tonight." If only I would have known it was our last hunt together. Oh well, what then? What would that have helped me? I just wish sometimes that this big empty feeling would get less. Oh yeah, it's getting better, you know, but sometimes I hardly can see my way through. Next Sunday will be a half year that you've been gone. How can it be? "Strengthen my faith." I'm so glad I can have this chance to hunt with your brother Gideon now this year. He seems to be excited about it. I know he has to force himself sometimes, but he sure is trying very hard to go on. My heart nearly breaks when I look at him sometimes and think, yes, you are our only son now. When did all this happen? I'm so proud of you now, Gideon, for staying strong through all of this "thing". I am so looking forward to seeing you grow up, and yes, I do want to say all in the Lord's plan. You know I had such big plans for Mervin, or should

I say dreams of a wife and little children. That was not to be, so I want to say, Lord, thy will and not mine be done. If I could only give myself up and realize that your plan is the right plan. You know with my small mind, I just can't see into it. In my way of thinking I still wanted Mervin. No way, I was not ready to give him up. What are your plans for us, Lord? Help us to go on with whatever you throw our way. Strengthen our faith!

Tucked away in our minds is a nice vision. We see ourselves on a long trip that spans the continent. We are traveling by train. Out the windows we drink in the passing scene of cars on highways, of children waving, of smoke from a power plant, of rows of corn and wheat, of mountains and rolling hills, of city skylines and village halls. But uppermost in our minds is the final destination. On a certain day at a certain hour we will pull into the station. Once we get there so many wonderful dreams will come true and the pieces of our lives will fit together like a completed jigsaw puzzle. How restlessly we pace the aisles waiting, waiting and waiting for the station. When we reach the station that will be it! We cry. When I'm eighteen, when I have paid off the mortgage, when I get a promotion. When I reach the age of retirement, I shall live happily ever after. Sooner or later we must realize there is no station. The true joy of life is the trip. The station is only a dream. It is always just out of reach. "Relish the moment", is a good motto. It isn't the burdens of today that drive men mad. It is the regrets over yesterday and the fear of tomorrow. Regret and fear are twin thieves that rob us of today. So stop pacing the aisles and counting the miles. Instead, climb more mountains, swim more rivers, watch more sunsets, laugh more and cry less. Life must be lived as we go along. The station will come soon enough. Now go play more with the children and stop worrying so and put your trust in Jesus.

Here I am again, Mervin. It's now over six months that you're gone. I just came back from the graveyard. I was weed-eating and cleaning up around there and watering your tree. I don't know what is going on, Lord. Why do I have such an empty feeling? What's going on? I could just scream again. I wonder am I missing something or is this normal? My, oh my, that hole inside me is so big right now. I wonder will that "thing" get better soon? I just do not feel like doing anything and have such an "aw, let me alone" feeling. I just wish I could enjoy life a little more like it used to be. What are your plans for me, Lord? Thy will be done! Sometimes I get bad thoughts about all this and wonder what's going on. Was this true? If it was, why? I must find something to get in a better mood and have a better attitude of this "thing". It seems nothing wants to help. Yes, we have friends coming from Indiana and that has me cheered up somewhat, but, but. . . Is this how I am supposed to feel, Lord, or what? If so, why?

As you do your work each day,
Painful memories cross your heart,
And you often think back sadly
To the day you had to part
From your dear departed loved one.
Even now it brings the tears.
Will it always press so strongly
On into the coming years?
Oh, they say time heals the sorrow,
And we're glad it is that way,
For God knows we could not carry
Such a burden every day.
So He sends a day of sunshine
After many days of rain,
And we find with moments passing,
That we can endure the pain.
Though at times we feel we cannot,
And we think our hearts will break,
Then we hear a tender whisper,
Fear not, child, I'll not forsake.
So we wipe our falling teardrops;
Meditate on memories sweet.
We no longer think of parting,
But instead when we shall meet.

Yes, there are so many nice verses written up and they do help some, but how long, Lord, will this hurt be so big? For a child who has lost its parents we have the word "orphan". For a husband and wife whose mate has died, we have the words "widow" or "widower". But language has never invented a word to describe a parent who has lost a child. Apparently the grief of losing a child is so profound that no society has developed a word to describe it. Yes, I came up with a word, but it really does not make sense to you all, I'm sure. It's that "thing". That's as close as I got to describe my feelings. Tomorrow is always a new day. Am I maybe stuck in grief? Good grief is accepting the fact that our loved one has died, and accepting the sorrow and the pain. Then why don't I? I guess, just getting through the days, the months and maybe the years. Yes, Lord, just help me get through the first year. If I keep thinking the sun will shine again, just maybe it will! You know, Mervin, I have no choice—you're gone. Yes, Lord, I really did not want a new life. I liked my old one just fine, but I know going back is not a choice. So then, Lord, I will try to move forward. Teach me to understand this "thing". I read of what bad grief really can be like.

A woman convinced her husband to go to a party that he did not want to go to. So he went along and was killed in a car accident. For fourteen years she went to his grave every single morning, regretting the fact that she convinced him to go to something that he didn't want to go to. I read that kind of grief is not of God. We must let go and let God. I want to humble myself before You, God, and please forgive me for not wanting to let You have Mervin. "Cast all your cares on Him for He cares for you" (1 Peter 5:7). Yes, help me to cast my cares on You. I just can't help it; when I look back I get really sad. No, I can't go back and say, I should have done this or I should have done that. It doesn't help me to wish it would have been different, so "thy will be done." I guess I should start reaching out to others more. Maybe that way I can get away from this "thing". Lord, help me to stop worrying and just let You take control. "Seek first the kingdom and His righteousness, and all things will be given you" (Matthew 6:33). Is that the answer? Sure it is, for all of us need to seek "first" the kingdom of God. My, how many of us do it backwards and take our way first? No, no, seek first the kingdom of God. I am convinced that this life is not planned to give us everything we want and be so comfortable and problem free. So, Lord, help us to be content with what we have. I read the difference between depression and sadness is that sadness does not last as long. It's not as intense and it does not stop you. Depression lasts longer and it does stop you. With sadness you can still go about your work, but with depression you only get about 70% out of work. There are so many new things that we find out through a death like this. It's about like being back in school, like first grade and learning. Satan knows when we are weakest, I'm sure. He knows when to come. He is so full of lies and makes me believe stuff that is not good. He, Satan, the devil, was a murderer from the beginning, not holding to the truth, for there is no truth in him. When he lies he speaks his native language, for he is a liar and the father of lies (John 8:44). Forgiveness is a choice, not a feeling. It's not possible to say, "I can't forgive." What you're really saying is, "I won't forgive." You are the only one who can make this choice. Forgiveness leads to freedom. But if you do not forgive men their sins, your Father will not forgive your sins (Matthew 6:14-15). I'm kind of let down sometimes on the direction I'm going. Sometimes I think I'm getting somewhere and then, boom, backwards I go again. I think I was past this part of the "thing" and then it comes back again the next week. I feel like I'm not making much progress right now. Lord, help me to replace my bad thinking with good thinking. You're okay, right, Mervin? I must remember it's always too soon to give up! I'm tempted sometimes by the devil to just give up, but he is a liar, we know. Yes, I know people can not know what we are thinking or feeling if we do not open up and tell them. But you know, how am I supposed to tell other people how I'm feeling when I don't know myself. The bottom of this "thing" is a lot deeper than I ever imagined. Sometimes I feel so hopeless that all I see is shattered dreams. But I know, Lord, they were just my dreams. You had other plans. Yes, Mervin, you're gone, but maybe this is the beginning of something very important in my life. Something that could not be without you, Mervin, being killed. Wow, that word just makes my heart skip a beat. It's true, right? I just wish I would be better at giving comfort to your sisters and your one and only brother. How am I supposed to comfort them when I need all the comfort and encouragement I can get? Lord, help me to keep pressing on. I would like to help other people get ready just in case something like this happens to them, but how? Yes, Mervin, your death seems so wrong to me, but not my will but thine, Lord.

No, I'm not blaming anyone, and even if I could, what would that help? I must live or have a living hope, a godly hope that I will see you again, Mervin. Oh, how I long to see you again. Oh yes, I'm glad for those 23 years we had you with us, only as a gift from the Lord. The Lord gives and the Lord takes away. One thing I am so thankful for with you, Mervin, is all the good memories you left back. How would this be if I would have bad memories of you? I really can't see how I could get through that. I should be more like David (in the Bible) was when his child was dead. He got up and washed himself and put on lotions, changed clothes and went into the house of the Lord and worshiped. "Now the child is dead. Can I bring him back again? I will go to him, but he will not return to me" (2 Samuel 12:15-23). David made the decision to go on living, so help me, Lord. Sometimes I wonder where God was when you were killed, Mervin. But we know He was probably at the same place as He was when His own Son was on the cross and died for our sins.

New Friends Reaching Out

HELLO, HELLO, MERVIN. My, oh my, time just slips away. Yes, our friends from Indiana were here for the weekend. It was a great pleasure to have them here with us. Things like that help us to go on without you. Yes, we really do not have a choice, right? As difficult as it is, our life must go on. No, I will never feel the same again. And that hurt "thing" in my heart will never fully heal. Oh Mervin, this is a new life. The other chapter is done, but the book goes on. We had such a nice time with Vernon and Darlene Miller, but it was much too short. I read that 78% of marriages do not survive the loss of a child. Yes, that's 78%. Yes, it is something that needs to be worked on very hard. Sometimes I'm here at one point of this thing, and it seems like my wife is way over there. To meet in the middle seems so out of reach. It seems like months since we met in the middle, but I know we really have to work on it to get back to the same level of communication. It's really tough, but I also feel that because of your death, Mervin, and our grief, it brought a bond for life between us. I really believe that even if we are going in different directions sometimes, if we keep our eyes on God we will surely meet again. Knowing the percentage of marriages that don't make it, makes me more determined to survive this thing. We need to read 1 Corinthians 7:14-15, and we also know that the Bible says what's in your heart comes out of your mouth. It also says if we confess it, He takes it away as far as the east is from the west. I have found that this grief puts an awful strain on a family and, Lord, help me to understand that each of us is grieving in his or her own way. My, Mervin, sometimes I'm sorry you can't be here to have a part in this. Aw, no, does that make sense? Satan knows when to get us. Take a back seat, you nogooder. Get away from us.

"Therefore encourage one another and build each other up. Live in peace with each other, encourage the timid, help the weak, be patient with everyone. Make sure that nobody pays back wrong for wrong, but always try to be kind to each other and to everyone else. Be joyful always, pray continually, and give thanks in all circumstances, for this is God's will for you in Christ Jesus. May God Himself, the God of peace, sanctify you through and through. May your whole spirit, soul and body be kept blameless at the coming of our Lord Jesus Christ. The one who calls you is faithful and He will do it" (1 Thessalonians 5:11,13-18, 23, 24). We *must* know that we have to give this "thing" over to Him and realize that we have no control over life or death. We know there are so many comforting verses in the Bible. We must read and believe! I have to think of Paul, how he wrote in 2 Corinthians 2:4, "I wrote you out of great distress and anguish of heart and with many tears, not to grieve you, but to let you know the depth of my love for you." Yes, Mervin, I really am getting on or moving on out of this "thing" one step at a time. I see other people getting back to their everyday living and quite often wonder if they forgot. I really wonder sometimes how I will ever be a part of that life again. I guess I'm forgetting sometimes to thank God for bringing me this far, always asking and not thanking enough. I need to thank God from the bottom of my heart for getting me to this point where I feel like I can handle this "thing" a little better. Surely God has a purpose for all of this. The pain I feel will be with me forever, but I do want to try to focus on the future. I really do want to be careful not to let the past control the future. We know God is greater than everything we face and greater than anything we will ever go through. Also, I feel without the church this would be almost impossible. I do not have to feel so alone. I need to focus less on this hurt or this "thing" and look around to see if there are other people, and yes, there always are people we can cheer up. I really need to put all self-pity behind me. I know it's a dead-end street that can only be won by me. "Do nothing from selfishness or empty conceit, but with humility of mind, regard one another as more important than yourselves. Do not merely look out for your own personal interests, but also for the interests of others" (Philippians 2:3-4). Each one should use whatever gift he has received to serve others faithfully, administering God's grace in various forms (1 Peter 4:10). Yes, Mervin, the day is here where I am starting to feel better and soon it will be 7 months that you're gone. How can it be? That better feeling is the grace of God working, I guess. His ways are so far beyond our ways. We can't even imagine. We know God loves us no matter what, and we also know that all things that happen are for our own good. God makes no mistakes. I know we must be very careful when things are going so good for us that we don't just put God on the back burner. We need God every minute of our life! So if through our suffering, grief, or whatever, that "thing," I guess, we come closer to God, then "thank you, Lord". Sometimes I try to go back and remember the guy I was and long for those days. But no, life has changed. I feel sometimes like my job is so much less important, but so be it. We can read it is better to go to a house of mourning than to go to a house of feasting, for death is the destiny of every man. The living should take this to heart (Ecclesiastes 7:2). We know that we feel sometimes like we should be tough, strong and independent, but we must remember God wants us to lean on Him. God's way is right! Yes, Mervin, more than ever you reminded me that we only have one life to live and we really do need to make it count. One thing about this is that when I talk to someone that has lost a loved one it's not that I'm telling them something that I have had no experience with. It really feels good to be able to share with them. We should always take time to approach people who seem down or troubled. Yes, I really can have compassion for others because I know that sick feeling in the pit of my heart that I thought was never going to go away. I know too, that some people want to be left alone in their grief sometimes and other times want to talk. So bear with us, please! I really can not explain all of this "thing". But I do know that it seems like the last 6 months, since you were killed, Mervin, were a big, big, big part of my 52 years here on earth. Does that make sense? Sometimes we doubt that God is everything He says He is, then we must tell Him our doubts. Read the book of John or Mark in the Bible. Yes, sometimes we get to where it seems like the whole world is against us. We can either turn away from the Lord, and walk away from the only hope that we have, or we can fall on our knees and say: Have mercy on me, oh God. I do not understand, but I do believe that you are a forever God and I commit my soul to you. We can do all the good deeds we want, but that will not get us to heaven. Just by going to church and having Christian parents is not good enough either. We must confess and really mean it that Jesus Christ is God's Son. This is not from ourselves, it is the gift of God, not by works, so that no one can boast" (Ephesians 2:8-9, John 3:36). When our old habits and patterns of thinking try to come back we must turn them over to God. This journal of you, Mervin, lets me express my feelings and also lets me look back over the time period and think, yes, progress is taking place and healing is a word I can now use more freely.

Here I am again, Mervin. How are you doing? My, time just keeps going. He heals us ever so slowly; it seems not in our time but God's time. I just have such a hard time thinking of going hunting again without you, Mervin. Fall is coming, and yes, that's when you would always be here, target shooting with your bow and arrows. Why didn't I realize? You so much looked forward to hunt archery. Gideon is starting to act like he can get into hunting, so maybe I should just move on. Another church Sunday went by and we heard about the writing on the wall in Bible times. Your death was like the writing on the wall, a wake-up call for us all, I guess. Will it last and do we all take it serious enough? I asked your little sister Rosanna the other day what she misses most about you. She said she remembers how you would play the Uno game with her at the table. She has good memories of you, Mervin, playing with her. She said one time she had her little doll baby on the table and one of the other children said she should take it down, but you said, "No, that's okay. You can leave it there." Her little 8-year-old mind has lots of memories of you, Mervin, but also maybe I should be more like her. It seems like she really misses you, but she does move on and seems happy. Oh well, yes, I'm happy, I guess, but what's wrong? Please, Lord, help me to give myself up to what you have for us. Job 8:21 says, "He will fill your mouth with laughter and your lips with shouts of joy." So I guess it is important to laugh and have a sense of humor. Yes, Lord, I need a good laugh and maybe I can move up one more step. I really can say when I think of you, Mervin, that I have such good memories and do not have things that try to make me think anything else. We are to focus on things that are pure, right and true according to God's Word. So thank you, Mervin, for giving me all those good memories. One of the best things I know to do is to open to the book of Psalms and read those great Psalms where David, with probably the same feelings that we have, cries out to God. Psalms 5,23,31,40,57,61,69, and 86 are a few to read. I really had a hard time waking up in the morning and facing the day. It sort of felt sometimes like that "what do I have to live for" feeling. But yes, slowly my joy is coming back. I do have more of a peaceful feeling now than what I had, so just maybe! I must praise God from the bottom of my heart even when tears are streaming down my face, because we know He is a "God of love". I know that everyone needs some kind of help, and yes, someone needs us today. So look around! I need to help as many people as I can and not think we have nothing to offer. That's just an excuse. I really do not want to just back away because I'm afraid to get involved. "Serve one another in love" (Galatians 5:13). Sometimes I get the feeling that some people might not want to ask me how it's going, because as much as I like to talk about it, they might think I will actually tell them. I feel so much better when I talk about you, Mervin, and also when I write to you. Also, I know that I am not the same person I was before. So much has changed inside and outside. I am going to try to fit into this new pattern of my life and maybe quit thinking so much of the old pattern. Lord, help me, please! There is one thing that we can never say and that is to tell someone we know exactly how they feel. That would be telling a lie because death is different for us all. I really want to be a good listener from now on. I know when it seems like someone is really listening to me it feels so good, and yes, brings healing for me. We might be tempted to say other people that are grieving don't want us to interfere or help them. In this "thing" just step in and help. People like us need other people, even though you might think differently. You might think, wow, doesn't he get tired of telling his story? No, I must tell my story over and over and over again. Just please bear with me!

I will close with my writing today with this "teenager's prayer". God in heaven, I am young and don't understand what it is like to be a parent, but it must be very hard because so many people are failing at it these last days. I pray for Mom and Dad, God, that you will help them to be good parents, strong in the ways you want them to be, so I can look up to them and feel confident that their instruction is right. Help me, dear Lord, to understand my parents. Remind me that when I don't get my way it is because they love me, and not because they want to be mean or keep me from having a good time. Help me, God, when I become stubborn and refuse to listen to accept the fact that they have wisdom and experience because they were once teenagers too. Put in my heart the respect they deserve, for their years of hard work. Help me that I may help along and save my money as we work along and help each other. They raised me as best as they could. Let me not repay them with grief or shame. Rather, help me to give them obedience, respect, forgiveness and love. Most of all, God, while I still have my parents here on earth, help me to appreciate them and let them know that I do.

A New Beginning

MERVIN, I JUST have to talk to you. I'm in Maryland on our deer farm for the first of bow and arrow season. I'm up in a stand that you and your cousin Sam built. I'm writing from about 25 ft. up in a stand, looking down over the woods and out over the cornfields. You know that spot well. Oh, how I miss you today. Your brother Gideon and I are here all alone today, thinking of you. I don't really know what's going on in my mind but that song, "Praise God, I'm on the other side" keeps coming into my mind, over and over. Is it you, Mervin? Are you over there singing and praising God? Tell me! I'm writing up here on this stand, thinking about you and not really caring about the deer. Every now and then I will glance around to look for deer. It has been so hard leading up to this hunting season, but I want to go on. Lord, help me, please. I still really can not believe you will not be hunting with us this year. I miss you so much right now. I am glad that your brother is trying so hard to stay strong. Is that you in my mind singing, "Praise God, I'm on the other side"? It is so real to me. From up here I can see over the field into the shack. My last hunt with you. What a memory! I miss you so. I just think you have to come walking under this tree and wave or something. I probably won't even be able to shoot my bow if any deer come. My tears are so, aw, so rolling. I'm thinking now, so what if I don't see any deer tonight? I'm with you in my mind so much right here on this stand. Is that you singing, telling me you're over on the other side? My, I hardly know which way to turn right now. Is that you, Mervin? I love you so. You seem so happy, so please just wait for me. I can hardly wait to see you. I don't want to miss it. Please, Lord, help me to stay strong and keep my eye on you. I just keep looking out over this field and the sun keeps going on down further and further. I have been here an hour and haven't seen any deer, but so what. You're here with me and I'm all alone up here in this stand. So much this last while, I just want to be alone. The birds are singing, so why can't I feel it too? You're still here, saying I'm over on the other side. The evening shadows are here and it's so peaceful up here. I'm alone except for you, Mervin. It just seems like you are right here with me. It just seems so awfully long since I've seen you and talked to you. Are you okay? You're singing, so you must be. Tell me you're okay. Yes, this is September 15th and cooler nights are here and time just goes on. Sometimes these last 6½ months seem just like one big daze. I have such a big hole in my, well, where is that empty feeling? I guess in my heart. I'm still up here, Mervin, and have about ¾ hour to hunt yet, but I just don't feel like it. I guess I will just quit for today and hope that feeling comes back again someday. I love the outdoors and love to be with nature, but I have such an empty feeling tonight. Lord, help me to go on. I guess any day now our Lord will come. I have such a longing to be with you, Mervin. I would gladly leave these trials here below if we could just all go to you as a family. Lord, help me to leave it to your timing. This journey is so hard and I feel so weary. I'm still here at the shack in Maryland and wonder what I'm doing here, but really need to sort things out in my mind. I really did like to be here still, but now I feel so, oh so……. I was thinking this morning when I was on the stand, Mervin, that you put these nails in this tree. I still just can't believe that you were right there on that spot and everywhere else I go down here. I really need to give myself up, but am having such a hard time right now. What can I do to make this "thing" go away or get less? I just hardly know my way through right now. What's wrong here? Just let my tears drip on this paper and don't even try to hold them back. I need to cry right now, then maybe it will get better.

Hello. Hello, Mervin. Here I am again. My, oh my, I can hardly believe the nights are getting cooler and the fall season will soon be upon us. There is so much happening, and yes, your birthday is next week. You would have been 24 years old already. It just does not seem all that long that I took you along to market and was so proud to have you as a son. We finally divided your clothes the other night. It was a very touching evening for us all. Step by step we are on this journey. Slowly but surely we are doing things like this and just realize you are gone! Are you okay? You know, Mervin, I keep thinking of you and think you are doing alright and that you are okay. You know, I am actually starting to believe that you are okay, even though I have such a longing to see you again. You remember your friend Todd? Well, his mom and dad stopped in this week for a visit. They were out in Wyoming to the hill where you were killed. You know that is an honor to us to know that people do want to go there and see where your "accident" happened. I have such a longing to go there soon, but have no plans as of now. I am so thinking that to go to that hill in Wyoming for myself will be another big step, but do realize that when I leave there, yes, it will still be true. You are gone! I was going through some of your school books this week and found more hunting stories that you wrote. I also found a note from your 9th grade teacher. She wrote, "We will miss you in class but are glad that you are now out of school. On the other hand, the school of life never ends as long as we breathe. May success and God's richest blessings be yours in the unknown future. Your teacher." How little did we realize how much those words, "the unknown future," really mean. Yes, Mervin, how I meant those words in that card I gave for just being who you were. It read: As long as we remain open with each other we'll grow together. I know sometimes you think I don't understand you, but I do remember how difficult being a teenager is. I know it is not easy working through all the feelings you are experiencing and I hope that you will always feel free to turn to me about any subject. Your teenage years should be filled with wonderful experiences, and I want all the times in your life to be fulfilling and enjoyable. I know sometimes you think I am being too nosy about your private life or too often it seems like I am telling you what to do, but

I am not trying to make you feel as if you have no independence of your own. I know you need your own space at times and I understand you need room to grow. But as your parent I want you to be healthy and happy and have every opportunity in life you deserve. When I put my foot down or make a few rules for you to follow, I'm doing what I think is best for you. Still, I want us always to be able to work through any of our differences and communicate openly with each other. Just as any relationship has its ups and downs, so will ours as parent and child. We have always had a good relationship and I think we can grow and learn together in all the years ahead if we both work hard at listening and respecting each other. You are very important to me. I hope you know "I love you" with all my heart and I am proud to be your parent (From Dad). My, oh my, when I said all the years ahead I sure did not think it would be only till you were 23 years old, Mervin. Shattered dreams! Thanks so much for being who you were. I know I really am blessed with all that your sisters and your brother Gideon do for me. I wish I could show it more. They are really trying hard, I can see. Dear God, please help them through these trials and temptations. They and we need all the help you can spare to give us. We really do want to meet Mervin some day. How will it be?

When the shock of loss is upon you, do not hide or deny your normal human feelings. Express all the grief you feel. Talk about your loved ones. Relive old experiences. Shed tears unashamedly. Remember that at the grave of Lazarus, "Jesus wept". To be sure, we are all different in our emotional reactions and no two people will respond in the same way to their loss. But whatever expression is natural to you, let it come. To hold back grief will do you more harm than to express it. A period of mourning is both natural and necessary. You may try to lessen your pain by pretending everything remains as it was before. Perhaps by keeping the loved one's room exactly as it was when he was last in it or by saying to yourself, he is only away and soon he will return. How much wiser David was at the death of his beloved child. "Now he is dead," he said, "so why should I fast? Can I bring him back again? I shall go to him, but he will not return to me" (II Samuel 12:23). Admit the truth of your loss. Accept it for the tragedy it is, and realize that life will not be the same. Life still can be good, but it will be different. We must hope our loved one is in fellowship with Christ, the Savior and Lord. Paul was sure that to depart and be with Christ is far better. We must think of our privilege under God of having our loved one as long a time as we did. Nothing can take away our memories of the grand person he was and of the nice things he did. These memories are a part of you. I miss Mervin, but I haven't room in my heart for anything but thankfulness to God. We had 23 years with Mervin. I really wonder sometimes how we can go on without our loved one. It is not easy to take on life again after losing a child, but God has made the human spirit that we can make adjustments to the most difficult situations. This God-given capacity is within you. It works most effectively when our trust is in God for daily guidance and strength. Say over and over again, when the going gets hard, "I can do all things in Him who strengthens me" (Phil. 4:13). I really hardly knew how I could live, but through the help of God I was brought this far. Paul wrote, "I am sure that neither death nor life will be able to separate us from the love of God in Christ Jesus our Lord" (Romans 8:38-39). We are promised this loss has come, not because we have done anything to deserve it, but because we are all involved under the Providence of God in that total life process which begins with birth and ends with bodily death. "It is appointed for men to die once" (Heb. 9:27). The exact cause and time of anybody's death are determined by factors too hard for any human mind to understand. But if we could see everything as God sees it, we would be content to say, it is the will of God. Remember what Job said. "The Lord gave and the Lord hath taken away; blessed be the name of the Lord" (Job 1:21). Often when a loved one is gone, we wish we had done or said something other than what we did do or say. If only I hadn't made that sharp answer. If I had only been more patient! The chances are that your quick word or slight impatience was just part of the normal give and take of life. But if you continue to be troubled by feelings of this kind, remember the forgiving love of God. He understands the strain of everyday family relationships, and He is ready to forgive you for any way in which you fell short in your life with your loved one. "If we confess our sins, He is faithful and just and will forgive us our sins" (1 John 1:9).

We say it has come so suddenly. If I had only known, had some warning. Here was our loved one and now he is gone. But how many people pray that they may be spared long illness. This was the privilege of our loved one to have, in place of long, painful illness. We were mercifully spared the pain of seeing our loved one suffer. How hard that would have been for me. How do we get comfort for the loss of a loved one that died so young? In the eyes of God length of life is not the important thing. It is enough that a man do his duty as he sees it for whatsoever time is allowed to him. Beyond time is eternity, and whether one's life is gone at eighteen or eighty, the difference as God sees it and counts time is very slight. "I am going fishing," said Peter after Jesus was crucified and after His first appearances. In his distraught mind, unable to adjust himself quickly to all that had happened, this was the wisest thing Peter could have done. There will be comfort for you as you return to familiar tasks and keep busy doing something useful. It takes determination at first, but with lots of effort will come the rewards. There were interests, activities and causes that were dear to your loved one. He would be happy to have you carry them on. By doing things he liked to do, you keep his memory fresh. Think of how you can help others. In doing so, you will find some comfort and relief. Take lots of time to make any changes. I am told at least for the first year you should not make any major changes. Paul said, "Do not grieve as others do who have no hope" (1 Thessalonians 4:13). It is natural and necessary to grieve for a season, and a great love can never be forgotten. But for our soul's good we must face forward with hope and expectation, for "If God is for us who can be against us? He who did not spare his own Son, but gave him up for us all, will he not also give us all things with him" (Romans 8:31, 32)? Yes, ahead of you, if you walk with God, there will be deepened spiritual comfort and new experiences of which you do not now dream, and beyond time there is eternity with reunion with your loved ones and closer fellowship with God. "Money is like fire, a good servant but a dangerous master."

I just heard another young girl was killed yesterday. She fell off a horse. How I wonder still, do you see them come, Mervin? Are they with you? A daughter of John and Sadie Stoltzfus (Sara Ann). How my heart aches for the parents, just to know what lies ahead. My prayer is that God would help them through this pain and grief that will surely come. One by one we are going down the valley, one by one heading toward the setting of the sun. My first thought is, how can I make it easier for them? Just by being there, friends, church people and a caring heart. Just to be with them will help. How I can remember, oh, how glad I was for all those people who stood by us. Surely we must realize that God has a reason for it all, way beyond our understanding. I can now say, one day at a time, and really mean it. That is what it takes, and life will go on. When things go wrong, as they sometimes will, when the road you're trudging seems all uphill. When the funds are low and the debts are high, and you want to smile, but you have to sigh. When care is pressing you down a bit. Rest if you must, but don't you quit. Life is queer with its twists and turns, as every one of us sometimes learns. And many a failure turns about when he might have won had he stuck it out. Don't give up though the pace seems slow. You may succeed with another blow! Success is failure turned inside out. The silver tint of the clouds of doubt, and you never can tell just how close you are, it may be near when it seems so far. So stick to the fight when you're hardest hit. It's when things seem worst that you must not quit. Do all the good you can, by all the means you can, in all the ways you can, in all the places you can, at all the times you can, to all the people you can, as long as ever you can.

Light in the Shadow of Death

Your Birthday—This Too Shall Pass

HEY, MERVIN, I have not written to you for almost two weeks. So much has been happening. I really had some hard days the last while, but I'm feeling a little bit better again. That sinking feeling has got me and I miss you so much. Oh Mervin, the table was full of flowers on your birthday. People did not forget us, so what's wrong then? I feel so, so.... alone. You would have been 24 years old. My, I did not realize that would be such a hard day for me. I went to Indiana to our new friends Vernon and Darlene's daughter Joann's wedding. It was nice to be there, but am I trying to rush into things too much? What's wrong? Lord, how much time do I need before I can get back to doing things again? No, I do not want to complain, but yes, Lord, I know your time is the right time. Strengthen my faith! Seven months have come and gone, and no, Mervin, you are not here anymore. Oh yes, you are in my thoughts almost all day long. I'm trying so hard to get a little normal again. You know, sometimes we must force ourselves to do things and then that's another step through this thing. I just could not force myself to go archery deer hunting this week. What's wrong here? I did not miss the first week of archery season for maybe 20 or 25 years. I'm so mixed up. I even packed my suitcase and did not go. I just left my suitcase packed, and now here I am at home with a sinking feeling in my heart. Should I have forced myself to go? I don't know. Gideon went on Saturday and left me a note saying, "Hi, Dad, I have been thinking about this a lot and I'm not sure how it is going to go walking up Mitchell hill." That was a hill that Mervin walked up every year. When I read that I just cried and cried. Gideon wrote on, saying, "I know Mervin would want us to go on." He also wrote, "We can only be what we give ourselves the power to be." Oh, how true. Well, Gideon came home again and I did not go. I just cannot explain how I feel. I really did not expect a roller coaster ride like this. Lord, help me! Please, not my will but thine. I really want to move on out of this thing and try or force myself to do things and continue to carry on. If I hold myself tense and refuse to let go, I know I will probably be in for trouble. So help me to move on, Lord! Sometimes I know you might think I have lost my mind or something, and my writing does not make sense. Sometimes I get a feeling of deep depression and feel so alone. It even feels like God is not even there sometimes, as if He just does not care. I know other people have grieved like this, but I feel like I am the only one sometimes. I know these dark days will not last forever. God has said He will help us. This too shall pass! I find myself thinking other things sometimes, but so soon I'm right back where I started. When something as important as a child has been taken from our midst we can think of nothing but that, sometimes, but we do know it's gone forever. So help us, Lord, to go on. Sometimes this last while I just feel like running away. Away from what? I guess life, I don't know. We know we must go on; we can think of all kinds of reasons to stay home and be sad, rather than go out and be forced to be nice to people and think new thoughts. But we must move on. We must go on. It's a full-time job for me. I really do want to move on, Lord, so please help me. I do not want to be angry and resentful. Please take my anger away and give me strength to rise way above it. I need to be careful that I do *really* want to get back to my usual things. Sometimes I just think I can hardly go on. My, oh my, Mervin, I miss you so. Yes, I still like to hear Mervin's name, so let's talk, please. Do not worry that you will reopen the wound. No, people, it's open. Tell me stories about Mervin. Let's talk about things he did. It's such a wonderful feeling when someone mentions his name. You might think, "I did not bury a child. How am I supposed to talk to him?" Give it a try. You might be surprised what God will speak through you. Every now and then these clouds begin to break up and the sun comes shining through. Thank you, Lord, for my better days and help me to be patient with the cloudy ones. Yes, there are times when we might not talk much when you ask, but just try again, please. I do realize when we go through a grief process like this we do come out a different person. What do we want to be? Depending on the way we respond, we will be either stronger or weaker, either healthier in spirit or sicker. We know if God is with us we do not have to face the present and the future alone. We need to rely on our faith more than ever with all our might, with all our strength, right now at this very moment and all the days we have left. We must not grieve as those who have no hope, but please, God, let me grieve. Even though I continue to really struggle with this grieving thing, I really, truly want to move on. So help me, Lord! Looking back, I really think of all the church people, friends, neighbors and, most of all, brothers and sisters who have stood by us through this "thing". All my life I lived as if the world would just stay pretty much the same. The children would go to school and come home again. I would go to work and come home again. This world that I was used to has drastically changed. Shattered dreams! I know that God cares, because sometimes He will let this calm feeling come over me and lift me up. I so much try to be a better man and a good father. I guess I should quit worrying so and let God. If we as parents don't mess things up too much and allow God to step in, our children will grow up and maybe become the person God wants them to be. I need the prayers of those I love. Help me, please, as I am walking through this valley. I realize there are no easy answers. I need the comfort from those I love. For those of you that have not passed this way, I have something to tell you. Read your Bible and learn all you can now before a "thing" like this happens. When this happens it is too late to really concentrate. Do so now before the great big storm. Study now and become familiar with the Scriptures. I can only now after seven months really start to concentrate. We know when God chose to take you, Mervin, was most likely the time God thought, "If I take him now it will make more of a difference in all who are left, in their lives." So then why do I question it? It was the perfect time, that's God's time. Some questions have no answers. God has promised to be with us. The light of God surrounds us. The love of God enfolds us. The power of God protects us. The presence of God is with us. Wherever we are, wherever our loved one is, "God is". If I would just let God, He longs to mend shattered lives. We must let Him! People say you're going to be okay. Yes, I know the pain does get less. My heart does ever so slowly heal. But what happened when it was your birthday, or the first day of hunting? My, that made the sharp pain come back again. I hurt! Each of us is going in a different direction still and sometimes I become upset. Lord, help me to be patient. Lord, help me to face this "thing" and not try to run away or around it. But Lord, you know nothing ever came close to this in my life. The shock and not really believing it just go ever so slowly away from me. I must follow and do what feels right for me, so I can move on. The pain gets less, but, Mervin, it seems so incomplete without you. Many times I look back and remember certain people who were here the first couple weeks or even the first week. Just a couple of words like, "I am so sorry" or just a touch or warm handshake I remember so well. This "thing" is a big wound, but with time it does heal. Job said, "If a man dies, will he live again?" We know for the Christian that question was answered 2,000 years ago through the death and resurrection of Jesus Christ. My concerns are sometimes almost more than I can bear. So help me, Lord. My, oh my, Mervin, I really did not expect to write so much today, but yes, I do feel better after putting my thoughts on paper again. Good night.

A rainy good morning to you, Mervin. How are you doing? Tomorrow will be eight months since you're gone. Eight months! I am not writing so often anymore, and yes, I do feel like I am making progress. That sinking feeling is starting to let go somewhat. Thank you, Lord! Oh Mervin, this Thursday is the start of weddings here in Lancaster County. Yes, your friend Norman, who was with you when you were killed, is getting married to your cousin Anna Mae. I'm not sure how this wedding and all will go. I keep thinking how much you would have enjoyed being there. So many times I think of you and can hardly believe that this is true. Right, you're gone. On Sunday we had communion services and you were not there. It was really something for me to be there, because I could just see you so plainly in my mind all day. Church was at John and Fannie's place, and yes, you remember that is where you starting joining the church. How well I remember seeing you come in that door with your cousin Sam. It was one of the best feelings I ever had. Thank you so much for joining the church and being who you were. I just cannot explain to anyone what that meant to me. Sometimes I just think, well, yes, God knew at that time that you were going to be killed the next Feb. 28th. So right then, He put it into your heart to be ready. If we could just understand and believe that we were made by God and for God, just maybe life would make more sense. Lord, help me to believe and understand that Mervin was not really ours, just given to us for awhile to have and to hold. God works in so many ways, way beyond our understanding. You know, He turned a murderer named Moses into a leader. Yes, I really think if we would really, really understand what's going on we would say, oh yeah, that makes sense! So help me, Lord. We do know that no man has ever seen or even imagined what wonderful things God has ready for those who love the Lord. Lord, help me to think more of eternity. Help me to be content with what I have! Make me realize that this world is not my home. Lord, is this a test? Yes, help me to pass this test and give myself up to what you have for us. Psalm 39:4: Lord, remind me that my days are numbered. I am here for just a short time. I feel so unworthy sometimes to be writing all these things on paper and thinking, what am I trying to say? But I really do feel a need to share these things that happen when there is a death like this in your family. Lord, help me please to write only what will help other people. Mervin, you know we loved you so, and feel like a big part is gone, but yes, I am so glad for all the other children to help us go on. It really seems like we are all getting somewhere in this "thing." Thank you, Lord, for your healing touch. We know that we *must* give ourselves completely to God and give ourselves up to His plan. Yes, Lord, I'm working on this and am somewhat struggling, but do want to really, truly give myself up. I am your servant and am willing to give myself up completely to your plan. Maybe that will help to put it on paper! Sometimes I think now I am going to change and be a better person, but you know the struggle goes on, and no, I really do not think God wants us to try to be someone else or be different. He surely would want us to be ourselves, because He made us different than anyone else on earth. Does that make sense? So my prayer would be, Lord, just help me to be myself and not try to be someone I'm not!

Moving On

SOMETIMES THIS LAST while I wake up and wonder, where's that feeling? It's kind of scary sometimes to think so differently, and yes, move on, I guess. The presence of the Lord is so real sometimes when death comes into our home and does feel good, but then sometimes I wonder, Where are you, Lord? It seems like sometimes when I need you most, you left me. Help me please to stay strong! We know life is all about love, because God is love. I read that life minus love equals zero. I also read that we all have temptations, and that temptations are not sin, but yielding to temptation is sin. Yield not to temptation. Yes, we all stumble and fall sometimes and need help getting back up. I really do not know or can not imagine how we would have gotten through your death, Mervin, without all the times we were picked up by friends. I really wish sometimes I could better explain where I am coming from when I try to tell you about this "thing". I try so hard not to think of how far we must go from here, but look back over my writing and think about how far we have come. When I look back over my writing and think about it, my, oh my, I just can not explain how I really feel. I usually think, did I actually feel like that and then I say, oh yeah, I remember that day or that week. We are promised that the Lord is close to the brokenhearted. When we are about at our lowest points or when the pain is the greatest, I really think God wants us there sometimes so we remember Him more. It surely is in our darkest days that we turn to God the most. When life is real smooth we have that chance of slipping too much. I really hope that we can stay with God's plan for us and not dwell too much on our pain and our problems. If we look at the world, we will be distressed. If we look into ourselves, we will be depressed, but if we look to the Lord, we will be at rest. Satan, the devil, still does not let me go. He seems to want to make me think bad thoughts all the time. Sometimes he makes me think bad things about you, Mervin. He just doesn't quit! We know that he hates our prayers and we must not quit. So help me, Lord! With this "thing" we need to always watch and not let our guard down or Satan will make us think bad things. Sometimes I wonder, how much longer, Lord? But yes, I do know that you are always on time. I read that God never wastes a hurt. He will allow us to go through a painful experience on purpose to help us to minister to others. He comforts us in all our troubles so we can comfort others. I have asked God again and again what to do with this journal or this writing. Should I share it or just keep it tucked away somewhere? What is your plan, Lord, for me? I really think that a great message can come out of a deep pain or hurt like this, but why me, Lord? If by sharing our struggles, through this death, I can help someone, then why not? You know, Mervin, if just one, yes, just one person will be in heaven because of you, my, oh my, it will be worth it all. So if that happens, then your short 23 years will have been worth it all. Yes, we know many, many people have lost loved ones, but you know there is no other story exactly like yours, Mervin. So, if I do not share it, the story will be lost forever. We know that God loves us all and He loved you too, Mervin. The Bible says so. When we are tempted by the devil, we should maybe just think of the pain that Jesus went through with His arms stretched out on the cross, so wide; He must have been saying, "I love you this much." Yes, I also thought maybe if I write these things on paper, people can, or they do not have to, read it. One thing I know is that no one can stop us from praying for them. We also know that the more we read in the Scriptures and the more we learn, all the more we are accountable for our deeds. We know that anyone who knows the right thing to do and does not do it is sinning. At the end of our time it will not matter what other people say about us. The only thing that will matter is what God says about us. Our goal should be to please God. My, my, Mervin, I really did not think that I would write so much today. Oh yes, yesterday I was at the graveyard. I know, Mervin, I go there a lot, and yes, I have such good memories of you there. I was filling dirt in at the different graves. We had ten inches of rain last week, and yes, your grave did settle some. So I keep filling it in and thinking of you. Winter time is coming and the grass does not grow much anymore. I still mowed it yesterday one more time. Rest in peace. I have this thing about the graveyard. I just like to keep it looking real nice for you. I miss you so. You had so many friends, not at all like "Gossip" which is nobody's friend.

My name is Gossip. I have no respect for justice. I maim without killing. I break hearts and ruin lives. I am cunning and gather strength with age. The more I am quoted, the more I am believed. My victims are helpless. They cannot protect themselves against me, because I have no name and no face. To track me down is impossible. The harder you try, the more elusive I become. I am nobody's friend. Once I ruin a reputation, it is never the same. I topple governments and wreck marriages. I ruin careers and cause sleepless nights, heartaches and indigestion. I make innocent people cry in their pillows. Even my name hisses. I am called Gossip. I make headlines and headaches. Before you repeat a story, ask yourself, Is it true? Is it harmless? Is it necessary? If it isn't, don't repeat it.

Here's another story, on how to make a mountain. First you must have the right conditions. If you don't have them, perhaps you can make them. Try to find a few people who are hard to get along with. If you want to do this thing right, try to have one of these hired as a teacher, or second best put them on the school board. Do not spend too much time on this, however, for you can raise a real ruckus without having this type of person in an important position. You will just have to try harder. Rake up a good seedbed by stirring up all the old grudges and dislikes of the past. With a little cautious questioning, you can get a good idea what has been forgiven but not forgotten. Keep the gossips and the rumors moving, but be careful you are not caught. If you have followed this far, you now have a promising seedbed, a soil that is eager to sprout trouble. Keep your eyes and ears open. Listen to everything your children relate about school. Pick out choice bits and store them away for an emergency. Encourage them to tell you about the other children and teach them to criticize the teacher. It's surprising how much the children can help you once you've got a molehill growing nicely. You won't have long to wait if you've followed directions closely. Differences of opinions are sure to turn up before long. If you're lucky you can get one started between two persons who can't seem to stand each other anyway. Move smartly then, and you'll have a mountain made. Try to draw all the people into the dispute. Get them to take sides if you can have them evenly divided. Feed the flames by throwing on all the fuel you have dug up—grudges, insults, gossips, jealousies. Molehills mature in a few days if conditions don't let the two sides talk things over too much with each other. It is much better to have them talking behind each other's back. Don't relax yet; many a thriving molehill has been knocked cold by a peacemaker or two. Sometimes one side or the other repents and develops a forgiving spirit. Then you lose all you have worked to win and more. For as soon as people humble themselves and start asking forgiveness, your seedbed will be ruined for a few years. But, barring these developments, you can expect the teacher to be fired, or the school closed down, or the community permanently divided by the mountain of ill will. And, you can consider yourself a success at growing mountains from the seeds of a molehill. Once your crop is mature, you can move on to other fields. Here's wishing you anything but success! "Thoughtless words leave lasting wounds." My wish is that we can all still walk arm in arm, without always seeing eye to eye in everything.

Closing the File

HELLO, HELLO, MERVIN. My, how time is going. I just can not believe that we are in the middle of November and that it is going on nine months since you were killed. How are we doing? Well, not too bad, I feel. I do not have that deep down sinking feeling so much anymore. Thank you, Lord, for your healing touch. I think of you so much, but do want to let you go. My hunting is not going very good, but I am slowly getting there. I did not do any archery hunting in PA for the first time in, I think, 30 some years. I just did not feel like it. Your brother Gideon is in Kansas for two weeks to hunt. My, how we miss him here at home, but we do know he is trying real hard to go on. Oh my, yes, I was in Maryland hunting and I saw this big buck. You know, I really got excited and I don't know for how long afterwards I was thinking, "I can't wait to tell Mervin and Gideon." I really did not think of you, Mervin, that you were gone. What a letdown I had when I thought about the fact that you're gone. I just could not believe that I went for so long, and yet it was maybe only a minute or so, thinking that I must tell you. Tears just rolled when I thought about the truth. You're gone.

We are still getting mail addressed to you, Mervin. Today a letter came from the law office of Linda Kling, the attorney that settled your accounts.

Yes, we had to hire a lawyer to close out your banking accounts. It read "Mervin Beiler Estate". "This concludes all legal action necessary for this matter and I will be closing my file. Thank you for choosing our firm." Is that what we must do now, Mervin, close our file? Oh no, Lord, please help me to accept the fact that we must close our file. It's true; I guess this is it; no more, Mervin. The weddings are in full swing here, and yes, we do have quite a few. I just feel so, oh so, I don't know how at the weddings. There will be no wedding for you, right, Mervin? Are you okay? Where are you? I really am feeling lots better and am having pretty good days. So much time has gone by and so many good memories you left behind, so we must go on. It does all depend on how we look at life, I guess. Joy or misery, what will it be? Paul wrote in Phil. 4:8 that whatever is true, whatever is noble, whatever is right, whatever is pure, whatever is lovely, whatever is admirable, if anything is excellent or praiseworthy, think about such things. So, I guess it's up to us; we can look for the flowers or the weeds. We can look for the bright side or look for the clouds. We can only be as happy as we decide to be. We will never have all the answers here on earth, but we do know somebody that does. We must try to live as though Christ died yesterday, rose today and is coming tomorrow. We have another chance. We've got today. Every day is precious; we have no time to waste. Some days bring that sinking feeling and some bring joy. One day at a time. Tomorrow is a new day; help me to begin it right, Lord. Maybe if I would just do my part and give myself up and see what the Lord has for us, everything would be alright. We do read that God does not say grieve not, but He says not to grieve as others do who have no hope (1 Thessalonians 4:13). Help me to remember, Lord, that nothing will happen today that you and I can't handle together. That long tunnel that I was in really does have some light at the end. Every tunnel ends somewhere, because if it would not, it would just be a cave. I do remember when I felt as if there would not be any light at the end of my tunnel. Sometimes I could not sleep, so I went out and walked around and looked up into the night sky. The stars were there in the sky, right where God put them, and I'm sure God was there too, just where He has always been. Our tunnel seems to be getting brighter all the time. Thank you, Lord. We must take our broken dreams to Jesus. To get a fresh start, be born again, accept God's forgiveness, freely forgive others. Learn all you can from your mistakes, turn your weaknesses into your strong points, accept what you cannot change and with God's help turn it into something beautiful. Put the past behind, get up and begin again. Yes, Mervin, I usually think this was so final, no second chance, you're gone, but I do thank you, Lord, for letting me feel like going on again. That is such a good feeling to want to get up and go. When grief was so strong, I felt like I had a full-time job just going on. We hope that those who live in the Lord never see each other for the last time. Yes, Mervin, I really, really miss you, but I also want to thank the Lord for letting us be your parents for your short 23 years. The preacher said the other Sunday how Jesus did so many good things while here on earth, but He did so much, much more through His death. Is that how it was with you, Mervin? I want to think so. I do realize that we are all different and grieve at our own rate. My hope is to come out of this thing much stronger and more understanding of the problems of others. I really did not think I could ever feel this good again, but it sure is nice. If our faith cannot move mountains, it should at least be able to climb them. I really think happy times will come again if I let them.

Mervin, I hope this little story is for you. A farmer was taking his little boy to a faraway place. While walking, they came to a rickety bridge over a turbulent stream. The little boy became frightened. "Father, do you think it is safe to cross the stream?" he asked. The father answered, "Son, I'll hold your hand." So the boy put his hand in his father's. With careful steps he walked by his father's side across the bridge. They made their way to their destination. That was in daylight.

The night shadows were falling by the time they returned. As they walked, the lad said, "Father, what about that rickety old bridge? I'm frightened." The big, powerful farmer reached down, took the little fellow in his arms and said, "Now you just stay in my arms, and you'll feel safe." As the farmer walked down the road with his precious burden, the little boy fell sound asleep. The next morning the boy woke up, safe at home in his own bed. The sun was streaming through the window. He never even knew that he had been taken safely across the bridge and over the turbulent waters. "THAT IS DEATH TO A CHRISTIAN." Yes, Mervin, sometimes I look back to the happy times when we were all together. Oh yeah, not all happy times, but good times with family ups and downs. But I do find that I am in those painful stages less and less and for shorter times. Thank you, Lord, for your healing touch.

Thanksgiving Day

HAPPY THANKSGIVING 2005! Yes, Mervin, it is Thanksgiving Day, and no, you're not here. Oh yeah, you are here very, very much in our minds, but, but, but—broken dreams as children bring their broken toys with tears for us to mend. I brought my broken dreams to God because He was my friend. But then instead of leaving Him in peace to walk alone, I hung around and tried to help with ways that were my own. At last I snatched them back. And cried, how can you be so slow? "My child," He said, "what could I do? You never did let go." Let go and let God have you is what I want to do so bad, Mervin, but then, why don't I? This Thanksgiving morning is quite cold, and yes, a coat of snow is on the ground, just like when we took you and buried you in the graveyard. There was snow on the ground, remember? Last night I just cried and cried for you, and yes, I did feel better again. The pain is not so intense. You know, on Monday, it will be nine months and that is the 28th. In February, the day you were killed was also on a Monday, the 28th. You know, we hold our children's hands just for a little while, but my, oh my, we hold their hearts forever, I guess. Yes, you will be with us here for Thanksgiving dinner, Mervin, in our minds. It just seems so unreal. Sometimes I just can not even get close to grasp it all. "Death." Yes, Mervin, your mother and I tried our best for you, and no, we weren't nearly perfect, but we tried! We must love our children and hope that we give good enough training, and hopefully with God's help and the Scripture they will get their hearts right with God. We can not force it onto them. I only realize how important those years from birth to around two years old is. Parents, you might not think your child is old enough to know at that age. I really believe we can put more into our children in the first two years than any other time in their life. We must not just nag and nag, but be very firm at that age. "Train a child in the way he should go and he will not depart from it," we are promised. God's Word says so! We must pray and trust the Lord. So, Lord, help me to pray and trust You with Mervin! Yes, Lord, I know that You know all about those hard spots in our lives, so help me to let go, please! Yes, as parents our prayers should be that our children will stand clean before the Lord. If we do what we can with the Lord's help and then let God, I really think we must not blame ourselves for the actions of our children. Do not think that you will wait till they are maybe ten years old or sixteen years old, then you will take hold. No, no, that will be way, way too late. We do know that whatever choices we or our children make, we *must* answer to God. We have a choice, you know. I asked God to make my handicapped child whole and God said "no". He said the body is only temporary. I asked God to grant me patience and God said "no". He said patience is a by-product of tribulation. It isn't granted; it's earned. I asked God to give me happiness and God said "no". He said He gives His blessing; happiness is up to me. I asked God to spare me from pain and God said "no". He said sufferings draw you apart from worldly cares and bring you closer to Him. I asked God to make my spirit grow and God said "no". He said I must grow on my own, but He will prune me to make me fruitful. I asked God if He loved me and He said "yes". He gave His only Son who died for me and I will be in heaven someday because I believe. I asked God to help me love others as much as He loves me and He said "Ah, finally you have the idea!" Romans 8:38-39: For I am convinced that nothing can ever separate us from the love of God; death can't and life can't. Yes, all the powers of hell cannot keep God's love away. What a promise! Now just believe. I really do want to believe. Help me, Lord. Thy will be done. It seems like so many people are in a daze. We *must* watch our minds. Some signs of depression include feeling sad, bored, disappointed, lonely, lacking confidence, not liking yourself, afraid, angry, and guilty. Those with depression have a hard time making decisions and they are frustrated with life. You feel desperate, as though you have lost your faith, and life is meaningless. You may get careless about how you look. You may move more slowly and have drooping posture. Your face may sag. You may be easily irritated and want nothing to do with anyone, and communication with others is gone. You may have difficulty sleeping and a major change in appetite or weight. You will also be very tired and weary. For a depressed person, life drains away all energy. Even breathing becomes a problem. Yes, people, I really think most of these problems will surface one time or another during our grieving. We must fight hard to keep them in control. Do not let your guard down. I can say each one of those problems has at some time had a hold on me. All of them at once one could not handle, so keep your eyes on Jesus. He will see you through. Yes, many times I wonder how do we give this "thing" to God. It gets frustrating. Do we know what giving up really means? The dictionary says 1. To surrender a right. 2. To put aside a plan. 3. To loosen one's hold on something or someone. So help me, Lord, to loosen my hold. Help me to give myself up, please. Yes, today I really do want to let God take over. Oh, the pain of letting go. Help me to completely let go of Mervin and let these wounds of grief heal and help me get on with my life! Help me to think more of the rest of my family. Are they all hurting so much on a day like this (Thanksgiving Day)? Yes, Mervin, I failed many times to tell you that you did not have to prove anything to us; we were so proud to have you as a son. We are trying so hard to put one foot in front of the other and march forward. We miss you so, but do want to let you go. If we would have a time, say next week or next month, and say now it's over, your pain is gone. I do not know how long this will go on, but do realize that it is different for us all. I do know that shedding tears, talking and the passing of time does work wonders. I must say, thank you, God, for all you have given me, for all you have taken away from me, and yes, for all you have left me! Oh yeah, Mervin, we got a card yesterday from good friends and it was very much appreciated; a cheer-up for Thanksgiving. Thank you to our friends, Elmer and Katie. We treasure your friendship. Well, here I was again writing much more than I was going to. Please all join us in prayer for our Thanksgiving dinner. Thank you for listening once again. God bless you all for your kindness.

That Empty Feeling Again

DECEMBER 12, 2005. My, oh my, I hardly know where to start. Hello, Mervin, it's me again. How are you? I just can not believe Thanksgiving is over and Christmas is soon here. I'm just having such a hard time. I really don't know what's up. I just got back from the graveyard about an hour ago. I cried like a baby over there today, and yes, I felt better. There's snow on the ground and how the memories did flow. Remember the snow on the day of your funeral? It looked so…. I don't know, when I was leaving a set of footprints in the snow to your grave. It was your dad walking over to your tombstone. I have this big thing in my, well, where is it? An empty feeling has got a hold of me. I feel so down and should be happy, I guess; Christmas is coming. I really did not know what to expect, but not this. I feel so alone, so empty, so, so depressed, I guess, but I know I may not dwell on the past. I must look ahead, so help me, Lord. It seems like a big, big weight on my shoulders. I really don't know what I want or feel right now and think maybe other people wonder what's going on. I'm kind of moody, I guess high, then low. No, never really high for the last 9½ months since you're gone, Mervin. Yes, the time is here to move on, I guess. We have had no company the last two Sundays. So what's going on here? Didn't I say there is a limit to everything when we were getting so much company? Now what? Am I wishing for company already? I really don't know what I want. Lord, teach me your ways, and yes, please, please, help me to give myself up to this. Mervin is gone. My, oh my, I look at the other children so differently now than I did before. Thank you, Lord, for such good and loving children that you gave us. Help me to appreciate them ever so much. I have been reading so many books on grief and wonder sometimes if I maybe would be better off sticking to "THE" book. You know, the Bible. Yes, we do know all the answers are there. So, why do I question all this? Christmas is only two weeks away and I'm just not sure I'm ready. Will I ever be ready for Christmas again? Ever? Winter time is here and I feel about as frozen inside as it is outside. What's this going to be like without you, Mervin? This circle has been broken or shattered by your death, and my tears are the only thing that sparkle. How can we sing all these Christmas songs without you? I really feel like just forgetting all the gift giving and all that goes with Christmas, but no, that would not be fair to the other children. It just seems that big lump I was having at first about all the time comes back now again more than before. What's going on here? We know we need not walk alone, so, Lord, show me that you are there. It's so rocky and bumpy, but I did read that the bumps are what we climb on. Yes, the more bumpy the road, all the more we think of you, Lord. So why do I wonder? Why do I fret? The rocks and the bumps are what we climb on. We must realize that God puts bumps there for a purpose. If the road we are on would always be level and straight, then what? No, the rocks and bumps are put there for us to climb on. We don't have to read too far in the Bible before we realize that we are not the only ones ever tested. Abraham had to go through an awful lot. How would it be to think of putting your only son on the altar? Abraham didn't give up, so, Lord, just give me some of that strength that Abraham had, please! Help me to keep my life in balance, between the sunshine and the rain and laughter and tears. Help me to stay strong, Lord. Increase my faith; help me to look to you more and not so much at myself. Help me, Lord, to quit looking back so much at past mistakes and so on. Please help me to look back and realize how far we have come. Thank you. I keep thinking of my mother so much these last couple of days. Yes, Mervin, Grandma had a stroke and was in the hospital and is not the grandma she used to be. Life moves on and I guess each stage has its blessings and its burdens. We must take it all as the Lord's will. Sometimes I get to wondering whether God cares. Why sure, He does; the Bible tells me so. We were never promised an easy path, but He does promise to help us and see us through. Please give me faith, hope and love and help me to really thank you and honor you. Even though I really do not understand all of this, we know that you do and it is for our own good. Right? I really should be thanking you more for your blessing on me, Lord. So help me, please! I wonder sometimes if it's worth it, but yes, I know we must trust and go on. Lord, help me to rise above the broken dreams and live in victory. If I could just have some of the faith Jeremiah had in the Bible. What a victory he found! God does not promise to protect us from trials, but He does promise to protect us *in* trials. I used to wonder what Psalm 81:16 meant about honey in the rock. I read that honey in the rock means that you are going through experiences in life. I remember the song, "There's honey in the rock, my brother." So, Lord, do not let me be discouraged! We know that the Bible says, "The trying of our faith worketh patience" (James 1:3). Trials are not working against us; they are working for us. We must look for the honey that is in the rock. Yes, it is wonderful to have friends, and we know we are supposed to share each other's burdens, but we can't expect them to do for us what we won't do for ourselves. So help me to be stronger and try harder. I really do want to lift other people up and be strong. Lord, help me to win this race. I know one of the worst things a runner can do is look back. Jesus would say to us like He said to Peter, to keep our eyes on the road ahead. "What is that to thee? Follow thou me." One day our race will be over and hopefully we can say we have finished our race with joy. By the grace of God we can hopefully win this race. Grace means God does for you what you cannot do for yourself. Grace means that God gives to you what you could never earn or deserve if you tried for a million years. Lord, help me to stay strong. Help me to watch and pray after this victory is won. Please do not let me win this battle and lose the victory. Help me to be on guard all the time. Satan will keep on tempting us and we must stay on top. Remember, Paul wrote,

"Let him that thinketh he standeth, take heed lest he fall." Lord, help me to keep my life in balance. Proverbs 3:6: "In all thy ways acknowledge him, and he will direct thy paths." When you pray rather let your heart be without words than your words without heart. It seems like life is kind of pressing in on me and the future looks kind of dark, but after writing again I do feel much better. Thank you, Lord! Read Isaiah 40:31. "They that wait upon the Lord shall renew their strength." Wait upon the Lord. Help me to keep on going when I feel like quitting. Help me to mount up with wings as the eagle, run and not be weary, walk and not faint. My wish is to be strong through this first Christmas without you, Mervin. Rest in peace. Joy to the world, a King is born.

The First Christmas

MERVIN, MERVIN, MERVIN, it's Christmas morning. My, oh my, what's going on inside of me? I just have a very hard time the last while. Please, please, Lord, help me to give myself up to whatever comes my way. I just came in from the phone shack. It's Christmas morning, you know. Mervin, the message machine is about full this morning, wishing us a Merry Christmas. My, it is so nice to know that we are not alone. Many, many people are thinking and praying for us. Thank you all! Yes, the mailbox was almost full the last while again. I never realized before what kind of lift that is; all that mail picks me up. Yes, Lord, I need all the lift I can get today. Stay by me to keep me strong. It seems that big lump inside of me just has so little control. I cry so easily anytime and anyplace. This morning in the phone shack I cried more than I have in a long time. Those uplifting messages! I think of all the families that have their first Christmas without their loved one. Lots and lots of sad happenings this year. I was thinking, wouldn't it be a comfort if all of us grieving families could just hold hands and cry and pray together for strength to go on? Never would I have thought that I would cry so much at ten months. Yes, Mervin, before we know what's happening it will be a year that you were killed. A year! I really, really had a hard time at market over Christmas and sometimes I wonder, is this what I want to do anymore. Market used to be fun and I enjoyed meeting all those people, but now what's going on? I am totally convinced that, yes, Mervin, you were killed so that I would look at my life and change it. Try, try and try to be a better person. I'm trying, Lord, but You know I need Your help. Sometimes I think too that you were killed to prepare me for something in the future. What is it, Lord? I guess it really doesn't matter what it is as long as I stay strong and try, try and try to be a better person. So many times I think now I can be a better person, then that old whatever it is comes back. Why do I have such a struggle? Yes, Lord, I really am trying. Can't you see I'm trying? Never did I realize what you folks that buried children went through. Before this, I just went on my merry way, not thinking, I guess. It does help to know that we are not alone, but would wish this on no one. Although, this might just be the best thing that ever happened to me. If ever we learn how to give ourselves up, it is now. We do not have a choice, you know. I do know that lots of good things came to us these past ten months that never would have happened without you being killed, Mervin. How is it up there where you are? Are you happy? I'm hoping this can be your best Christmas ever. Is it? So I should be happy, right? Talk to me and tell me what's going on. Send me a sign of something, please. I do want to be happy, but—but! How is this going to be today at dinner time when we sit down to have our Christmas dinner? I really want to be strong, Lord, so that the rest of the children can see that I am accepting the fact that Mervin is gone. What about when we exchange gifts? Christmas is a time when we think of Jesus, yes, but shouldn't we always keep Him in the foremost part of our lives? So help me! Yes, a time for joy, but my, how our loved ones are missed. Precious memories, how they linger, how they ever flood my soul. Lord, we know You will provide our every need as we go through this homesick feeling. Comfort us and help us to comfort others. I really do want to trust, hope and believe that someday we will meet you, Mervin, on that heavenly shore. Jesus is the reason for the season.

A letter from Jesus! As you well know we are getting closer to My birthday. Every year there is a celebration in my honor and I think that this year the celebration will be repeated. During this time there are many people shopping for gifts, there are many radio announcements, and in every part of the world everyone is talking that My birthday is getting closer and closer. It is really very nice to know, the celebration of my birthday began many years ago. At first people seemed to understand and be thankful of all that I did for them, but in these times, no one seems to know the reason for the celebration. Family and friends get together and have a lot of fun, but they don't know the meaning of the celebration. I remember last year there was a great feast in my honor. The dinner table was full of delicious foods, pastries, fruits, assorted nuts and chocolates. The decorations were very nice, and there were many, many beautifully wrapped gifts. But do you want to know something? I was not invited. I was the guest of honor and they did not remember to send me an invitation. The party was for me, but when that great day came, I was left outside. They closed the door in my face—and I wanted to be with them and share their table. In truth that did not surprise Me, because in the last few years all close their doors to me. Since I was not invited, I decided to enter the party without making any noise. I went in and stood in a corner. There were some who were drunk and telling jokes and laughing at everything. They were having a grand time. To top it all, this big, fat man all dressed up in red, wearing a long white beard, entered the room yelling Ho-Ho-Ho. He seemed drunk. He sat on the sofa and all the children ran to him, saying, "Santa Claus, Santa Claus," as if the party were in his honor. At midnight all the people began to hug each other. I extended my arms, waiting for someone to hug Me, and do you know, no one hugged Me. Suddenly they all began to share gifts. They opened them one by one with great expectation. When all had been opened, I looked to see if maybe there was one for Me. What would you feel like if on your birthday everybody shared gifts and you did not get one? I then understood that I was unwanted at that party and quietly left. Every year it gets worse. People only remember the gifts, the parties, to eat and drink, and nobody remembers Me. I would like this Christmas that you allow Me to enter into your life. I would like that you recognize the fact that almost two thousand years ago I came to this world to give My life for you, on the cross, to save you. Today, I only want that you believe this with all your heart. I want to share something with you, as many did not invite Me to their party. I will have my own celebration, a grand party that no one has ever imagined, a spectacular party. I'm still making the final arrangements. Today I am sending out many invitations and there is an invitation for you. I want to know if you wish to attend and I will make a reservation for you and write your name with golden letters in My great guest book. Only those on the guest list will be invited to the party. Those who don't answer the invitation will be left outside. Be prepared, because when all is ready you will be part of My great party. See you soon. I love you! Jesus. WOW, what a letter! Thank you, Jesus, for Your love for us. I am so hoping I can just go through this day trusting in You.

The children are singing this morning so—so. . . Yes, Mervin, you are greatly missed, but I wish you sweet rest and joy, joy, joy. I am so glad and feel so unworthy to have a nice family like this and really want to appreciate what we have. Thank You, Lord, for Your blessings on me. Let us remember the reason for the day. The newspaper or whatever they had when Jesus was crucified could have read like this.

Jesus Christ, Jewish activist, dies on cross. Jesus Christ, 33, of Nazareth, died Friday during a crucifixion at Golgotha (the place of a skull), near Jerusalem. Pontius Pilate, the Roman ruler of Judea, had ordered the execution at the urging of local citizens during a public hearing. Born in Bethlehem, He was the son of Joseph, a carpenter, and Mary, both of Nazareth, and both descendants of the line of David. A well known traveling teacher of spiritual knowledge during the last three years, He has gained a large number of followers, who believed He was the prophesied "Messiah" of the Jewish people. During His travels and teachings there were numerous reports of miraculous events and healings, including the restoration of the sight of one, and possibly two, blind men in Jericho last week. He was baptized by John the Baptist in the Jordan River. He had preached His gospel to large groups of people, including some 5,000 which gathered near Bethsaida. He reportedly fed the entire group with only five loaves of bread and two fish. Other alleged miracles included turning water to wine at a wedding in Cana, Galilee, raising a man from the dead in Bethany, and walking on the water near Gennesaret on the north shore of the Sea of Galilee. Besides His mother, He is survived by four half brothers and several half sisters.

The body was released by Pilate to Joseph, a man from Arimathea, who interred it in a local tomb. No memorial services have been planned.

Note: Shortly before press time, reports were received that the body of Jesus was stolen from the tomb, despite a guard placed at the entrance by Jewish priests. Rumors that a man who looks like Jesus has been seen with some of His disciples are being investigated.

Yes, because He lives we celebrate Christmas. Oh, Mervin, I almost forgot to tell you last Sunday church was at Dannie and Annie's. Remember, that's where you were baptized. I really, really had a hard day there, but also when I thought of the words that you said there on your knees, "I believe that Jesus Christ is God's Son," how could I not also be happy for you? Mixed, mixed feelings. You know, you were so—so plainly in my mind all through church services. I even thought I could hear you say those words. I could also just see you walk through the crowd after church services were over. You went over to Mother-in-law and said hi, and also said thank you for coming. Yeah, I watched you walk over to her and thought to myself, Mervin what was that all about? I even remember looking around and wondering did anybody else notice that? It kind of went through me, that feeling I can't explain. Thank you for being who you were. You even went to the bishop and said thank you for what he and the other preachers did. Precious memories! We will always love you. I hope to meet you someday. Merry Christmas to you and God bless you!

No, Not Last Year!

chapter 21

IT'S ME AGAIN, Mervin, your dad. Here it is the first week in January 2006. How can it be? I have such a hard time. Now, you know, I must now say it was last year that you were killed. No, no, not last year! We had our Christmas family gathering at my daddy-in-laws. My wife's brothers and sisters and your cousins were there. When we all sat around singing those Christmas songs, the tears just flowed. It will never be the same again. I thought of you almost all the time the whole day through. I remember last Christmas when you were ready to leave, you came in to all your uncles and aunts and gave your hand for a firm handshake of good-bye. Yes, Mervin, when you went around giving your hand to them all for a good-bye, did you know? Did you know you might not have another chance to do that? I remember thinking, well, Mervin, what was that all about?

Yes, Mervin, New Year 2006 is now here, and again friends showed us they care. We had our supper brought by friends and they will not know how much that meant to us. We feel so unworthy of all the kindness that was shown to us over these last ten months. Yes, Mervin, it's now going on eleven months. No, no, not one year, I keep thinking! But yes, I know the year mark is coming fast. I really don't know how to explain this, but I do not want to say it's been over a year. No, no, not over a year!

We keep getting such beautiful letters and lots of cheer-up cards. Thank you, friends! Just this week a real nice letter came from Ohio, the Enos Barkman family, whom we have never met, but do write back and forth quite a lot. Yes, their Sammie was killed a little while before you were, Mervin. A bond between people like that can not be described. You know, Mervin, in the year 2005 there were twelve Amish young people who died in Lancaster County. Twelve! I think you, Mervin, were maybe the oldest one at 23 and the youngest one was 13. That is more Amish young people dying in one year than ever before in Lancaster County. Are we awake? Are we listening to God talk? You know, the Barkman family sent a nice letter and in the package was this daily calendar with a verse for each day of the year. Of course, I went straight to February 28th, the day you were killed, to read that one. It read, "There is no safer place to be than in God's loving hands." The chills went through me and the tears started rolling down my cheeks. You know, people like us are always looking for something somewhere to give us a boost. Could it be that God talks to us like that? Could it be that Mervin was saying he is safe? Could it be that you, Mervin, are saying you are in God's loving hands? Also, sometimes when I get all these questions I think back and try to put myself at the age of 23. How responsible was I or what were my thoughts? You know, here I am at 52 years old and have so many questions and different kinds of struggles than I did at 23. My wish for you all is that you could have a better understanding of life and eternity than I do. I try to imagine how things are going to be, but then must quit and "let God". I so much do not want February 28th to come, but—but—you know, time waits for no one. Yes, Mervin, you remember, my birthday is February 27th, the day before. How, oh how, can I ever have a Happy Birthday again? Lord, help me to hang in there and be strong. Oh, how I wish sometimes I would not have been so busy and wrapped up in my work when you were young. We need so much to keep a happy-medium. If we could only slow down and smell the roses and take time for our children. It's such a short time that we have them, so we should make every moment count. I read of a Vince Foster, who worked for the President Clinton administration. Vince had a very hectic schedule, and on July 20, 1993, he took his own life. Just eight weeks before he died he was asked to speak at a school.

This is what he said, "A word about family: You have shown that you are willing to learn and work hard, long hours and set aside your personal lives. But it reminds me of the words that no one was ever heard to say on a deathbed. I wish I had spent more time at the office. Balance wisely your professional life and your family life. If you are fortunate to have children, your parents will warn you that your children will grow up and be gone before you know it. I can say that it is true. God only allows us so many opportunities with our children to read a story, go fishing, play catch and say our prayers together. Try not to miss a one of them." This was written just eight weeks before he committed suicide. Yes, folks, while we are climbing the ladder of success, we must not forget our family. The years that I spent with Mervin and the other children seem like now they're here and now they're gone. I'm not sure how to say it, but we must do whatever we can to grab those precious moments. It might mean changing jobs, or turning down big exciting jobs. Take time to smell the roses. Nothing is worth losing the children, I mean nothing. Lord, help me to see my past mistakes and try from here on to learn from them. What is our first duty to our children? It is very important to provide support and love and teach them in the Scriptures. But I really think there is another duty that must come first. It is the duty to make the children's mother happy. All that other stuff cannot take the place of a happy home. Lord, help me to be a better father. Help me to do my first duty, to make the children's mother happy. With all these deaths this past year, it causes me to stop and think. Think about life and what the meaning is of it. Money, big houses and all that mean so little to someone on his deathbed. We know that we come into this world with nothing, and that is exactly the way we will leave this world. I guess when it comes down to it, the only things that really matter are people. Lord, help me to treat all people alike. Help me to do something nice for someone, and not expect anything in return. Help me to remember that this could be my last chance to do something nice. We never know which day will be our last here on earth, and we never know when another person's last day is here on earth. We must then forgive one another. Time spent hating and being angry is time wasted. Forgiving someone, truly forgiving, can be a wonderful thing. We never know when our time is up.

Light in the Shadow of Death

210

The Longest Good-bye

JANUARY 20, 2006. Here I am, back again. Hello, Mervin. Lord, I just want to thank you first of all for all you are doing in this recovery, coming out of that deep, dark tunnel. Yes, I am ready to be used by you in the lives of other people who are hurting. Show me the way, Lord! Lead me to someone who needs a word of cheer. Lord, help me to say the right words to them. I do realize that by reaching out my healing is on fast-forward. I really do want to remember that we did not have our grief alone; you sent lots of people at just the right time to share with us and walk us through. I want to help others, and do realize as I do, I become stronger. I know, Lord, that I was not prepared for what came and what still comes and realize maybe nobody could be ready for anything like that. Amen!

Yes, Mervin, that is my prayer, and yes, I do feel like I have come a long way. The date, you know the one, is fast coming to be February 28, 2005. How that rings in my ears. How can it be one year already coming up? Oh, I don't know how I feel about it. Sometimes it seems like a long, long time since you went away. And then the next time, I can not understand where the time went. Mixed feelings! It's January and seems like my mind goes with the weather, so dreary sometimes and feel so—so—well, lonely, and homesick for you, Mervin. But I do want to move on. Slowly but surely, I must say good-bye to you, Mervin, and really mean it; yes, the longest good-bye I ever had. I try to make the most of each day and live again. I guess what comes so hard is the fact that this good-bye has changed my life so much, and no, it will never be the same again. We read, "Blessed are those who mourn, for they shall be comforted" (Matthew 5:4). I have mourned, Lord, and do feel your comfort. Thank you, Lord! Step by step through this "thing" I go. How can it be? I wonder sometimes, if the steps would come too fast, we surely would stumble, so help me to slow my steps and surely someway come out of this dark, dark valley. I realize that sometimes we are heading in a different direction from what God has planned for us, so He adjusts our way. Hopefully through this adjustment He can get us going in the right direction. It seems like when it was so dark, I felt like I could never see bright light again. Things are looking up and the deep, deep pain is getting less. Thank you, Lord! If this is what it takes for us to learn more and be a better person, then I do want to say, "Thy will be done." I realize that if we look for the good in everything, it's there somewhere! I would say to you all, if this dark, dark valley has increased your faith, then be joyful and praise the Lord. Oh Mervin, sometimes I think back over my life, my teenage years, and think to myself, Lord, never let me forget about the pain of trying to fit in and the worries of being liked and all that goes with being a teenager. My wish is that when I talk to teenagers to try and turn back to their level. The things that seemed so big like finding a girlfriend, or fitting in, are now bygone things for us older people, but we must never forget they are very, very real to teenagers. Yes, Mervin, when I think of you, I hope upon hope that you are so happy now and must not worry about these earthly things anymore. Help me, Lord, to listen to younger people and really care, and just maybe make a difference in their life. Yes, you young folks, do not forget to ask the Lord to guide you and surely He will hear you and help you. You are precious in His sight.

Praise the Lord, praise His Holy Name. It's January 27, 2006, and here I sit at the table in the shack in Maryland. I'm all alone here, Mervin, thinking of you and talking out loud to you. Yes, I do hold a one-sided conversation with you. There's no answer from you, but I just think sometimes maybe you would hear me. Your memory is so fresh when I sit here, and it's one place where I can just let everything flow, my thoughts, my crying and the tears falling down my cheeks. Lord, is that alright? I still get so much homesickness sometimes that I hardly know which way to go. We realize, Mervin, that one year since you're gone is coming so fast. Paul wrote, "To die is gain" (Phil. 1:21). Help me to believe. I feel somewhat like Paul. "For I am in a strait between two, having a desire to depart and be with Christ." I really want to use my life that I still have to the fullest, but—but...We know that those who die and are with the Lord are the winners. If we could only get it into our minds that we are losing out here and you, Mervin, hopefully are the winner. Help me, Lord! Sometimes I just think I have to know what you are doing, Mervin, or how it is wherever you are. Are you walking beside those crystal clear rivers? Are you saying I won, I won, and the race is over for me? I so often wonder many, many times if you knew what was happening. Did you know you were going to die? Did you realize that you were going home; did you see the heavenly glory shine in front of you? What did you see, Mervin? Help me, Lord, to not always think of our loss, but, Lord, help me to think more of Mervin's gain. I just feel so helpless sometimes in my thoughts. "Precious in the sight of the Lord is the death of his saints" (Psalm 116:15). Death seems so much more real to me and I think on it a lot. Sometimes I get greedy and I think, no way, I want to do this and that and want to go here or there yet. And then I think, what does all that matter? Let me be ready when He comes and not think so on this earthly stuff. Help me to remember that we are only strangers and pilgrims on this earth. Help me, Lord, to desire a better country. Well, Mervin, thanks for listening again and making me feel better. Lord, thank you for your healing touch and thank you for giving me a more peaceful feeling about all this that happened to Mervin. Now, Mervin, come with me for a walk in the woods. See the birds, look at the deer and help me to enjoy the moment.

I'm back, Mervin; I was out in the woods here in Maryland with my bow. I was hunting in your stand that you built. It's late archery season here in Maryland and there are still lots of deer. I counted about 33 last night. None came close enough for a shot, but, you know, that didn't really matter this year. I feel so close to you out there on my stand and cannot really explain how it is. Yes, Mervin, when I'm up there sitting on my stand I think more of you than I do of deer. Oh yeah, I still like to hunt, but feel so different about it. The birds were singing and the squirrels running around and I was in my own little world with you, Mervin. You know, I have lots of time to think about you and all when I'm sitting there for hours at a time. Do you hear my still voice talking to you? Rest in peace!

Hello again, Mervin. It's February 4, 2006. February 4th? I am not afraid of storms, for I am learning how to sail my ship. Yes, I was at the Maryland shack again last night. I need to talk to you again. Sometimes I just need someone to listen to me. I really want to be a good listener when other people need a listening ear. It means so much to me when people listen. I guess this grief thing is something that we will never fully understand until we walk through it ourselves. We need someone to listen to us, please. Sometimes this deep sorrow and an empty feeling just want to take over. That empty hole in my stomach is getting smaller, but is still so very, very real. You know, Mervin, when you went, a part of me went with you and now that part is missing. I was over to your grave the other night again. I really do want to let you go and surely do not want to go against God's plan. We are all hanging together as a family and the new normal seems to be okay. Sometimes I think back and think maybe God was trying in other ways to get my attention, and then He saw that I didn't listen, so He really wanted my attention now. Yes, Lord, not my will but thine. I think God wants us to feel good and comfortable in the situation we are in, just not too comfortable. He wants us to depend on Him. He surely does not want us to love the comforts more than we love Him. Help me, Lord, to let go and be willing to go in this new direction. Help me to surrender my old dreams and go after the dreams that you want me to. Help me, Lord, to surrender all of them to you. Thank you, Lord, for taking me through this deep, dark tunnel, so that I can depend totally on you. Show me the light! I really want to walk step by step into this new normal and say, look at all the good that has come! I do not want to deal with this grief myself, but want to surrender it to you, Lord. I want relief of the big empty feeling if it is your will, Lord. I know that the healing touch of God is the only way to heal me and restore my soul. Sometimes I do not want to tell people about you, Mervin, because it puts them in such an awkward situation. They just do not know what to say and I feel sorry for them. I know we must let them say whatever they want and not criticize them if they do not do it just right. They mean well. I guess nothing that anybody says can even come close to the healing power of God's love for us. Yes, Mervin, those waves of grief come and go so—so when we least expect them. So often something will suddenly jump out at me about you, Mervin. The pain just shoots through me for a second. It's not that life has stopped; it's just the life that we knew that stopped. Thank you so much for listening again. See ya!

February 9, 2006. Hey, Mervin, I have to talk to you. Yes, today it's one year that I last saw your living body here on earth. My, how memories flow! How it hurts! Love ya!

February 11th. Mixed, mixed feelings! Today you went on your vacation to the West. Why do I feel so...... so, well, what a long vacation it is. We miss you so much. Did you know when you left? I just can not get this hole in my heart to go away today. I am here at the market and think maybe nobody or at least not many people know what's going on inside of me. One year that you said good-bye. One year that we heard your voice for the last time while we could see you. Yes, I did call, but that was later. This was a rough, rough journey, but thanks so much for God's presence. He helped us through. Are we through? Yes, Lord, help me to live my days in joy and hope, because someday I know I will have to give account of how I spent the rest of my life without you, Mervin. It seems like I'm doing okay, but this grief thing sometimes just drags me along. The last talk, the last days, months, weeks and moments that we had together are now gone and there is no turning back. Starting from here, I want to keep keeping on. Thanks for the prayers from those we love.

February 17, 2006. Hello again to our firstborn. How happy we were to have you, our first baby. How well I remember the joy, joy, joy. Now you're gone, but thanks, Mervin, for being a part of our lives. It's leading up to February 28th, the day you were killed so suddenly. One year. Oh yeah, Mervin, your buddy bunch was here to sing the other night. How nice it was to hear them sing. My mind is so full of things to tell you that I can't even think straight. I really do feel okay this last while and am moving on. My, oh my, if last year this time we would have known what was in store, could we have gone on? We still did not have a clue what the Lord had planned.

Sleep On and Take Your Rest

THIS SONG JUST keeps ringing in my mind today.

Sleep on, precious one, and take your rest. There now waits for you a great reward; we loved you, but Jesus loved you best. Enter now in the joy of the Lord. You fought the fight and won the victory, an inspiration on the battleground, you were a light for everyone to see. And now it's time to lay your weapons down. We'll keep our memory of you day by day. And often we'll be calling out your name. Lord, help us to remember on life's way, that our loss down here is heaven's gain. Jesus Christ said, "Because I live, ye shall live also." We do not see Jesus Christ with our eyes because He changed his form. He lives, and because He lives they live. It follows that our loved ones are not lost to us merely because we cannot see them. They have merely changed their form.

There is a parable about a butterfly, who before he was a butterfly was a caterpillar, and he crawled on the ground with all the rest of the caterpillars. They had discussions in their own caterpillar manner. They observed that the caterpillar comes to a time when he wraps himself up in a silken cocoon and they never see him again.

So they agreed among themselves that the next one was to come back and tell them about it and clear up this mystery. The one appointed rolled himself up into a silken cocoon, died a caterpillar death, and while he was in this cocoon, a marvelous thing happened to him. His form changed and when he burst the cocoon, he was in the form of a beautiful butterfly. His silken wings glistened in the sunlight as he flew, released between the earth and the heavens. He saw down below, but he said to himself, "They wouldn't understand. I cannot communicate to them what will happen to them, but what is the difference anyway." Now they crawl close to the dark earth under bushes, but it is only a while until they, too, shall have silken wings and be released.

So help me, Lord, to wait on my silken wings and be released. Oh yeah, some glad morning help me to "fly away". I'll fly away, oh glory, I'll fly away. You all know that song. Won't it be wonderful there, having no burdens to bear? Those old songs still are as meaningful as ever. "What a friend we have in Jesus."

February 22, 2005. Hello, Mervin, it's me again, Dad. Talk to me. I'm so much thinking about you. One year ago today we had our last words on the phone. How can it be? I remember it like it was yesterday, you saying it's just beautiful out there. My heart so aches for you, but I am wanting and trying so hard to move on. What a beautiful candle we got through the mail today from good friends, Vernon and Darlene Miller from Indiana. I just can not believe that you will not know them, but I really do believe that you know their son Joas. He is with you, right? I can picture you two walking down the streets of pure gold, talking and feeling no pains and not having to worry anymore. Take care till we meet again, hopefully up there on high. Yes, we are trying as a family to hold our heads up high and go on. Last night the barn was ringing with singing again. My, what those walls could tell us out there in the barn! The *Daily Reader* that was sent to us from the Enos Barkman family in Ohio read like this today, "Comfort and prosperity have never enriched the world. Out of pain and problems have come the sweetest songs, the nicest poems, the most gripping stories. Out of suffering and tears have come the greatest spirits and the most blessed lives." Yes, today I think I was asked a question that no one had asked me yet. A man asked me, "What do you think was the most outstanding part of this last year?" Well, I thought for a while and then said, "You know, I think I would have to say the fellowship between all the new friends, the grieving friends, church folks, brothers and sisters. Also, right in line with that was the closeness or comforting feeling of knowing that there truly is a God. He's there and there's no doubt." I thought I was probably asked all the questions already, but that was a new one. Well, I will talk to you again soon, Mervin. We have our supper coming tonight from a true friend, Linda Riehl. Oh yes, you had known her, Mervin. My, oh my, there would be so much I would want to tell you, and yes, you know all about it. I talk to you a lot when I'm alone. We loved you so!

February 24, 2006. Here I sit writing and thinking again. There are so many old songs going through my mind. What's going on? Lord, teach me to wait on you. Come home, come home, it's supper time. It's supper time in Heaven. Come home, come home, it's supper time. No, Mervin, you just don't come home for supper time anymore. Come home, come home, it's supper time. I've got a mansion just over the hilltop. How I long to be with you sometimes in that mansion just over the hilltop. Life is like a mountain railroad. Sometimes it will get bumpy and not so smooth. We must make the run successful from the cradle to the grave. Keep our hand upon the throttle and our eye upon the rail. Blessed Savior, thou wilt guide us, till we reach that blissful shore, where the angels wait to join us in thy praise forevermore. A favorite of my dad was always I'll fly away. I'll fly away. What a friend we have in Jesus. Take it to the Lord in prayer. Farther along we'll know all about it. Farther along we'll understand why; cheer up, my brother, live in the sunshine; we'll understand it all by and by. Help me to understand this lonely feeling, Lord. Help me to kneel at the cross so I can meet Jesus there. Help me to leave every care. Yes, Lord, just bring things into my life that bring me closer to you. Where could I go but to the Lord, seeking a refuge for my soul. Needing a friend to help me in the end, where could I go but to the Lord. Take my hand, precious Lord, take my hand. Hear my cry, lead me on. Guide my feet, hold my hand. I am so tired. I am weak and my mind is in such a turmoil. Take my hand, precious Lord. Lead me on. Death is an angel sent down from above. Gathering flowers for the Master's bouquet. Beautiful flowers that will never decay, gathered by angels and carried away, forever to bloom in the Master's bouquet. I hope these old songs will never fade out of our singing. Life here is lonely since the old friends have gone home. Sometimes I would so much want to tell my dad about all of this. I think about him so much this last while. Dad has been gone for nineteen years now and I so often wonder if you see him, Mervin. Dad died at age 59, and now to me seems not very old. You know, Mervin, my birthday is the day before you were killed. This Monday, February 27th, I'll be 53 years old. This is Friday, February 24th, and in only four more days it will be one year since you were killed. One year! I am weak, but thou art strong. Jesus, keep me from all wrong, I'll be satisfied as long as you let me walk close to thee. Just a closer walk with thee, granted, Jesus, is my plea. Daily walking close to thee, let it be, dear Lord, let it be. Where He leads me I will follow, where He leads me I will follow. If we never meet again this side of Heaven, as we struggle through this world and its strife, I will meet you on that beautiful shore. Precious memories, unseen angels, sent from somewhere to my soul. How they linger ever near me. How they ever flood my soul. In the stillness of the midnight, precious, sacred scenes unfold.

February 26, 2006. Hello, hello, Mervin. It's early Sunday morning and I'm so in a turmoil this morning. No, not that you're gone; yes, I'm finally starting to realize that. It's just that I lay awake most of the night last night thinking about you. I thought about a year ago, Sunday, in church. My birthday and how happy the whole church had been that day. I thought about you a lot that day, kind of expecting a phone call from you saying happy birthday. My mind went to Sunday night, how I was surprised with a birthday party by neighbors and friends. I thought of some of the words in the sermon that day. "Evil words bring bad thoughts." I thought about the snow the next day, and yes, I got to the part of finding out that you were killed and started crying and crying. I thought about the house full of people here afterward and how they supported us. I thought about this mountain we tried to climb this past year and how this was put at us, no, not something we chose to go through, but something God chose for us. I thought about how I thought the world will end, but here we are one year later, trying to put one foot in front of the other. I know I should still be sleeping this morning, but sleep is far out of reach just now. I am so wide awake. Mervin, I heard that some of your friends are planning to be in church today. It has gotten me all excited. Is that what you would call it, excited? Or maybe anxious or touched by their kindness. Sometimes I try so hard to write my feelings down and it just does not come out right. I would rather sometimes sit or walk with someone for hours and talk instead of write, but I do feel so much better after I write. Sometimes I do just want joy again instead of dragging this heavy heart around day and night. I guess I'm not trying hard enough to say and mean, "Thy will be done." And just maybe it's not like this for other people. Just maybe they are so much stronger in faith than I am. I did find out that our hearts are larger than we think, so what if I cry like a river; that's my way, so just let it come. The bumps are what we climb on, remember? I took a walk this morning and it's such a crystal clear morning with the stars so bright and everything seems so fresh, so why can't I feel refreshed? I can hardly wait to go to church today and be with all the church folks and feel that comfort only they can give. I'm so hoping I can hold up today in church and keep myself together. The fear of not holding up sometimes is worse than being there. Well, Mervin, daylight is peeping over the mountains to the east and I will see what the Lord has in store for us today. You will be right there by my side all day. I'm not near finished talking to you, so I'll probably talk to you tonight.

Answered Prayers

HERE IT IS Sunday evening after church and lots of company. My, how I feel so... so, is it good? Or is it mixed? I don't know. I do know, as I lay awake last night I was thinking how I need a lift and wouldn't it be nice if our neighbors would be there at church? I asked God to just give me something out of this day that will lift me up and help me through this day. Sure enough, God still answers prayers. Give all the glory to Him. I knew I would have a hard time, but like that! No, not that way. I must admit I am weak, but thou art strong, oh Lord. I took a handkerchief out of the drawer this morning and then I thought just maybe I better take more than one. Yes, then I grabbed four of them, and when I came home they were totally soaked. What is wrong with me? Where is my faith? We heard so much in the sermons for comfort and it seemed like just what I needed. We were told that God does not want us to get weary in our struggles. He wants us to keep on keeping on. Help me, Lord, to keep on the right path to you. Yes, Mervin, we had such uplifting company today and I do want to thank the Lord for that. How great is our God! Lord, help me to let go and by doing that maybe I will be still nearer to you and for sure not farther away. People that came did offer comfort today and some with the same experience knew just what to say because they were also comforted at one time. We do know where our greatest comfort comes from though. "Jesus Christ, the Father of compassion and the God of all comfort, who comforts us in all our troubles, so that we can comfort those in any trouble with the comfort we ourselves have received from God" (2 Corinthians 1:3,4). This journey has taught me that those in grief, no matter what kind of loss, have so much in common. I do realize that I am most likely through the darkest part of this grief journey, but sometimes I just fall so fast. I do realize that life is short and that death comes to us all, but hope it will all be even in heaven, no more sorrow, no more pain, just joy, joy, joy. It seems like I'm gaining so little ground sometimes in this "thing". No, Mervin, I do not want to let you down by all my crying. What would you say? Don't cry for me! It would maybe be more of an honor to you if I were happy and joyful. I'm trying so hard, but just maybe not hard enough. The knot in my heart or soul just gets so tight sometimes and then there is release again at times. Thank you, Lord, for that better feeling. Help me to take advantage of this storm and use it to sail my ship. I do realize that all the kindness from friends and strangers, the wise words and prayers, even that purple martin flying around here last summer, was God's hands reaching out with love and comfort for me. Please, Lord, I ask, please let me grieve with hope; hope that I can see you, Mervin, someday. It seems like the world is pressing down on me sometimes and is trying to question my faith, trying to discourage me. My wish is that our ministers and bishops can see a way and not get discouraged. Sometimes I think they would feel like their work is in vain and they are accomplishing very little for God. Yes, we are in days when we can get discouraged. We need to stay strong and help build the church and surely not try to bring it down. Whenever we find ourselves getting discouraged we need to turn to the Bible and ask God to encourage us. Fear and discouragement will destroy our faith. We must trust God and wait for His help and know that He will never fail us. Each of us knows by reading the Bible that we are very important to God, because Jesus died for you and me. Lord, help me to have that forgiving spirit; we know an unforgiving spirit doesn't hurt the other person, it only hurts us. Help me to not think that I am better than other people. Help me to have a forgiving spirit. "And be ye kind one to another, tenderhearted, forgiving one another, even as God for Christ's sake hath forgiven you" (Eph. 4:32). Help me, Lord, to win and have victory over this journey. I ask you, Lord, to give me a satisfied mind. Sometimes it looks so dark and dreary and then we must look for the joy which can be found if we just look for it. We know that we should never fear the future. God knows and controls the future. No matter how confused things may be on earth, God is on the throne of heaven, guiding our every footstep. God has the future in His hand, and we know that for the Christian the best is yet to come. Well, Mervin, I am going to go to bed and try to keep on keeping on. Tomorrow, you know, is my birthday. I guess it will be up to me how happy it will be. Good night!

Happy Birthday to me. Oh yeah, it's here, my birthday, February 27, 2006. What am I making out of it? The day seems to be dragging on and I really do not know how I feel. I do realize that the year mark is here, and yes, some of you would say, "Time has a way of healing our wounds." Sure, I think as time goes on, we learn. But I really do not think time has anything to do with our healing. It's what we learn about this grief journey that helps us along the way. Our thoughts and beliefs are what control us through God's helping hand. We must learn to sail this ship. I really am filled with hope that I will survive this big missing part inside of me. It has been very hard work for me, but I am realizing more and more that this will not last forever in the state I am in just now! So I will look for the next stage and so on and on. I'm sitting here in the middle of the day and just can not get started with anything, so I just write to you, Mervin. I am thinking so of the other children and hope they are doing okay. They most likely feel like what was written in a letter to us this week of a family that also buried a son and brother. This person wrote that when I dropped off some candy and other things, she was so happy to see her mom and dad happy and smile for just that little while. So, yes, I do not want the children to think I just can't be happy anymore; I'm going to try very hard from here on. We do have such a great reason to be happy, with friends and supporters everywhere. God is good, God is great! Yes, Mervin, you know, I really did not realize how much I lost till you were gone. So now here I am and I have this privilege to have such a loving family. Help me, Lord, while they still live, to be a great parent. Lord, this journey has taken some real effort to be a survivor, and to live again, but I do know that you are my lean-to and my helper through it all. I realize, Lord, that life has changed in our family and also do realize that things like this do not always happen to other people. I'm sitting here thinking faster than I can write today, and thought if a death like Mervin's was coming wouldn't it be nice to have a day's warning, just so we could still say "good bye" and tell them how much they meant to us? But I do realize that is not God's plan and am sure if I would have had a little time all I would have asked from God is for more time. How could we ever get ready to let go? Sometimes I wish all of the other children would write their feelings down for me to see. I do realize for me it's very, very hard sometimes to put my feelings into words. Looking back, I think sometimes maybe I should have involved us all more at different times through this thing. We would most likely all have a different opinion here and there. Yes, but I do realize there is no real right or wrong way. One thing that I really do not want to do is make the children feel like Mervin was perfect. He was not. He was human like all of us. He gave us great joy to be his parents, but so do all the other children. We love you all with all our hearts. In God's eyes we are all the same. Remember, He loves us all. Dear Lord, my wish is to be a better father to our children. My great wish in this life is that we as a family can all see Jesus. What a day of rejoicing that will be. I also really hope and pray that our children can keep the faith and feel God's protecting arms around them through their life. The privilege we have here in this life can not be bought with money. Stay the faith. Well, here I am and feeling so much better again after writing in this journal and just telling it like it is. Thank You, Lord, for Your blessings on me.

One Year

chapter 25

THIS IS THE day the Lord has made, let us rejoice and be glad in it. Mervin, Mervin, Mervin, yes, here it is, "February 28, 2006". I was awake a lot last night thinking, thinking, thinking. I almost just wanted to stay in bed this morning till nighttime comes and then start over tomorrow. But, Lord, I do not want to get weary, I want to go on. I got up at my usual time, and then went back to bed but couldn't rest anyway, so I thought, Lord, just help me one step at a time to face this day. There's snow on the ground this morning. Oh my, remember the snow falling last year at the time you were killed, Mervin? What is God trying to tell us? Am I listening? The cool crisp morning and the beautiful sunshine making the whole earth sparkle here this morning. Lord, help me to sparkle and be a light today. Strengthen my faith! I went out to the barn, upstairs to the window, and on my knees looking to the east, I prayed for strength. Guide me, please, today and always. The jet streams, oh yeah those jet streams. Now we see them and now we don't. They were so bright this morning. Did you hear me talking to you, Mervin? What are you doing? The message machine on the phone is full again and again. Many birthday greetings and songs are being sung for us. Thank you, thank you, all you friends. That song, "Praise God, I feel like singing", was ringing in my mind this morning and then I went to the phone shack and it was on the message machine. I cried and cried when I heard it and felt relief again. That song so many times comes to my mind and it seems like you are singing it, Mervin. Are you? Praise God, you're saying I feel like singing I'm on the other side. Wow, you feel like singing I'm on the other side of life now. How is it? I so much want to go to the graveyard this morning, but I just don't know. I really do not feel like doing anything, just let the memories flow if they want to. I have such good memories of you at the graveyard, you know, with the snow on the ground and your face shining so bright. That is so clear in my mind when I think of you there. Oh my, what a precious time we had last night. Your friends brought supper and we sat there after supper just talking and talking about you, Mervin. It was once again one of those moments, times that we can not plan. Moments can not be planned. They happen, you know. So many times when we least expect it, here are some of the best moments just happening again. God's way of giving us comfort. Lord, I'm hoping you give me comfort for today and let me look on the brighter side of life, please. Maybe tomorrow, let me have a fresh start again, and onward I go step by step. Help me, Lord, to not be too weary. Help me, please, to have a song in my heart and a smile on my face. Help me to not go around with a long face and a miserable look that brings all around me down into this pit or valley. Christian people should be joyful people, right, Lord? Help me to be joyful. Help me to remember that if I accept You, Lord, that You have a home waiting for me when my life is over. "Rejoice in the Lord always, and again I say, Rejoice" (Phil. 4:4). Help me to study your Word and in so doing increase my joy. "Ask and it shall be given you" (Matt. 7:7). Help me, please, to fill my heart with joy. We must not forget about all the feelings and everything that other people feel too. Sometimes we think it's just us or me. All around us are people who are hungry for love and joy; help me to pass it on, Lord. I am so mindful of people watching me and seeing what I make out of this grieving thing. It seems like I am being watched at work and everywhere. Maybe I just imagine it, but am I? People watch us because we are Christians, and yes, this gives us the best opportunity to show them what a difference Christ has made in our lives. Help me, Lord, to be a light to all those around me. Help me to look for the joy which is everywhere. Help me to show the world there is hope. Help me, Lord, to fill my heart with Your love and joy. No matter what, Lord, how difficult this life will be, let me not fear, but let me hold my head up and be joyful. Help me, Lord, to not look back so much that it keeps me from looking ahead. Help me to make the right decisions in this life, so I can somehow help others. Help me to be more like Paul in the Bible. "For I have learned, in whatsoever state I am, therewith to be content" (Phil. 4:11). Help me, Lord, to not surround my life on daydreaming about Mervin. Help me to know, no matter what, I cannot bring Mervin back, and I cannot control the world around me, so just help me, please, to control the world within me. I wonder why, well, no, we shouldn't wonder why. Paul said he has learned. He learned through experience, I guess. He was also human just like us. He said he has learned to be content. To learn we must go through troubles and trials, difficult situations, and face the changes the Lord has for us. We must watch so we do not become too comfortable in the state we are in. Help me to accept the changes in this life. Help me to take with joy what You have in store for us in this New Year ahead. Before us lies a New Year, like an unopened package, an unread book or an untrod pathway. It is new and it lies in our hands, to use to His glory or for our pleasure. God has placed it there and we are accountable, responsible to Him, for how we use it. We may choose whether we will waste its minutes or fill them in His service. But when it is gone it will never return again. We can never bring it back. It will fade into the past, so let's cherish this gift, and let us use this year to shape our lives for His glory. Let us seek to be perfect in Him. Yes, before us lies a new year, a new year that will never return. I guess the sooner I realize what that word "never" means, so much sooner can I get the comfort that will surely come, if we let it.

My, I did not expect to write so much again, but am so full of—what? It is now very close to the exact hour and minute that you were killed, Mervin, one year ago. It just seems so—so, I don't know, you were still living and breathing at this moment last year. My, oh my, I can't grasp it all. In a split second you were gone. Is this all true? Time just now seems like it is standing still. Lord, spread your loving hands over us and protect us, please. "Thy will be done."

I'm so restless. I was to the phone shack again and the message machine is full. Beautiful, beautiful encouragement. Thank you, thank you! I'm so going in circles. The cardinal is singing without stopping outside the window all morning. What's going on? I feel something's got a hold of me. That cardinal was singing so much last year over your funeral, Mervin. He is back in full force this morning. Praise God! I feel like I must keep moving, but which way, Lord? Lord, just give me that calm that only You can give.

I'm back, Mervin. It's now 1:00, February 28th. I can't think straight; nothing wants to go on just now. We are all just kind of sitting around doing nothing and feeling empty. I am writing every hour or so as the day drags on. Now, 1:00, Mervin, you were gone, but we still did not know. I can't explain this day or this feeling. I did not know what to expect, but my, I do know I can feel the prayers of those we love. It seems almost every hour today here comes a bouquet of flowers and I just brought the mail. My, oh my, we are so blessed, Lord, to live in a loving community like this. There were 38 cards in the mail. 38! I am so overwhelmed and it seems like we all just cry and then cry again. Lord, I want to thank You for that feeling of love, joy or what do I call it? Help me, Lord, to do my part in making other people feel wanted and good. I just wish I could find the right words for how I feel just now. I try to explain, but it does not want to come out right. It kind of feels like I want the world to stop for a little bit and let me get on. I'm floating! I'm just now thinking of those poor friends of yours on that hill when you were killed, Mervin. You left them there to do and think the best they could. I'm trying to realize how that would have been at this exact time one year ago for them. Thanks so much for all known and unknown prayers that we can feel on this day. I didn't get anything done yet today and you know, I don't really care. Just let me think. The one verse reads today, When the believer dies, the body goes into the grave, the soul and spirit go immediately to be with the Lord Jesus awaiting the body's resurrection, to be forever with the Lord in eternal bliss. Yes, Lord, I realize just the body goes to the grave, but I can not get the graveyard out of my mind today. I just want to go there. 5:15,

February 28, 2006. Oh my, the time is here so close to exactly one year that we found out you were killed, Mervin. I did not know what to expect today, but I do know it was the most unusual day of my life. Almost like a sacred day, a holiday or something. I did not get anything accomplished today by way of work. I cannot explain the feeling. The same flower man came again and again last year and now here he was today again. Thank you, friends, for all those beautiful bouquets of flowers. They really do mean a lot to us. Friends, neighbors, are bringing supper tonight for us. It is very close now to the exact time son-in-law Daniel and daughter Lydia Jane came to tell us the life-changing news. Mervin was killed! Mervin was killed!

Light in the Shadow of Death

Rest in Peace

IT'S ME AGAIN, Lord, March 1, 2006. It's over a year! One year! The house was full last night with your friends, Mervin. Precious memories. Up to your room they went and let the tears roll. They miss you a lot. They will never know how much they mean to us. It seems today is just kind of like yesterday, no get up and go for me. You know, Mervin, it seems kind of like a sacred holiday of some kind. What could it be called? Oh yeah, I'm so looking forward to tonight when all these friends of yours come again to sing. Again I say precious memories, how they linger, how they ever flood my soul. Words cannot describe the feeling of support we have over this time. I really can feel the prayers of those we love. Thank you!

Today March 1st, same day, a little later, 4:30. Today I will not imagine what I would do if things were different. Things are not different, so I will make a success with what I have! Is our child really gone? In our memory he still lives on—. Rosanna and I just got back from the graveyard. Why did I want to go there? Just because! Oh Lord, take this will of mine which wants to have its way and lead it into paths divine where you would have it stay—. Lots of cards again today. Precious memories!

March 2, 2006. God has promised strength for today, rest for the labor, light for the way, grace for the trials, help from above, unfailing sympathy, and undying love. What's going on, what is happening, what's wrong? Oh my, I don't know. I'm okay, I guess. I just hardly know which way to go. Singing was ringing through the barn again last night, but you know, I barely heard it. My mind is tossing and turning so fast I can't get with it. Yes, I do like singing, but I guess I'm so mixed up. Thinking, thinking, thinking of you, Mervin, one year ago. I would recommend to maybe not have a singing this same week you were killed. My mind has plenty enough to do without too much other things going on. I just cannot believe how far I fall again and again. Lord, I'm trying, but maybe I'm trying too hard. Just let the memories flow and let the tears roll.

Well-meaning friends say, "How are you doing?" You know, the people that have been down this deep, dark valley, I do not have to tell how I'm doing and those that have not gone this way I could try to explain all day and would not be able to explain. How can I explain it to someone when I don't even know how I feel? I'm here at my desk at the market and all I can think is that I want to go home. I want to go somewhere away, way far away and be alone. I don't know what I want, but I do know I do not really want to be here at the market. Are the other children having such a hard time, I wonder. I'm asking you, Lord, to help me to stay strong, to help me realize this is how it is. I feel so alone! Mervin, Mervin, at this time last year we were talking to your friends that came back from Wyoming. I can't find words to put on paper just now. I really don't think there are any words for how I feel. I just want to run. Run where? Somewhere for relief, I guess. Somebody please take me home. Lord, I'm coming home!

March 3, 2006. About now is when you came in the driveway, Mervin, in a casket! Oh my, how can all this be? One year ago!

> Lord, let me put my hand in thine,
> This is my humble plea.
> I cannot find my way alone.
> Please help me walk with thee.
> You know the way that I must go.
> You know what's best for me.
> I only ask you for your hand.

Lord, help me walk with thee.
Sometimes I've stumbled by myself,
And fell in deep despair.
Do not let me fall again,
This is my earnest prayer.
I need your guiding hand, dear Lord,
I beg on bended knees.
Lord, lift me up and hold my hand,
And help me walk with thee.

Here I sit at my desk and am wondering why or how did I fall so far again. I just can not seem to even think straight. I just did not realize this journey would be such hard work. Lord, You know my thoughts, You know my ways, and I need You so very, very much to get me through this week, You know. Please, please, don't let me down! I'm so mixed up! Mervin, what would you say about all this? Please, Mervin, just give me a little more time, then I'll be okay. I feel like I'm going against Your will, Lord. Help me, please, to stay strong. Tears are just rolling and I am thinking of you, Mervin. About right at this time last year we were opening your casket for the first time to look at your body. Oh my, my, my, I just cry and cry. You looked so at peace lying there, so why don't I say, peace be with you. Peace come to me, Lord, if it's Your will. I'm in such a turmoil, Lord. You know my thoughts. Help me, please, to find rest in my soul. I guess what's getting me more than anything is how I had made up my mind the last couple of weeks to move on and be strong. I just can't figure it out. Don't I really have more control than this? Am I rushing things? I guess I just have to add a question mark again, because I don't know; I didn't have training for this. I'm just asking, Lord, one more time; guide me one minute at a time, today, tomorrow and then—. Maybe more peace will come to me tomorrow at the time we would have laid you down in that deep, dark grave, Mervin, tomorrow! Your friends asked me this week if I would go with them to the grave tomorrow. So yes, sure, I'll meet them there. I was so touched by their concern. Your friends, Mervin, mean so much to us now. Just for today I am going to try to live through the next 24 hours and not expect to get over your death, Mervin, but instead learn to live with it, just one day at a time. I'll talk to you later today, Mervin. Rest in peace!

Here I am, Mervin. It's the evening of your viewing. Oh, can it be? I think of all the people that came to show their respect to us. Friends that we didn't even know you had, Mervin. You know, Mervin, I'm thinking your death has made a much, much greater difference in other people's lives than I could ever come close to. I'm thinking of how at this time last year we were standing beside your open casket and felt like that's where we wanted to be. Precious memories! Rest in peace! Sorrow can lead us into one of four lands: the barren land in which we try to escape from it, the broken land in which we sink under it, the bitter land in which we resent it or the better land in which we bear it and become a blessing to others. Lord, help me to enter that better land and accept your comfort that you so freely want to give. Just for today, Lord, help me to remember Mervin's life, not his death, and live in the comfort of all those treasured days and moments we shared. Thank you, Lord, for your blessings on me.

Good morning, March 4, 2006. Today is the day the Lord has made, let us rejoice and be glad in it. Well, mixed, mixed feelings, but more of a satisfied feeling this morning, I guess. Today one year ago was your funeral, Mervin. One year! I was awake a lot last night, thinking, thinking, thinking. Tears were rolling onto my pillow and I can't remember a dream or anything that would have made me cry. Just my mind going on and on, I guess. I thought about last year how I got up real early the day of the funeral and was sitting with you, Mervin, by your casket for hours talking to you. I was many, many, many times so glad I did that. It was such a peaceful good-bye feeling just sitting there talking to you. I really do think I have or will have a joyful, peaceful feeling after today. I don't know, one day at a time. I really do want to lay you down into that grave and move on. I really want to praise God in everything. It's just that deep, deep longing that has ahold of me. It seems truly impossible sometimes for life to go on, and the pain is almost unbearable, but I know God is the God of all comfort and a healer of our broken hearts. Lord, please help me to be comforted by thoughts of where Mervin has gone. Help me to think his journey is over and he has won the victory. Help me to not even for one minute wish you back, Mervin. Rather, Lord, help me to prepare to meet him someday. Praise God!

March 4th, evening. We just got back from the graveyard, my wife and I, and your friends, Mervin, were there with us. How precious it was, talking with them, thinking about you, Mervin. My mind is so full tonight I can hardly write fast enough. I'm thinking this writing or journal must sometime come to an end. My, oh my, am I going to quit writing or maybe I'm thinking just a little bit more, Mervin. Sometimes I think of quitting writing and then I think, no way, isn't this just the beginning? I do feel somewhat of a peace tonight as I sit here knowing that one year ago you were buried in that cold, dark grave. Yes, it almost seems after this year mark, that we buried you again today. I really do want to praise God for all the good that has come to us through this death. Let me be more like little Rosanna, our youngest daughter, singing tonight in the shower, not knowing we were outside listening. She was singing, "NO TEARS IN HEAVEN, no sorrows given, all will be glory in that land. There'll be no sadness, all will be gladness. When we shall join that happy band. (Chorus) (No tears, no tears up there. Sorrow and pain will all have flown, no tears in heaven fair, no tears, no tears up there, no tears in heaven will be known). Glory is waiting, waiting up yonder. Where we shall spend an endless day. There with our Savior we'll be forever, where no more sorrow can dismay. Some morning yonder, we'll cease to ponder o'er things this life has brought to view. All will be clearer, loved ones be dearer, in heaven where all will be made new." Matthew 18:3: "Verily I say unto you, Except ye be converted, and become as little children, ye shall not enter into the kingdom of heaven." I opened the Bible today and this is the page that came up: Psalm 67: "God be merciful unto us, and bless us and cause his face to shine upon us. Let the people praise thee, O God; let all the people praise thee. O let the nations be glad and sing for joy, for thou shalt judge the people righteously and govern the nations upon earth. Let the people praise thee, O God; let all the people praise thee. Then shall the earth yield her increase, and God, even our own God, shall bless us. God shall bless us, and all the ends of the earth shall fear him." Paul wrote in Romans

12:3:"Because God has given me a special gift, I have something to say to everyone among you. Do not think you are better than you are. You must decide what you really are by the amount of faith God has given you." Proverbs 3:5-6: "Trust in the Lord with all thine heart, and lean not unto thine own understanding. In all thy ways acknowledge him and he shall direct thy paths." I guess I could say with Paul in II Corinthians 2:4: "For I wrote you out of great distress and anguish of heart and with many tears, not to grieve you, but to let you know the depth of my love for you."

In Memory of Mervin Jay Beiler

Day 1, Monday, February 28, 2005

5:45, Monday evening, Lydia Jane came over crying loudly with the sad news, my namesake and nephew, Mervin J., was killed in a snowmobile accident near Square Top Mountain in Wyoming. How do I describe this feeling on paper? Hopefully, I could make some notes here on these couple of sheets with the memory still fresh. I'm writing this on Saturday, March 5, 2005. The funeral was yesterday, Friday, March 4th.

Well, here we were, sitting around the table just finished with supper. We were reading a Bible story to the children Marilyn (age 7), Johnathon (age 6), and Amanda (age 4). Reading out of Bible Story Book #1, the story "The Girl with a Kindly Heart", where Abraham sends Eliezer to find a wife for Isaac.

I got my boots and coat and walked with Jane over to her house to take care of five-month-old Michael, while she and Daniel walked up to tell Aaron's. I should have gone along to tell them; I just didn't think that far ahead. Esther and the children came over to Daniel's and we all waited until Daniel and Jane returned. Then we got dressed and went up to Aaron's. Neighbor Steve's Susanne stayed with the children.

"Falling snow." It had snowed since 11 o'clock this morning, with a total accumulation of about 7 inches. We met Aaron outside at the front door steps towards the drive. Can this really be happening? Everybody seems to be in shock. Between prayers and sobs we greet the family and my dear old mother. Dad had passed away eighteen years ago from a heart attack. So a sudden death isn't something our family has never experienced before, but oh, the ache in our hearts. Bishop Jake King said a prayer out of "Lust Gartlein" soon after everybody got together. Then we said another prayer before going home around 1:30 a.m. We need the prayers of those we love!

Aaron's Gideon, and Elmer's Anna Mae and sister Mary are in Florida with their friends. And the other four boys who were with Mervin are still so far away. Those who were with him on their trip were John King's twin boys, Johnny and Jake; they lived in White Horse along Rt. 340; Amos Smucker's David, Peters Road, and Mel D.'s Norman, Talmage. Their plan was to be away for three weeks. They left February 4th to go snow skiing and snowmobiling. The area where they were was close to the Nobles Ranch in Pinedale, Wyoming. I was there when I was 20 years old, making hay on their ranch.

Now I will describe the day that the accident happened and how it happened, as I gathered from Norman, David, Johnny and Jake, his friends that were there when it happened. They had left the lodge, named "The Place", where they were staying, around 8:30 that morning. They were heading out for some sight-seeing. The way I understood it, Mervin was leading the way most of the time as he carried the maps. His sled had problems with the heater in the handlebar not working. He had cold hands, so he and Jake traded for a while. Then two miles before the accident they swapped back to their original sleds, which they had borrowed at the lodge. This means that Mervin and Jake were now traveling last, picking up speed to catch up with the rest. Never having snowmobiled in the West, I can only make a picture. I hope I can give accurate details. This is only a remembrance for our children, family and friends. Norman, who is now going first, following tracks from the day before, goes over the top to what they said was a 10' or 12' drop on the other side. It had only looked like a small knoll coming up on it and the main trail stays to the right and goes around the crest. Johnny goes over and David stays to the groomed trail around the right side of the hill and he stopped on the other side, knowing Jake and Mervin would be coming soon. Jake goes across and comes down sled nose first and is thrown, flying 10 feet from his sled. Not far behind comes Mervin on the same trail. Now here is Jake's sled standing on end, nose down. Mervin comes over the top and drops right before the upright sled. As the front of his sled hits the upright sled, it throws him up against it, with his head taking the blow. Funeral home "Furman" said it was an instant death from a broken neck, caused from an impact on top of his head causing the spinal cord to shut off all nerves running between the vertebrae. Now they gathered around Mervin. He was still sitting on his sled, snow up to the handlebars. They couldn't find a pulse. So Johnny headed out for help, while the others stayed there. They started to pray the "Lord's Prayer" out loud, and about halfway through, Mervin let out one breath. Soon after that, five other snowmobiles came along and stayed with Norman, Jake and David till one and a half hours later when Johnny came back. They didn't take the body out till four hours later because of an investigation by the sheriff. This happened at 10:30 a.m. Wyoming time, 12:30 our time. A two-hour time change.

Day 2, Tuesday, March 1, 2005

Sent Marilyn off to school. Johnathon went along to Aaron's. Amanda stayed at Daniel and Jane's. Their mother Katie was taking care of them. Fah-geha were Butter Jakes Squeaky and Fannie, Poofly Aaron's and Jaky B.'s. The family gathered around the table and made out the Leicht papers. Brother JR did the morning prayer ("Lust Gartlein," page 177) before we made out the Leicht papers. We ate dinner around 11 o'clock; people were coming and going all afternoon. We ate supper around 4 o'clock each day. Gideon came home from Florida around 1:30 in the afternoon and I met him at the front door with Daniel and Jane. Aarons came outside with the other girls. What a reunion, only one boy so soon. Sister Mary, Dads and Sadie came about 4:30. Now the Florida people are all back. Thank the Lord for bringing them all home safely. Esther and I sat with Aarons while they gave information to Phil Furman. He called out to Pinedale to find out when the body will come back. Oh my! Not till Thursday morning?

He would arrive in the Philadelphia airport at 11 o'clock Wednesday night and they don't open until 6 o'clock in the morning to pick him up. Heavy, heavy hearts. Prayer in the evening was by Yonie King. We left around 9 o'clock and went to Mom's overnight, talking till 11 o'clock. What would our Dad say?

Day 3, Wednesday March 2, 2005

Slept pretty good. Awake every couple of hours; we're all going through this together. Johnny King stopped in this morning just to talk to Mom. So we decided to get them to take us to Aarons around 8 o'clock. I walked down to Brother Elmer's to see if the boys who were with Mervin were back. Lydia Ann said they were. So I went upstairs to talk with Norman, as he was staying there. They are planning to get married this year. After embracing, I started to ask a few questions. Of course, we were all anxious to know all the details. Then we went downstairs and Mom came down and Elmer came in. They had gotten home from Wyoming around midnight. They drove straight through. It took about 28 hours, he said. Then Sara King came, so we went back to Aarons for the day. When we pulled in the drive, Ike Huyard was sitting in his minivan waiting on Aarons to go to pick a grave site. He opened his window to say he could come back later, as the four boys that were with Mervin Jay on the trip had just gotten there. We started talking to Ike Huyard, Mom and I, as his parents, Bud and Lydia Huyard, were good friends with Dad and Mom. Ike (Furman's helper) said he was going to Philly the next morning to pick up the body. Not thinking twice, I just said, "Well, can I go along?" He said, "Well, yes, I'd be glad to have you along." Imagine my surprise. Are you serious? Can I handle this? So he said he would pick me up around 4:30 a.m. Thursday morning, as we would not be able to pick up the body until 6 o'clock when they open. He was scheduled to arrive at 11 o'clock in the evening. So okay, plans were on. I'd go along! Then we walked in to meet the boys. Fah-geha were cleaning up the floor and doing dishes. Praise the Lord for these people in a time like this. They did such a good job. The family was slowly gathering again. Aaron and Mary Ann are sitting in a circle with these precious friends of Mervin to share the events of their trip. Oh, the tears just want to flow as they explain in low tones how it all went. Now it is starting to sink in. Or is it? Aaron explains how their last conversation went on the phone. They were near Afton, Wyoming, and Aaron had been there hunting mule deer and elk when he was single. Mervin was on a cell phone and didn't have good connections. He says, "Are you there? Can you hear me? So, okay, good-bye, Dad." Then the boys talked again about how they just had a perfect trip. Clean fun, and no regrets. God must've been guiding the way, still so many things to be thankful for. The thing that kept coming to my mind was the choice that Mervin had made last summer to join the church, such an important step in life. Oh, when we look back on our own lives, thank God for the gift of His Son Jesus. We have so many good memories of Mervin; we want to accept this as God's will. Not put a question mark where God has put a period. One of the Scripture verses that have been a comfort for Aarons was Psalm 147:11. "The Lord taketh pleasure in them that fear Him, in those that "hope" in His mercy." Where would we go if we couldn't go to God and the Bible? I guess the one that really kept going through my mind throughout the first few days was Psalm 84. "For a day in His courts is better than a thousand." Read that chapter now to try and stay with what we were on before. As we all got to meet the boys, it seems like almost everyone had a question for them. Then Mervin's dad, Aaron, said he used to think that parents were supposed to raise their children. Here he said it was the other way around. That boy raised me; I learned many a lesson from him. I don't think it was anything we did, God raised him and he was only borrowed to us for these short 23 years. Then Norman handed Aaron Mervin's wallet, and another flood of memories came rushing back as Aaron explained how not long ago he had given him a lot of money. This was all planned. I used to wonder what it was about him. He just kept on talking while rummaging through the wallet as he got up to go out. He handed it to Mervin's special friend. There was one picture in it of her and her friends. We will never know, Mary, how it all might have been. May we all strive to meet where there will be no more partings. Well, they went to pick the grave site. Lots and lots of young folks were in and out all day. I guess with the body not being there to view, people needed other memories, so there was often a crowd of people in his room upstairs. There's the picture of him and the buck he got in Potter County this past fall. In rifle season, the first day, he and I were about 3 or 400 yards apart. I helped him drag out the trail in the evening, partways, then he said we'll come back with more guys. So we hid him (the buck) along the trail. After supper the cooks and those that had their deer went with him to bring the buck in. There are his baseball trophies standing on his desk and the group of friends on the team. Now what do we do with them? There's the 9-point that I chased up to him in Maryland. We could see each other when he shot. I asked what he's shooting at, as I thought the drive was over. I thought he said a fox, but he had said a buck. Imagine my surprise! I guess he had his share of trophies by the looks of his room, but he always carried his shoulders low.

After rounding up all the young folks in the evening for prayers, the upstairs was full and some were in the basement. Willie Riehl said the prayer, page 138 "in Gebet Buch". I hope that I never forget that when the prayer was ended, all those people and young ones together sat in a long, long silence. How sacred. I went home overnight with Mother again.

Day 4, Thursday, March 3, 2005

I set my alarm for 4 o'clock because I was going with Ike Huyard at 4:30, even though I didn't need an alarm. Don't know how much sleep I got. Well, he was right on time (4:30). I called good-bye through Mom's bedroom door. She said, "Good-bye." So here we go, Ike and I, to the Philly airport. We had no problem getting acquainted, even though we never really knew one another before. We talked about our families and our parents. He talked about some things his dad used to say, and I could still hear my dad say those stories. One was when someone asked him what he knows. I know that my Redeemer lives. This was old Bud Huyard. Another one was when he'd meet my dad he'd tell him when they were parting, "Now don't wait to come till you walk by my coffin." Then say, "Al aau goot alver vie sei selbert." That's how those two were when they were together. One minute they were laughing and the next minute they were crying. Now they've both been gone for so long already. I guess that's why I'm writing this about Mervin Jay. Time goes so fast and we just don't want to forget these 23 years he had with us. Arriving at Philly at about 6 o'clock, he tells me we're looking for the sign "Cargo". I'm thinking how cruel this sounds, but I guess we have to face it. When the body and soul separate, isn't that just about what it is? Now we're asking directions. The signs were not very clearly marked and we're looking for the Delta Airlines terminal. After stopping and asking three times and making a few loops, we find it adjacent to the huge Fed Ex warehouse with one small entrance door and one small overhead door with Delta Cargo in small writing. Ike's trying to keep the moment light by telling me we're doing alright for a couple of little Amish boys. It took us 20 minutes to find. My heart starts beating a little faster now. What do I expect? We walked in the small door together. He showed the lady behind the counter a piece of paper and told her the name of Furman Funeral Home. He paid her with a check for $536.00 from Furman. Then we walked outside and they opened the small overhead door and pushed out this cardboard box on a four-wheeled dolly. Two colored boys and an older white man (how strange this all seems) lower the ramp and we gently slide the cardboard box into the back of the minivan. Now we're climbing back into the van with this box that has two straps going all the way around on both ends and a paper on top that says "Mervin Beiler" in big black magic marker letters. I remember thinking that's my name. After we got out on the freeway again, I asked Ike if it would be alright if I talked to Mervin. He said that would be alright. So I just turned back to what was just a cardboard box with a wooden frame for its bottom and said, "Rest in peace, Mervin. Your friends are all waiting to see you." On the way home we talked about some Scripture and how it really is with death. The body and soul separate; this is how we agreed. The soul goes to its eternal destiny and the body goes unto the dust. Then according to Scripture we get a new body at the end of time that is reunited with the soul. Driving up Rt. 1, I thought of some of the jobs down in Chester Co., where Mervin Jay, Sam, Mahlon and Gideon did work over the years. Now here we were coming home in a hearse. I could think of one Saturday coming up through there on the way home from work, although I didn't have too many memories of working with them. Then Ike wondered if I wanted to go along to the funeral home. Well, I said, I didn't know that I'd be allowed, so I decided to go along. We arrived at Leola around 8 o'clock. We had made good time. We didn't stop for coffee or waste any time. We backed up to the overhead door. He pushed the button and it went up. We rolled out this dolly that adjusted in height and we slid the box onto it. Till now I had been brave, but could I take this? He cut the two bands holding the lid to the top. "Go on that end and lift," he directed. So I did. We set the lid aside. There was my namesake's body. Ike said he was going to the restroom and I could take a few minutes. Yes, it was Mervin! He looked so real. Furman said they did a good job out there. His left elbow was banged up a little, but his face and the rest of his body didn't show any injuries. Now his boots and bag of clothes that he had were also in the box. Ike told me to load them into the minivan while they took the body into the back to touch it up and put it into the coffin. Then he called me into the room to help put his shirt and pants on. They had his clothes because it was going so long until the funeral. So that was another new experience, to help put his clothes on, and his shirt was mine. I had worn it three times or so. They cut the back open from the collar down to the bottom and then just slid the arms into the sleeves. After closing the top and putting the screws into the top we pushed the dolly to the back of the minivan and loaded it again, this time taking it to the house and arriving at about 9:30, earlier than they were expecting. That was good, not so many people were there. I went into the house, clearing a path to carry him into Aaron's bedroom. Aaron started calling the children, Suzanne, Verna, da Mervin isht da. Komit, Rosanna, Esther, Gideon, Lydia Jane; aw, Gideon isn't up yet. Well, I guess we will carry him in. Aaron wanted Gideon to be there to help. Over and over, Aaron kept saying, "Mervin, Mervin, Mervin, Mervin, welcome home. Welcome home." Those to carry him into the house were Aaron, Dan, Bro. Jr. and me, with Mary Ann and the girls walking alongside. We carried him into the bedroom and set him down. Aw, Gideon isn't downstairs yet. They all want to be there when they open the coffin. Aaron went upstairs to get Gideon and hurry him along. I trailed along behind Aaron. Now calm down a little, Aaron. The better you take this, the better the rest of the family will take it. Now Mary Ann comes upstairs too. The children are all downstairs in Aaron's bedroom with the coffin still closed. Now Gideon comes out of his bedroom and the four of us walk downstairs too. The immediate family is all here. Ike Huyard slowly loosens the latches and opens the lid. There he is, "still". Looks like the same sweet boy, but the life is gone. Oh my, our brother, our boy, our nephew, our friend. Many, many cries and tears were heard. Now the week is wearing on as people come and go through the viewing. So many young ones, so many friends. My, my, Mervin, I didn't know you had so many friends. I guess it's because you made everyone feel important. They said when someone used to stand in the back, that's the one that you would befriend. Well, I'm sure they probably would all have a story to share. Evening prayer was led by Yonie King and then silence. Thank you, friends and family, for your great respect. We left Aaron's around 9 o'clock both evenings. I went home with my wife and her sister Mary and our children. How do we explain to these young hearts? My heart stirs a little when I think of their future, but it's all in God's hands. Trust and obey, for there's no other way, to be happy in Jesus, but to trust and obey.

Day 5, Friday, March 4, 2005

We awoke at 4:00 a.m. to prepare for the funeral day. We got to Aaron's about 6:30 a.m. We took our horse and carriage so we could go along to the graveyard. I went in to view soon after we got there. Aaron had a chair beside the coffin, and he said he had been in there since 3:00 a.m. with the Bible and a kerosene lamp, reading and saying farewell to his oldest child. He had Psalm 147 open, then I said, "Well, Mervin, I guess I'll make my farewell: Rest in peace, Mervin. Thanks for all the fun times together. May we meet on Heaven's happy shore." Aaron read some of Psalm 147, then Jonas, Mary Ann's brother-in-law, suggested those that were there just join hands and say the Lord's Prayer out loud, so that's what we did. Aarons ate breakfast and soon there were more and more people coming. The small funeral started at 8 o'clock. The pallbearers were Samuel Beiler, Norman Stoltzfus, David Smucker, Jonathan King Jr., Jake King, and Johnny King. Willie Riehl preached first in the house, talking about how that morning he went into his little boy's room to cover him with a blanket before he went out to the barn to do chores. Then he thought about these parents covering their child today for the last time. But we want to think further than the grave. Samuel Smoker read (Page 442, Lied #29), "Wer weisz, wie nahe mir mein ende." "If a man lives to be a hundred years old it's still just a short time compared to eternity."

We follow the family and the coffin out to the barn where the funeral was to start at 9 o'clock. Everyone was seated and waiting as we all took our seats. All is so quiet. Bishop Jake King tells the other ministers that they will have a part in the service. Aufang Steffs, Eli Stoltzfus main part, or Leicht predige. Soon after he stood, he said he didn't know if he had ever stood up in front of so many people. Five hundred (+) and so many young ones, we all took this sermon to heart. He said that if the most educated evangelist in the country were to stand and preach it wouldn't be a louder call than what we have right here in front of us in this coffin. Do we realize that it could be any one of us. And he said how he worked with Mervin over a period of seven years, when Mervin helped Steves on their farm. He never heard Merv complain from the age of eight until he was 16 years old. He thought he would get to repay him sometime, but he guessed he had waited too long. Mervin had sometimes gone to work there early in the morning before school and in the evenings when he came home. And in the sermon it was stated that if we all sent a letter the same day, the mailbox couldn't hold them all, and if we all came to visit the same day, the house couldn't hold us all. And there were quotes from Scripture about giving thanks to God in everything.

Jake King "Leicht Predige": Talked about how Mervin had led seven young people last summer along up to Abrott and confessed, "My beger ist fa frieda macha mit Gott und die gma." And how they took pleasure in helping them join church, then how Mervin Jay came and said thank you to the ministers. Jake just looked down onto the coffin and said, "You're welcome, Mervin." He said when he stood up he felt like the weakest person there. Also mentioned about this sled that they were riding, that they probably would have talked to him about it, but that he can forgive him and he thinks the church can too. And that he could just imagine that

Jesus would just be pleading with the Father on behalf of Mervin. And that when speaking to Aaron he would often say, "Ya, Dat, Abba Father," meaning, Yes, Father, and that is how we should respond to Jesus. Talked a lot about baptizing and how when they baptized them in September, that day the deacon being Brother Jr. He said "in zeigness" that it spited him to pour the leftover water out onto the stones and how there were others there that day that had the age to join the church. While he was at home thinking what he was going to say at this funeral, his wife was softly singing out in the kitchen, "Gone to Bloom Above" (page 626 in the *Christian Hymnal*). "Oh, gentle one, we miss you here."

John Riehl (page 437 #24), "Weit hinweg ich bin dein Mude."

Now the funeral is over. Everyone walks by the coffin. For some it will be the last glimpse of Mervin here on earth. Those that go along to the graveyard will walk by the coffin again. Now we gathered our clothes and prepare to leave. A long line of teams, numbering up to 55, and probably 20 cars, will travel one mile to Ridge Road Cemetery for our last good-bye or should we say good-night? With bleeding hearts the loved ones gather around. Now Furman closes the lid and they carry him in and lower him into the grave. This is our children, Marilyn's and Johnathon's, first experience and they have lots of questions. Yonie King read Lied (page 473 #2). Absheid Bishop David Esh then the Lord's Prayer in silence. He also said that when they buried their son that he wished the Lord would return and they could all fly to heaven together.

Mervin Jay Beiler

"Son of Aaron F. and Mary Ann Beiler"
Born: September 30, 1981, Died: February 28, 2005
Age: 23 Years, 5 Months

In Loving Memory of our dear friend, Merv

Our hearts were nearly broken.
We thought it could not be,
That a boy so young was taken
Away from friends and family.

Oh, sometimes it seems it cannot be
That he has left us now.
No more his happy voice we'll hear,
Nor see his happy smile.

When we arrive at your house, dear friend,
How we miss your friendly hello.
There seems to be such a vacancy.
At times we wonder, is it really so?

God knew it best to take him away,
We know we are not here to stay,
So let us do our best and try,
And hope to meet him by and by.

We do not want to wish you back
Into this sad world of care,
But we think you are with Jesus,
And we hope to meet you there.

But God has promised He will help us
With the trials that He sends.
So our thoughts are lifted upwards,
Keep us Savior to the end.

How we cherish happy memories
Of joyous times we had,
While he still lived here with us
And joined us in the crowd.

Beautiful memories woven in gold,
This is the picture we tenderly hold.
Down in our hearts his memory is kept
To love, to cherish, to never forget.

Precious memories....
How they linger!
—by friends, Benuel and Sadie Stoltzfus

Mervin Jay Beiler

"Son of Aaron F. and Mary Ann Beiler"

Born: September 30, 1981, Died: February 28, 2005

Age: 23 Years, 5 Months

"Through You, Through Me"

I didn't know, Lord,

my life would be over in 23 short years,
or that my last breath would be taken
far away from home…
with not one more chance to say
good-bye to my loved ones.

I didn't know, Lord,

that the sunset I admired
or that the beautiful land I saw
while traveling…
would not later be shared or described
in words, by me.

I didn't know, Lord,

I would never eat another
of Mom's home-cooked meals,
or talk to my dad or brother…
or see the sparkle in my sisters' eyes
when we played games together.

I didn't know, Lord,
I would never be called "Husband"
or know the joy of going home
to my wife…
or have a little girl or boy say, "Hi, Daddy."

I didn't know, Lord,
I would never climb a ladder
again to put on a new roof,
or thank my uncle for my paycheck,
or enjoy putting in a hard day's work
with the guys who knew me like a brother.

No, Lord, I had no idea,
no inkling of what You had planned for me.
The last prayer I whispered,
the last song I sang,
the last sermon I heard…
I had no idea!

I did know, Lord,
I enjoy life; looked forward
to good days ahead,
was thankful for my loving parents.
(Did I know the depth of their love?)

I did know, too,
it was a joy to me to have a good brother,
the sweetest sisters
anyone could wish for,
my grandmother who lived close by was
any boy's dream,
my grandparents, too. I did know
what love was!

I did know, Lord,

my uncles, aunts, cousins and friends
gave me utmost joy,
and I knew, I had a reason
For living, for giving, for loving.

I did know, Lord,

my dad and mom answered my questions
about being baptized,
about salvation and Your love,
forgiveness…
the truth concerning spiritual things.

I did feel, Lord,

the peace and contentment of making
the decision of joining church,
the sacredness of being baptized,
the holiness of communion,
the love overflowing coming from my
bishop, my ministers… and You.

I would thank You

daily, for all these gifts.
But, Lord, I didn't know I wouldn't
have a lifetime to do it.

Through You, through me, Lord, please,

may my life have touched some hearts,
some souls.
Through You, through me,
Your glory, Your honor lives on and on!

Samuel S. Esh

"Son of David and Annie Esh"
Born: December 4, 1981, Died: June 18, 1993

We do not know why these things happen. We need to consider the words of our Lord, "God's ways are not our ways, and His thoughts are not our thoughts." Do you think it will be like the song goes, "Farther along we'll know more about it. Farther along we'll understand why. Cheer up, my brother, live in the sunshine. We'll understand it all by and by." A few verses of another song. The title is, "This life is hard to understand." One of the verses goes like this. "When the hand of death reaches in our home, we are made to weep for a dear one gone. We shall learn to know what the Lord has planned. And by and by we'll understand." Chorus: "This is hard to understand. And the way seems rough to the pilgrim land. We are pressing on to a better land. And by and by we'll understand."

There will be times that you have a deep longing to talk to him. There will be times that you want to be all alone and go down on your knees and just pour out your feelings to God. There will be times that you want to go outside and just look up toward heaven and the beautiful floating clouds. The beautiful sunsets and the sunrises will mean more to you than they did before, and don't forget those beautiful rainbows. How great is our God.

There will be times that you will get so much "Zeitlang" that you almost can't see your way through; the way looks dark and the mountain looks steep. It is then that we need to step aside and let the Lord lead the way. We do not want to ask to remove the mountain, but "Please, Lord, help us climb that mountain."

Well, it is getting late. The rest are all in bed, so I have a longing to write of our happening on June 18, 1993, with our Samuel. Your Mervin and our Samuel were born in the same year, just a few months apart. That Friday morning started out as usual. We did the milking and the rest of the chores and went for breakfast. Samuel and I came in from the barn together. We ate breakfast with the family, then my driver came. I said "good-bye" to the family and left. We only went about one mile, then I happened to think that I forgot my tools. So I came home again, got the tools and went into the house to tell them what I wanted. I said "good-bye" again, never thinking this would be the last time I would see Samuel. We went to Brandywine to do some work. Soon after 9:00 A.M., our driver came and said I am to come home, as our house is on fire. Right on the spot I took my nail bag off and got in the car and we headed home. I asked the driver what happened. He said he didn't know. Maybe it was just a false alarm. We came up 340 through White Horse, and I was thinking maybe it is a false alarm, although I also thought if we would have a bad house fire, White Horse would surely respond. As we went through White Horse I looked back at the fire station and saw all the doors were open and the building empty. "Oh my. I guess it is not a false alarm. "Coming on up 340, I saw the smoke. Coming in West View Drive, I noticed it is not the house; it is just the shop. What a relief, but not for long. I think there were around 12 different fire companies there, the police were there, the ambulance was there, the helicopter was on standby. I got out of the car. Pud's Sim and neighbor Mervin's Sam were standing up from the drive beside the house. I walked up to them and asked, "What happened?" They said, "There was an explosion." I said, "Is anybody hurt?" Sam looked at Sim, and Sim looked at Sam. I sensed something is wrong. "Oh, my." They didn't say anything right away, then after a bit Sam said, "It took Samuel's life." I said, "Do you mean our Samuel?" They nodded their heads. I was not prepared for something like that. "Oh, please, please, God, help me." I felt so weak and helpless. They said Samuel is still out in the building. I wanted to go see, but they said it would be best not to. The undertaker took him away Friday a.m. and brought him back Sunday a.m. in a disaster bag in a casket. The boys, Jr. 17, Steve 16, and Mervin 7, helped to carry their charred brother to the house, into the bedroom. The casket was kept closed all the time. We, the family of eight girls and three boys and four sons-in-law, gathered around the closed casket and just cried for awhile. We would have liked so much to put some nice white clothes on him, but we couldn't.

Oh, I thought your son Mervin's clothes were so nice and white. The clothes fitted so nice, with his nice white vest and his nice white bow. He looked so peaceful in his coffin. I think he deserves a good bed.

Our loss is their gain. "The Lord hath given, the Lord hath taken. Blessed be the name of the Lord."

Samuel's funeral was Monday at 9 a.m., a small funeral in the house and a very large funeral in the barn. The casket wasn't opened. The people all walked past the closed casket in a very quiet, mannerly, and respectful way. We took him to the Gordonville cemetery. Our team was also marked No. 1. Oh, Aaron, I know exactly what you mean by that in the *Botshaft*.

After Samuel was buried, while we were still in the cemetery, I was wishing Jesus would come and take us all with him. When we came home, the benches were all loaded and the house and barn were in order, but that partly burnt building where Samuel was killed looked so _____, I can not think of words to describe it or words to express the feeling how it felt the next morning when I went into the shop. I must admit the future looked so dark and desolate. Please, God, help us to go on. I just knew the only way we as a grieving family could go on was through the grace of God.

Friends and neighbors came to tear down the building and build a new one. Many, many words of sympathy and encouragement were given. We are thankful to live in a sharing community and in a church where there is Christian fellowship and under an Almighty and loving, caring Savior and God. He sent His only Son to pay for our sins. "Amazing Grace." We wish you all *fiel gedult,* peace and love.

This letter is meant to lift some traveler's load. *Aus liebe*, let's pray for each other.

Mervin Jay Beiler
"Son of Aaron F. and Mary Ann Beiler"

It broke our hearts to say good-bye
To a friend we loved so dear.
And now as we meet to play again,
We wish you could be here.

When you first came to play for the Rebels,
We called you "cherry knob".
We liked the way you played the game,
We gave you a starting job.

You were young and very talented,
And the guys all liked your style.
But the thing that we all liked the most,
Was your joyful laugh and ready smile.

You went along to Nationals,
I can picture you sitting on the bus.
You sat there grinning at everyone,
But you never made much fuss.

The Nationals were in Florida,
And you were singing, "I'm gonna soak up the sun,"
And now you're soaking up the Heavenly light~
Because your work on earth is done.

Light in the Shadow of Death

You had a winning personality,
You stood out from other guys.
You seemed to have time for others,
There was always a twinkle in your eyes.

We count it a privilege to have known you,
And to have had you play on our team.
Your life was short, a reminder for us all,
But you always are someone we see in our dreams.

You gave your life to Jesus,
You could see it in your face.
So we know that you're in Heaven,
Because of God's life-giving grace.

And now that we have said good-bye
To you, our teammate and friend,
We're looking forward to the day
When we at last see you again.

RFF/05

In Memory from the Rebels
—Your Baseball Teammates

A Letter from Wyoming

March 12, 2005

To the family of Mervin Beiler,

I am so sorry for the loss of your son and brother. While I did not have the good fortune to know your son during his life, his four travel mates made it abundantly clear to me what a wonderful young man he was.

I work as an EMT (medic) for Sublette County, and as soon as we had our ambulance en route I said a prayer for the unknown young man we were headed for.

After snowmobiling in to Mervin's accident site, we checked him for vital signs and ran a cardiac strip to be sure, then I walked over to his friends and they talked about what a good mood he was in all the time. How much fun they had had on this trip West. They told me about all of you, and how he was especially close to his littlest sister. (I think they actually said one of his little sisters.)

When I remarked on what a beautiful location we found him in, they told me that Mervin was always the first to notice the beauty of the places they visited. (The sky was robin egg blue and the sun was drenching us in sunlight.)

My fellow medic Kris asked if they would like to say good-bye while we waited for a sled to arrive to carry Mervin to the parking lot, and those four young men gathered around and quietly prayed. It was so respectful and right.

We were without radio or cell phone contact until Sublette Search & Rescue arrived with a satellite phone, and there was an extended time period before we could clear the scene and get Mervin's friends back to where they could get your number and give you the worst news you'll ever hear. They were concerned about getting word to you as rapidly as possible.

As a mother, I want to let you know that when I arrived at Mervin's side his face looked peaceful; he didn't look as if he had had time to register fear or pain.

I couldn't wait to get home to hug my boy and girl, and I regret that you will not have your son to enjoy on earth any longer. May your memories be many, and your remaining children live a long and healthy life.

Sincerely,

Jacque S.

I hope when my boy starts to roam that he chooses his friends as wisely as your son did!

Testament of Joseph:

Written to his children; how his faith was tried and he remained faithful in the most severe temptations. His brothers hated him, but God loved him. They sold him as a servant. God exalted him as a king. While I was being slandered and hated, the Lord comforted my hurt heart.

Gen. 39: When Potiphar's wife of Egypt came by where I was for resale, her husband asked me where I was from. I said I was a servant of the Ishmaelites. He did not believe me and had me whipped without mercy. I tried not to betray my brothers' wrongdoing. But O how I suffer! When different ones of my brothers were trying to kill me I hid behind my sympathizing brother Issachar as we were both bitterly weeping and pleading for my life. Potiphar's wife told her husband to buy me regardless of cost and he paid 80 guilders for me. Her goal was unknown to me.

My dear children, note how much I suffered while I was trying to hide my brothers' sins. So you should also forgive each other's sins. I loved them so much that I wept bitterly at the reunion meal and said to them, I am Joseph, your brother! Their pain was my pain. Their need my need. My land, their land. Their souls I loved as my own and felt least among them.

I had been 12 years old when I was sold. And Potiphar's wife, beautiful by nature, favored me with friendliness and promises and told me that she loved me as her own, and hoped that some day I could be the master of her household. She often came to me at night with the appearance to see if I was all right, and would tell me how much she admired me and respected my pious behavior. As her appreciation seemed to increase to be in my presence, she became more bold and tempted me to sin with her. As the Lord had comforted me in the loss and sorrows of my dear ones I feared Him greatly, so that I did not want to sin against Him. She would relate how handsome I was, and more virtuous than her husband. So by her fanning the flames of passion, I often fasted of food and wine to withstand the temptation. I prayed and wept that God would keep me from sin and enlighten this woman to discontinue her sinful desires. She suspected that I feared her husband's wrath that I would not yield. So she assured me that I not fear him, as he would not believe any ill report of us as she has often told him of my piety. As temptations heightened by her seducements of partly undressing in my presence, I put on sackcloth and lay upon the ground in earnest prayer that the Lord would deliver my soul from this sore temptation and bodily affliction. As the Lord sustained me, and her lustful efforts failed to allure me, she changed her method by coming to me and saying that I was more righteous than she was. She then asked me to instruct her in God's ways and promised she would put away her idols. I instructed her that God forbids adultery. As I told her this, it seemed she had tears in one eye, and with the other she was trying to entice me over and over again. She offered the suggestion if I fear God to commit adultery with her, then she was willing to kill her husband, then it would not be adultery if we married. But I answered her that if she did so I would report her, and she would be punished by having her life taken. Then she began to shower me with gifts. I was well aware of her intentions and in no way yielded to her offers. She tried another way by preparing me an elaborate meal mingled with sorcery. The man that brought it to me appeared to have a sword in his one hand. This was an indication of danger to me, so I did not eat it. The next day she came to visit me and found I had not eaten her meal and asked why I didn't. I said her meal is mingled with death. After she saw that her scheme had failed again, she seduced me to sin, as often before. Then her countenance fell and her husband saw that she was sad. He asked her what it is that makes her sad. She said her heart hurts and breathing is hard for her. She needs a physician. After her husband left to attend to his affairs, she came running to me, saying that she will drown herself in the well or jump off the cliff if I do not consent to her will. But I told her if she takes her life, her husband's concubine will get her children and may abuse them. She said to me, that concern is hers... I expressed concern for her children, and she still had hope that someday I would consent. I prayed all night with tears that God would deliver me from this woman. That morning she came again and took away my clothing so that I had nothing to wear. Then she told her husband that I had molested her, and she kept my clothing as her proof. So her husband had me put in the prison stocks, as he was third highest to Pharaoh. As I was in prison thanking God that

He had delivered me from this temptation, she appeared on the scene and heard me thank the Lord. She again offered to free me from prison if I would now consent to her will.

My dear children! Esteem the words of your father Joseph! And walk in his ways; serve the Lord with fasting and prayer, so that He will keep you in the hour of temptation. I was 28 years old when my 12-year prison term was over and never yielded to these temptations which had hounded me over the years. May I praise the Lord in eternity. Children, learn and be wise from your father's painful example. In prison I not only suffered the pain of hunger and stocks, but my name was cast out as an evildoer before all that knew me, and my father thought I was dead. So I covered my face with a sack because of loneliness and shame, with all the untruth heaped upon me. Yet God did not forsake me.

When Joseph's brothers humbled themselves and admitted their cruel deeds, Joseph's heart was moved to compassion and he said, "I am Joseph, your brother," and began to weep. A figure of Jesus' love for those who come to Him and are sorry for their sins.

The Lord showed Joseph in a dream that in Judah there would be born a virgin that wore a white robe, and through her there was born a perfect Lamb, which all other animals attacked, but the Lamb overcame them all. This was a foreshadow of Jesus the Lamb of God. And His mother Mary. It was given me to see into the future when Egypt would no longer fear God, and would oppress Israel as slaves. Then the Lord will lead you into the land of Canaan. I request you take my bones with you and lay them in a grave beside my mother Rachel's grave. Joseph knew that Jesus would die for the sins of the world, and that many would rise up from the grave at the time of His death (Matt. 27:52-53). And Joseph desired the grave of his bones to be in that number of the saints, as Abraham, Isaac and Jacob with his eleven brothers, whose remains were all carried and buried in Hebron the land of Canaan. Joseph died when he was 110 years old. He had patiently endured the false accusations, and had loved his brethren to the end. He had suffered the pain of rejection and disgrace and was innocent in prison for years.

This testament can be found in an old German Bible, 1735 page 265.

Translated into English in concise form. "Though your sins are as scarlet, they shall be as white as snow" (Isa. 1:18).

The attached note was sent with the above testament: I am 71 and had never found the Testament of Joseph to his children or never heard of it. I made a concise translation from German into English.

I feel certain that probably none of your readers have ever seen this and I feel it would be of interest to young and old if printed.

WE REMEMBER MERVIN at our wedding. Now as parents we can't figure out why we invited Mervin (a 9-year-old boy) and didn't invite Aarons (his parents). But I can still picture him on that day. Mervin and Eli Jr. were together all day. I even remember he gave a cake.

We can still picture Mervin shoveling feed out the barn windows into the feed rack outside. The first years he had to struggle to lift the shovel to the windowsill, and he couldn't open the barn windows by himself. But then in a couple years there was nothing to it.

Wonder how many times he helped tie cows! I can't remember him ever getting mad at them. I know we sometimes had quite a time of it, to get some of the heifers in their stalls. Dairy farming has a lot of dirty work daily. But Mervin never complained. He scraped, swept, put barn dry on, fed the cows, helped milk, whatever there was to do, sometimes running, always on the ball.

We always liked to have our own chickens, sometimes letting them hatch their own chicks. One time it happened that we had 4 or 5 big roosters running around here. We caught them often and put them back in their pen, till they were as wild as deer. Then there was no way we could catch them. Oh, they were so disgusting, digging in the flower beds, etc. So we got Mervin to bring his gun. We knew he was a good shot, because the rooster's head was always moving and he got him in the head. And how he laughed to see that rooster flop around without his head. Another time before that we butchered chickens, and that was the first time he ever saw a chicken flop around headless. Oh, how he laughed!

I enjoyed cooking for him too. It's a good thing farming gets up an appetite!

No matter how quick a meal it was it always seemed to be appreciated. He even asked for a recipe one time. As a young married, inexperienced cook, I was flattered. I still remember it was rhubarb crunch.

And I think I worried as much the first time Mervin took the team out in the fields as I do now when John does.

I still remember when Mervin was around 14 years old. We went to the Green Dragon one Friday night. Aaron's took off from the market and went along, too. We really enjoyed that evening. I still remember Aaron saying that soon (when he's running around) he will have other interests and won't want to go to the Green Dragon.

At Christmas he always came with gifts for the children. John was just asking if that blue truck Mervin gave him is still around. It's in the attic. We need to get it down and also a big doll he gave Suzanne. It was a big doll named Suzanne. Sometimes I wish I wouldn't have let her play with it, because now its hair is all raggedy. But it was a favorite.

Mervin also liked to play ping-pong. We had our table set up at one time and Steve and Mervin played after dinner sometimes.

—Written by Martha, Steve's wife
Mervin worked for this family in his younger days

Life of a Hired Boy—Age 8 to 15
(My first hired boy)

IN 1989, SOME thought I needed a little helper to feed the animals and help with small chores around the farm. I didn't really know Aaron and Mary Ann, but one day I decided to walk out and see for myself. A little nervous, I walked up the road and in the lane to Aaron's, partly hoping no one would be at home! I managed to get to the door and knock. Here comes Mary Ann. She was friendly enough, and I soon forgot I was nervous. I managed to get out what I was here for, "my first hired boy". Mary Ann said he is just 8 years old. So Mervin started helping with the chores; giving calves bottle, feeding heifers, feeding horses, scraping grates, etc. It didn't take long to see that I have a real hired boy at 8 years of age and a very willing little chap with a beaming smile.

We invited him to our wedding and I remember the smile I got for that. When he was a little older he started coming for the day and was here for meals. I soon saw that Mervin isn't picky, he is used to eating anything that's on the table. Martha did enjoy cooking for him.

One day it was time to butcher chickens. I told Mervin to bring the hatchet, asking him if he had ever helped. "No! I didn't," he replied. We caught the chickens and put the first one on the block and I showed him how it's done. I whacked it and threw it over the fence on the lawn. It started squawking and running and jumping up and down. I think Mervin was dumbfounded for a split second, then he started laughing. How can this be the rooster that is supposed to be dead? Right here is his head. "Aw no, Mervin, that's the way they do. They all do that!" "Really?" "Yes, really. Watch this one." I whacked another one and threw it over the fence. Now there were two. I think they knew they had an extraordinary audience because these headless roosters went at it like I never saw anything quite like it before. By now Mervin was really losing it. So I kept whacking heads off and he kept losing it. We soon had a half dozen roosters putting on a good show to make this a day for Mervin and us to remember. By now it was high time for Mervin to try his hand on the hatchet. It may be a little dull by now. Mervin hit it hard, whack! Oops, you just got part of it.

Hit it right, whack. That was better, but it's only half off. The third whack, and I sent it flying over the fence to join the rest. What an experience (something a little special about this one). We finished off the rest, and by that time he could do it with the first whack! Now, on with the butchering, pulling feathers, and finding the little soft eggs, etc.

Back to the old routine, the odd jobs that need to be done, the boring ones that take no skill at all, but just need to be done. Anyway, he had them done like all the other work he did, in short time and well done with never one word of complaint or any sign of dislike! Everything gets done the way it should be done to the T.

Soon he was big enough to ted hay. Of course, I felt a big responsibility here. This was a hired boy, but don't worry; he was alright and did a great job! We soon saw him raking hay—great job again. By now he really enjoyed being in the field, so we tried the big team, 6 horses, standing on the hitch. Small boy, but big talent. Then the disc-bine to cut hay and to bottom plow. This was great.

Sometimes when it wasn't as busy we played a couple games of ping-pong after dinner. Sometimes we went to the cow or horse sale or milk meeting and the yearly milk company picnic at Muddy Run or Overlys Grove Park or went fishing at the free fishing pond. Precious memories!

When our John was about 2 years old, he would follow Mervin around the cow stable. Mervin often had something in his pocket for him. He was like his big brother. He watched him clean the cow stable, put feed out the windows, which was about all he could reach at first, but with the willpower he had, soon it was an easy task. When he was about 13, he could harness and unharness the horses, hitch up the horses and unhitch by himself, and I could always depend on it that it will be done very thoroughly. When corners around the barn or anywhere on the farm needed to be cleaned up, he was the one I wanted to do it, because well, how would you do it any better?

We had some naughty roosters running around the farm. We used to get Mervin and John to catch them and put them back in their old pen, but sure enough, the next day they were out again. In the garden, in the flower beds, on the porch and everywhere else but where they were supposed to be. Before long John couldn't catch them anymore. So Mervin helped him catch them. This was getting a little competitive, as by now these five roosters were getting a little good at playing this game of "catch the roosters". Even though it was kind of fun for John and Mervin, it kept taking longer and they were out more often than in and it was getting very disgusting for the "gardener"! Well, guess what, when the pain gets big enough you might figure out a way to fix it! So the "gardener" mentioned something to me about asking Mervin to bring his gun along. Well, I didn't know. I guess Aaron's won't mind, hmm. We decided to mention it to Mervin." "Oh yeah, that will be fun. I'll bring it tomorrow!" "Okay, good! We'll get rid of these rascals and be happy again! Well, I guess we can't get much meat out of these things, but at least we will be rid of them."

The next morning Mervin comes and with him is his gun, Oh, good! This is on top of the list. They are in the garden and the oats are about 1½ feet tall. It may be a little tough here. Martha mentioned trying to hit the heads, so we don't lose as much meat. I said, "I guess that will be almost impossible because their heads are always bobbing from one side to the other. They don't hold still for even one second." But Mervin said he will try it once, if we want. Okay. I was thinking, yeah, this would really be a miracle now, the head is always jerking around, the oats are tall enough for a little cover for them, and we are going to try to hit that little round head. When BANG! And what, whheerre is—ooohh it was shot in the head. Good shot, Mervin! This one isn't jumping as much as the ones you whacked the heads off of! So, more shots and four more dead roosters met the canner!

So it was that we got a little spoiled with our first hired boy, which very rarely missed a day for cold or snow or rainy weather. If it was at all fit for him to come we could depend on it. He will be here. He had a pleasant and cheerful manner; how could we forget it?

I did not want to think about it that he will someday be old enough for a better job. But all too soon the time did come. Mervin mentioned it a little, but this may have been a little difficult for him to do. He hated it too much. But sure enough, one day it happened. We were eating supper when Aaron walked in and broke the news. Beiler Bros. Roofing needs Mervin. Aw no, I thought, how will we ever do without him? I wanted to hang onto him, but I couldn't do that, so I said, "Yeah, we'll try it," although, I really could not see my way through. He worked for us for 7 years and now this is it!

But Aaron said Gideon will be able to help out, and I sure never regretted it. Who would have dreamed that we could have two like them right back to back! Not I! But it was a good lesson for me. Although we will not be able to repay for this, we hope to pass it on as best we can.

Later Years:

Mervin gave us a deer several times. The most recent one was a nice buck, and I asked him if the horns go with it. "Oh no," he said, "I was planning on keeping those!" "Okay; that's alright! He delivered it to the butcher and picked it up again. He always had time to stop and chat a little when we met him. He was always very pleasant and friendly.

—Written by Steve
Mervin worked for this family in his younger days

April 28, 2005:

Hi Dad, it's just me, your son Gideon. I'm not sure where to begin. I miss Mervin a lot; this last while it's just really sinking in. You know we'll never hunt with him again. But just think of all the good memories. I was just listening to a song that went like this.

"I'll have eyes that will never fill with teardrops.
I'll have legs that will never ache with pain.
I'll have hands that will never age and wither,
And a heart that will never break again."

Just think about it. He is so happy. At work sometimes I just think he's going to come walking around the corner. But I think we're going to see him in heaven someday. I know I'm not always a very good son, but I will try to do better. This life is hard to understand. But I think the Lord has it all planned out. Keep looking up and praying. I can't thank you enough for everything you've done. I want to thank you for the trip to Maryland. I think it did us good to get out and enjoy what we both love to do. I'm sure Mervin would not want us to quit hunting. He would be so proud of you for getting two turkeys. I hope we can have a good trip to Potter.

I Love You,
Your son, Gideon

Memories of Mervin Beiler

MY MEMORIES Of Mervin are all good memories of hunting with him in Potter Co. all of his life and the last 2 yrs. in Maryland. Wayne and I talked quite often about what a fine young man he was, very agreeable and easy to get along with. If we discussed which stand we were going to hunt, it was never, "I'm going to this or that stand." It was always, "I'll go wherever you don't go."

A humorous memory comes to mind about last November in Maryland Archery. Sammy B. took Aaron, Elmer and me down Monday afternoon. Mervin was already there. We didn't get anything that evening. We all stayed overnight except Mervin. He had a wedding Tuesday. Mervin said he will be back Tuesday night. "It was the Rut". Tuesday morning Elmer got an 8-pt. That evening I got a 9-pt. Aaron hit a buck that evening that we could not find. Mervin arrived late that night after the wedding. We were already in bed. When he saw those 2 deer outside and Aaron told him about the one he hit, he made a cute remark. He said that he might as well have stayed home. Aaron asked, "Why?" Mervin said, "The big ones are all shot." We often had a good laugh from that comment. Later that week Mervin got a nice buck.

I will always think of him when we go to "the shack," the barn that Mervin so willingly helped to build. In Potter County there are too many memories to write. One stands out in my mind last year in buck season. Monday afternoon Mervin got a beautiful 8-pt. He was very happy when he came back to the camp. The boys went out with him after supper with the deer cart to bring him in. Wednesday morning of that week the weather was very miserable, pouring down rain and very windy. His uncle Mervin left his tree stand and stuff out at his tree Tuesday evening. Uncle Mervin was trying to get someone to go with him to get his stuff. Of course, Mervin went with him. I knew Mervin as a very friendly and kind person. (May you rest in peace, Mervin.)

To the family: May God bless you as you grieve the loss of your loved one. He will be missed.

—Lee Stoltzfus

Homesick

You're in a better place,
I've heard a thousand times.
And at least a thousand times I've rejoiced for you.
But the reason why I'm broken, the reason why I cry
Is how long must I wait to be with you?
I close my eyes and I see your face;
If home's where my heart is, then I'm out of place.
Lord, won't you give me the strength
To make it through somehow?
I've never been more homesick than now.
Help me, Lord! Because I don't understand your ways.......
The reason why, I wonder if I'll ever know.
But even if you showed me, the hurt would be the same,
Because I'm still so far away from Home!
In Christ there are no good-byes;
In Christ there is no end.....
So I'll hold on to Jesus with all that I have to see you again!

The Message Came One Monday

It said, "My brother—your son has passed away."
Oh, what a shock-could it be real?
What grief and pain our hearts did feel.
Yes, Mervin left with no farewell;
The grief it brought no words can tell;
And yet amidst the pain we know
God's ways are best. He planned it so.
He left behind his dad and mom.
Brothers and sisters he too did have.
Although we miss him we can say,
We hope to meet some glorious day.
His friends to him meant very much;
He loved to hunt and keep in touch.
He gave a smile to all he met;
His cheerfulness we won't forget.
We did not know that it would be
That he would leave so suddenly,
And as we gather round that place,
We bow our heads and plead for grace.
Time will heal is what they say,
But as for us and for today
I choose to pray and comfort seek
While thus I bow my head and weep.
For memory will serve us now
While 'neath the sod that tender brow
Was laid to rest so calm and still;
We trust full well it was God's will.
It matters not what we may do
From time to time the whole day through,
That memories come floating in
Of how it was…or might have been.
And yet we often think above
Where all is peace and all is love;
We wonder what he's doing there.

Our Compassion as We "Remember"

February 11, 2006

Hello Friends,

For those who know sorrow, there is a bond. Our struggles and our "low times" somehow shape us to become a different person than we were before. If we become better through this, then our sons' lives weren't in vain. If we become bitter because Steven and Mervin died, it would indeed be a loss that they lived.

We don't want that to be. We want to talk about our sons. We want to remember the good times, the valuable times, the asset they were in our lives—and we want to meet them again, having the fullness of love become complete! Indeed, as the hymn writer states, "What a Day That Will Be!!"

As we pass your home, our compassion and thoughts enter the outside walls of your house, knowing about the hole in your midst. But we also know about the healing which comes from Christ, the Man of sorrow Himself, and our supplications are that you continue (even midst the bumps) becoming filled with His love.

We do not always understand God's purpose. His ways are higher than ours—but we do know somewhere there is a reason. We also know God will help us become as He wants us, as He needs us, as He can benefit His kingdom. I totally believe somewhere is the reason that Mervin died. And that this occurred not by accident, but according to a Master Plan, and this needed to be when he was away from home.

We'll understand it all by and by! That which God causes or allows can somehow make us strong—if we consent to His perfect will.

Now time as we know it according to our calendar shows the date approaching when Mervin left. Even when we haven't "stopped" having our boys in our thoughts, it awakens memories and feelings. It almost creates urgency. And of course Zeitlang isn't less.

But let me tell you this, Aaron; don't wish to avoid the first anniversary of Mervin's going. It is painful perhaps, but also healing. We "re-feel" the peace that God gives. Time doesn't heal—not "time" alone—the healing is placed by Him who loves us, even as "imperfect" parents or partners (husband/wife) or teens or young children, or neighbors and friends. So—time doesn't heal but God does through Jesus who tells us of home where all tears will be washed from our eyes and we'll be led to living fountains of waters. Home together, never parting!

Not only the first death anniversary, but each year marks a special and important date and urges us closer to Him, who holds the future in His hands! 2006 will mark 12 years since we yearn to be a family complete. We know that will not be in this life, for we have here no continuing city, but seek one to come.

We keep talking about coming again—and we might!

A LOVING GOD AND A COMFORTING DREAM
—Mrs. Ruth Yoder

ON NOVEMBER 9, 1992, our son John Andrew (we called him Jay) turned five years old. About that time he started asking about the coming of Jesus, when the end of the world will be, and if he can be with Jesus. Jay asked these questions every few weeks.

Then on January 26, 1993, I was doing some sewing and his daddy was working on lanterns. Jay came to me and again asked these questions. "Mom, when will the end of the world be?" I assured him that we do not know when Jesus will come, but we want to live for Jesus and be ready when He comes so we can go with Him. Then Jay asked, "Will we be able to see the scars on Jesus' hand, where the nails were when He was on the cross?" I said, "Yes, we read in the Bible that we can see the scars."

Soon it was lunchtime and also time for the mailman. Jay went after the mail, but no mail was there. He started back, but a Blazer was hidden from Jay's view and he so suddenly was gone. Oh, where did he go? Life here was gone, but the soul never dies. Daddy was watching from the porch, but it happened so quickly. We saw the truck and saw Jay start to cross the road. It was out of our hands; it was God's perfect timing. Jay looked up and threw his hands in the air, and the men in the truck told us he had a big smile on his face. Oh, we wondered, why did he have a smile—what did he see?

The next morning my four sisters came, as well as the grandparents and many others, to spend time with us. Then my sister Carolyn said that their son, John Allen—who is six weeks older than Jay, his cousin and good little friend—told them that morning that Jay didn't die. She replied, "Yes, John, Jay died. A truck hit him," and so on. But again, John said, "No, Jay didn't die. I had a dream. I saw the accident and how it happened."

He explained how the truck almost hit Jay, but just before it hit him, an angel took Jay and flew up through the sky. He said he watched until Jay and the angel were real little (he showed how small with his fingers just a little bit apart), then there was Jesus and took them in.

What a wonderful dream for a five-year-old boy—oh, what an awesome God!

That first night I was so wishing for a dream, a comfort to know that Jay is with Jesus. I did not have a dream, but I thank God that He sent this dream to my young nephew … oh, so nice, such a good, comforting dream!

Now, ten years later, John Allen asked his mother if she remembers the dream he had. He said it was so real and he remembers it so well.

Sometimes death seems so harsh, but God is so healing, and He comforts us with thoughts and dreams and Scriptures which before we did not understand. We thank God for the dream and the questions he had asked before he died.

Jay had asked to have his bedroom painted red. The forenoon of his death he came and said he wants it all white, motioning with his hands, "white all over." We believe he got his wish—a white room and a white robe. Thank you, Lord!

This account was taken from the forthcoming book *Speak, Lord, for Thy Servant Heareth*. In the book seventy-nine people share their personal miracle stories.

The book will be available by writing Robert J. Yoder, 4622 TR 403, Millersburg, OH 44654 or call 330-852-3535.

This was John & Ruth Yoder of Topeka, Indiana. Their son was killed. They were at Mervin's funeral and are good friends of ours.

If you would like to write to them—John Yoder 6860 S. SR5 Topeka, Indiana 46571

No. 2 Writing Found in Aaron E. Beiler Estate

IF NOT EVERYTHING is exactly as you would wish it, accept it all in a good will. If you want to be holy, never excuse yourself, never be impatient, and never out of temper; accomplish everything in the sight of God. Life is so full of little troubles. We must be prepared for them. Think it could be worse. Do well what is given you to do. That is what God requires of us. Do everything simply, cheerfully, and completely. Never feel alone, whatever happens to you, and where He is, Heaven must be. Then pray more frequently. Early in the morning open your heart to receive God's grace. Then the daily trials will not hurt you so much. If you have not brothers or friends, God will be your brother and friend. Keep yourself calm and quiet, that God can see you are contented. Devote yourself to doing good to others. That pleases God, to see you laboring for Him. Let us live in Christ's strength, in His refuge and in His defense, and have Him for our protector. Show your love toward your neighbor. Help him in his difficulties. Strengthen and comfort him and pray for him. Do your duties as well as you can, as well as you understand it, and as well as God helps you to do it. God sometimes blisters you, to draw out inflammation. Like a doctor. He sees that too much joy, too much happiness, would not be good for you. It would make you careless and make you cling too much to worldly things and get careless in prayer, therefore He plants in you a few thorns that you feel for His help. Love your parents and grandparents, who will soon be with God. Give them a soft place in your heart. Surround them with gentle smiles and cheerful words. Let them know that you are still under their obedience. Then after their death, you have something to feel comfort with.

No. 3 Writing Found in Aaron E. Beiler Estate

I HEARD SAY of parents that had a daughter. I believe they were plain people. Then when this daughter grew up, she got proud and disobedient, dressed up and went out in the world and got married. But, not long afterward, she got sick, commenced to worry herself and died. But before she died, she said to her parents she blames no one else but them, because they did not make her obey. Who will answer for this? I will once more say, Make your children obey.

But parents can also give their children good advice if they themselves live together in righteousness, peace and love, reason with each other and pray together that the children will learn. But if it would work the other way, that the parents would quarrel with each other, what would the children learn then?

Oh, careless parents, why did you linger when your duties called you? This wants to show us that we shall not delay when our duty calls us to serve God. How do we get started not doing our duty toward God? Perhaps a trifling thing committed in our youth carelessly and not wishing it. Then the habit is formed. Perhaps some commandment is not kept. Perhaps thinking at some commandment is unnecessary to keep. It puts a germ in you that you get careless to do your duty toward your parents and toward God. Never think it is just a trifle or a small sin. Things formed in your youth are in later years easily done. So let us, whatever age we are, pay careful attention to the smallest duties.

No. 4 Writing Found in Aaron E. Beiler Estate
For young married people

OH, LIVE TOGETHER in righteousness, peace, love, and in Jesus. What is nicer in this world than if married people stay in their place? If you have children, raise them up in meekness and advising to the Lord. Make them obey. If children are obedient to their parents, they will also obey better in school and better in church. You can do a great part in your children to build the church up and make them God-fearing people. If a child knows so much to get angry, then is the time to commence, to make them obey. It will not take so much if you will commence in time. Make them obey when they are at home. I still think a mother can do a great part in her children to teach them to be good, because Mother's heart is the nearest to the children. If she tells little prayers, tells them about Jesus, that He is in heaven and that God had sent Him on earth to save us from our sins and the fall of Adam and tells them for what Christmas days are, and tells them if they are not good children, Jesus or the "Good Man" will see it. I believe it puts a feeling in the children that they will obey better. But a mother ought to be very careful that she will not get the children too much on her side. But teach them to love and obey their father. Teach them to pray and pray with them. I believe our mothers nowadays are falling short in that part. They sooner buy them playthings and give them all the worldly pleasure that they can. Take your children along to church. Teach them to be quiet and listen to what the preacher is saying. A child is like a small tree. If you want to expect good fruit, you have to pay careful attention to it. What children are taught in their childhood stays with them better. Good points have to be taught by the parents.

The Freedom of Forgiveness Received

—By Joel A. Kline

Note from CPYU: Joel Kime is a youth pastor and friend of CPYU. He has a very powerful story to tell and we've asked him to put it into writing for our website. We would love for you to use this somehow with your teens as a starting point for a discussion on a number of issues, including forgiveness, taking responsibility for our actions, and how we communicate with, and learn from, other cultures. Joel has also written a study guide with questions to go along with this story. Let us know what you think.

IN THE GOSPELS Jesus tells the story of a certain servant who owed millions of dollars to a king. When the king requested an accounting of the debt, the servant couldn't pay. The king ordered the servant, the servant's wife, children, and all his possessions to be sold to pay the balance. Horrified, the servant fell on his knees before the king, pleading for time. The king, filled with pity, forgave the entire debt. The man left rejoicing until he bumped into another servant who owed him a few thousand dollars. The first servant violently demanded that this other servant pay him immediately. When the man could not, he had him thrown into prison until the debt was paid in full. Word of this got back to the king, who called in the man he had forgiven. How could he have his enormous debt forgiven and then go out and choose not to forgive the small amount this other man owed him? The king, astounded and angry, reinstated the large debt and threw the man in prison until he paid every penny. Jesus concludes by remarking, "That's what my heavenly Father will do to you if you refuse to forgive your brothers and sisters in your heart" (NLT).

It is a story familiar to us; perhaps too familiar. All of us can share probably numerous personal illustrations of broken relationships, bitterness, and grudges. We wonder when we'll ever experience the full life that Jesus promised He came to give us. Jesus skillfully used this parable to illustrate that life should never include grudges or bitterness toward people for anything they do to us. Symbolically, and certainly in reality, forgiveness frees us. We see in the parable the joy of the first servant, who, if he had not received forgiveness from the king, would have remained locked in a prison, despairing for his lost wife and family and everything he had. Sadly, like us, he returned to that prison as a result of his inability to receive forgiveness and show it to others. I know from firsthand experience that this parable is true-to-life. I am that first servant.

The Crime

In the fall of 1991, just eleven months after passing my driver's license test, I thought I was the best driver in the nation. I remember how much fun it was trying to push the limits. My parents' drive to church, for example, took about fifteen to twenty minutes; I did it once in eight. It was a video game to me rather than the responsibility it should have been. I hadn't gotten into any trouble, no tickets for speeding, no accidents because of recklessness, though I had a few close calls. But don't we all? On Sunday, November 3, 1991, I went to church with my family and couldn't wait for it to be done so I could rush home, shovel down dinner, and leave to play football with the guys from church, our Sunday afternoon tradition. After lunch, my brother Jeff and I hopped into my parents' early 1980's AMC Concord station wagon. Yellow with imitation wood grain paneling on the sides, it is a model hardly seen on the roads now, twenty years after its manufacture. We picked up his friend Chad, my friend Dave, and sped over to Lancaster Christian School for the game.

I knew the back way to LCS very well because my brother, sister, and I all attended there through 8th grade. Part of that back way took us south on Kissel Hill Road, just to the east of the Lancaster airport.

It was a beautiful fall day, cool, clear, and crisp. I clearly remember driving on the section of Kissel Hill Road between Millport Road and Oregon Road. As I came over the crest of a small hill, I hit the gas and we felt the car lurch into high gear. Sounding like I knew what I was talking about, I made some inane comment about the car "doing good today because it hit third gear at 70 mph." Dave, who hadn't yet put on his seatbelt, responded that he'd better do so! Little did he suspect that his caution might have saved his life. As he fumbled with the belt, I saw an Amish buggy about 100 yards in front of us in our lane, heading the same direction as we were. I said to everyone in the car something like, "I'm going to blow by these guys." I thought I was so incredibly cool.

For those of us in Lancaster County, accustomed to the Amish community within our borders, the sight of Amish horse and buggies is commonplace. Lancaster is known worldwide as a hotspot of Amish culture. Thousands of tourists visit each year hoping to catch a glimpse of a horse and buggy on the road or of Amish families in their traditional black and blue outfits. Subject to religious persecution in Europe, the Amish journeyed to the New World in search of their own promised land. Their culture and customs have remained, for the most part, exactly as they were centuries ago when they first came to America. The Amish know English, for example, but talk amongst themselves in their Pennsylvania Dutch/ German dialect. All Lancastrians can tell you stories about how their culture is changing incrementally, but there is no denying that the Amish have maintained a traditional culture in the midst of a progressive one. The changes and pressures of a farming county that is rapidly blossoming into a wealthy suburban county have, however, over the last few decades, soured many Amish to their Lancaster County soil. As neighborhoods and business parks cover farmland, hundreds of Amish families have migrated to quieter farmlands in such places as Indiana and Mexico.

This small second exodus has done little to change the face of the Amish in Lancaster. Buggies are still regulars on country roads like the one I traveled. By and large, the American culture in Lancaster treats the Amish just as they do their slow-moving buggies, taking them for granted and passing them by. The standard legal practice for passing buggies is to slow down behind them, put your left turn signal on, verify that the left-hand lane is clear ahead, pull over the double-yellow lines into the left-hand lane, pass the buggy, put your right-turn signal on, and move back over the double-yellow into the right-hand lane. For some this drill is a nuisance: "They slow our progress. Their metal rims wear ruts into our roads, and their horses make a stinking mess everywhere." This minority view with its accompanying round of Amish jokes can be contrasted, as most Lancastrians will tell you, by the accurate description of the Amish as extremely hardworking, peaceful, and prosperous.

I stomped on the gas again, now doing about 70-75 mph and steered the car into the left lane to pass the buggy. As we raced closer to the buggy, I will never, ever forget seeing the nose of the horse turn out in front of me. Instantly I knew they were trying to turn in front of me. I hadn't looked for nor had I seen their turn signal or the small county road they were attempting to turn left onto. Instinct took over as I pounded the brake pedal with my foot. The brakes locked and the car skidded forward, tires screaming. We smashed into the buggy, and I heard the POP of my windshield shattering into tiny pieces of glass. The buggy flew over top of the car and we rumbled to a stop in the field to the left. My hands, gripped tight to the wheel, were streaming with blood, but only from shards of windshield glass that grazed my knuckles. I still have a tiny scar in between two knuckles on my left hand, a constant reminder that basically nothing happened to me.

Dave never quite got his seatbelt buckled. When I hit the brakes, he grabbed the shoulder belt and held on with both hands. The belt locked and swung him around like Tarzan and his left shoulder hit the windshield. Possibly his shoulder, but maybe the buggy, broke the windshield. Other than soreness, though, neither he, Jeff, nor Chad was hurt. Dave's father, who visited the scene that evening after it was cleared, later told us that the skid marks from the car quite visibly ran off the road, missing a telephone pole by about 12 inches. It all happened so fast, I do not even remember seeing a telephone pole.

After making sure everyone in my car was okay, I tried to open my door but the collision had jammed it shut. Just then an Amish man came running up to our car yelling frantically, "Does anyone know CPR? Does anyone know CPR?" At 17, I was the oldest in the car. I think Dave had a bit of training, but we were not prepared for what we saw after we got out. We walked down to the crash site, and there the Amish man was holding from behind the crumpled pile of what looked like his mother. She was severely injured, convulsing, and definitely missing teeth. I told Jeff and

Chad to run to the nearest homes, which in that area were all farms, to find a phone and call 911. They sprinted across the fields, so riveted on getting to a phone that my brother never even saw the Amish lady. He remembers that the fields were recently plowed, as though he was running sluggishly on a sandy beach. A very frustrating prospect when all you want is to get to a phone as fast as possible. My brother's race to the phone is the first instance of many in which I realize the extreme pain my sin brought not only to the Amish family, but also to my family. Imagine being a 13-year-old, running with all your might to get to a phone to call 911 because your older brother had caused an awful accident? Dave and I stayed and flagged down cars, hoping someone might have a mobile phone, which at that time was still a rarity. I tugged at his shirt in desperation, saying something like, "What do we do?"

Immediate Aftermath

Eventually cars stopped, and a policeman and an EMT/ambulance crew came to the scene. That was a huge relief for me. A family friend who was driving by picked Jeff up from the scene and dropped him off at our home. He was the first to inform my parents, and together, he and my dad returned to pick me up. On their way back to the accident they could see from a distance the car in the field, and the buggy was unrecognizable. Imagine the dreadful feeling of driving to the scene of devastation that your son caused. How that must have felt for my dad! As my dad and I sat in the back seat of the police cruiser, I don't remember much except fear and an overwhelming desire to tell the truth, to get what I knew was a weighty burden off my back. The officer gave my dad and me a few moments alone after I had blurted some initial details. We figured he left us to ourselves then, so we could go over the details of the story together, possibly to come up with a spin that didn't make me so culpable for the accident. I knew it was horrible, so I told him exactly what happened, even that I was going at least 70 mph. They were able to confirm that later anyway by the length of the skid marks. I came to find out in the coming weeks that the officer was really impressed with my honesty. At the time I was simply scared to death of any further trouble. Lying was not an option. I didn't know if I was going to jail, the local juvenile detention center, Barnes Hall, or some other awful place. But the cop let me go home with my dad, clearly stating that there would be follow-up.

I'll never forget what my dad said in response to my rather tepid apologies as we drove away, "You've been through enough. We're not going to make it worse for you." He was right, and I'm very glad for it. It was already bad, about to get worse. When we arrived at our house, less than five minutes away, my mom met me at the door. I must have spent the next half hour just crying on my mom's shoulder. As the news got out, many family and friends showed their love and support by coming over to do nothing and everything at the same time: be there. The friends from church who we were on our way to meet stopped their football game and came over, dirty and disheveled from the game. Gradually a herd of my school and church friends migrated to our house to show support. That in itself was meaningful, because I had rarely attempted to mix these two groups of people. I think they even prayed together.

As I was with my friends huddled downstairs in my basement, my parents called me upstairs to my bedroom to tell me that the police officer had just called with a report about the Amish lady who had been taken to the hospital. Due to permanent brain damage, she needed life support to stay alive. Since the Amish don't believe in life support, she died that night in the hospital. The horrible news began to pile on top of me. The Amish lady, the officer told us, wasn't the mother of the man. It was his wife. More than that, it was his newlywed bride, and they had been on their honeymoon. They had only been married for 5 days; he was 21 years old, and she was 19. Traditionally, November is the Amish marrying season, and they were on their customary Amish honeymoon travels, visiting a few days in one relative's home, then moving on to another and another and so on. In the midst of that bliss, she was dead, and I had killed her. It was, and still is, by far the worst day of my life. My mother recalls that she held me crying in her arms while my dad and brother sat next to me on the bed, and my 9-year-old sister, Laura, was convinced I was going to jail. Eventually, everyone left our house, but God and I talked long into the night.

The next day my parents let me stay home from school, and actually, one of my friends was given permission by his parents to stay home with me. He picked me up and we watched Monty Python videos to get our minds off the disaster. In the middle of Live at the Hollywood Bowl, my parents called. They had found out from my uncle, who had connections in the Amish community, that the viewing was going to be that day, and they told me that I was going. It was extremely frightening news. Yet it signals the depth of my parents' character. I know my dad later told people that it was the hardest thing they ever had to do. As a parent of a 6- and 5-year-old now, I can hardly imagine what I would do if I was in their shoes. How would I handle this horrible thing my son did? How responsible would I feel? And what would my reaction be? Step by step through the process of dealing with my sin, my parents did everything right. In a world where so many want to shift blame, especially when their children mess up, my parents stood by me and guided me through handling this situation in a God-honoring, responsible, and truthful manner.

That evening, my parents, my youth pastor (who had only been at our church for 3 months... it still amazes me that he came... another example of godly commitment), and I went to where we thought the viewing was going to be. I felt so nervous that there was actually pain ripping across my guts. I didn't know what these people were like (shows how much this Lancastrian cared about the Amish subculture as I grew up around it) or what was going to happen. Would they come pouring out of the porch of the house with shotguns? That was literally the image in my mind. We got to the house and it didn't seem like anyone was home. We had mistakenly been given the location, not of the viewing, but of the husband's family's home. Some of his relatives were inside, and my mom remembers his grandmother coming out to meet us, hugging me and expressing her forgiveness. This kind gesture I do not recall, most likely due to the fact that in my mind the worst was yet to come. Amazingly, the husband's father was there and needed a ride to the viewing. So we took him with us, and he led the way. The father, while very reserved, wasn't mean to us, and even expressed his forgiveness. But can you imagine driving to the viewing of your son's new wife with the family of the guy who was responsible for her death?

When we finally made it to the viewing, we saw Amish buggies parked all over the farm property, heightening my fear. This was a tragedy in the life of Lancaster's Amish community, drawing many to support the family and attend the viewing. A loss in what was supposed to be a joyful season made the front page of the local paper. Then the moment came. We got out of the car and walked into the dimly lit house. My mom mentioned that because the father-in-law was with us we didn't have to go through the painful process of knocking on the door, and we were immediately ushered into the house. I had never been in an Amish home and was surprised at how similar it looked to my own. The family, through the grapevine, knew that we were coming and met us in the front room. The parents of the Amish lady who died, Melvin and Barbara Stoltzfus, walked up to me and put their arms around me. Through tears I muttered how sorry I was, and they spoke some of the most incredible words that I think are possible to utter, "We forgive you; we know it was God's time for her to die."

Unbelievable. It was totally, absolutely amazing. But they went even further than that! They proceeded to invite my family to come over for dinner! And they wanted us to come soon, within a few weeks' time! I cannot express the relief that flooded over me.

Then someone led me to a back room where the husband, Aaron Stoltzfus, stood beside the open casket of his wife, Sarah. To my surprise, as I nervously glanced at her, I was looking at a beautiful young woman. Aaron, like Sarah's parents, came to me with open arms. I said, "How can I ever repay you?" He simply forgave me. We hugged as the freedom of forgiveness swept over and through me.

As I read and reread the previous few paragraphs, I feel extremely limited in my command of the English language to evoke the feeling of what took place. When I tell the story live, it seems to carry a greater impact. Maybe the audience reads my face. Maybe the emotion can't help but flow through me. All I know is that the Stoltzfuses' concise words of forgiveness rushed through me with power. Some people have said that Amish are able to forgive like that because their theology leans toward fatalism, meaning that they believe everything is determined, is bound to happen, so there's no reason to get all bent out of shape about something bad. God is in control. They become somewhat emotionless about all the pain and suffering in life and are much more capable of dealing with it well. I don't know how true that is for every single Amishman, but I do know that this particular family is very emotional. In a positive way. They are incredibly upbeat and warm people. And I know the accident, Sarah's death, was very, very hard for them.

My mom, recalling the events, said, "I will never forget what Pastor Jim told us the next day. He watched Joel during this entire night. He said he started out as a young teen with an incredible burden of guilt on his shoulder, but walked out of that house with a tremendous weight taken from him through forgiveness."

The Sentence

The Stoltzfuses did have us over for dinner sometime in that next month, an event I recall with wonder. There we were sitting in that same Amish home with Sarah's family, Aaron, and some from his family too. The table was loaded with delicious food, and never once did they show any kind of resentment. Never once did they attempt to make us feel bad. On the contrary, it was kind of a get-to-know-you session, an intentional beginning to a meaningful relationship. We exchanged stories, comparing and contrasting the Amish subculture with mainstream American culture. They were so kind. They had opened their home and hearts to us!

The larger Amish community in Lancaster was also very impressive to me. I still have the pile of at least 50 cards that I received from various Amish people across the county. They were constantly encouraging and pointing me to God.

It was also in this time that I clearly recall a striking visit from my soccer coach. I remember meeting him at the door one evening, probably just a few days after the accident. I will never forget what he said. "Joel, you will be compassionate from now on." How true. Since that time I have never had trouble forgiving people. Not that I have worked on it and have become talented at it. On the contrary, I think

God must have changed my heart, because I don't have to try to forgive anymore. It flows out as naturally as my heart beats without me having a say in the matter.

In the ensuing months, I did not drive again, handing my keys over to my parents. My trial was set for February 5, 1992. Because of the severity of the accident, I was charged with vehicular homicide, a charge that indicates an accidental but irresponsibly reckless use of a vehicle that causes the loss of life. I'm not sure where it falls on the murder/manslaughter scale, but I do know that if I was one year older, I could have been facing jail time, which is another facet of the whole story that points me to the grace of God. I was 17, a minor, and was therefore dealt with under the juvenile justice system, saved from a much harsher penalty in the adult courts. Soon after the accident, I was assigned a probation officer and a public defender to walk me and my family through the penal process prior to the court date. The standard punishment for juvenile vehicular homicide at the time was a suspension of the offender's driver's license for 3 years, 200 hours of community service, payment of all court costs (only about $100), and probation until the community service requirement was completed. To me, with Sarah's life gone because of my actions, it was an extremely generous sentence.

My trial and punishment served as another instance for the Amish family to demonstrate the freedom of forgiveness. They wrote letters to the judge begging for my pardon, asking that I be acquitted on all counts! Imagine the character it would take to write that letter! Because of the severity of the crime, however, there was no way pardon was possible based on the law. At the trial the only thing my dad asked the judge was if it might be possible for me to get my license back sooner because I would be going to college soon and would need to drive. I hoped that maybe I could have more community service in exchange for a short suspension, but the judge held firm to the standard. A wise decision that was completely rational and acceptable to my thinking. As we walked out of the courtroom, my probation officer met us in the hallway. I will never forget pulling out my wallet and handing my precious driver's license over to her that day after the court appearance.

From Forgiveness to Friendship

Our relationship with the Stoltzfus family has continued ever since (both Aaron and his in-laws' surname is Stoltzfus). Over the years they have come to our house and we to theirs, about once each year near the anniversary of the accident. Once when they came to our house, I remember playing ping-pong with Aaron. We must have played 10 games and I beat him every time, which was to me an awkward situation. Here I am, I thought, an irresponsible kid who killed his wife, and now I'm playing ping-pong with him. He really seemed to enjoy it and wanted to keep playing. I wondered if I should have let him win, but what would that do? I came to realize that our relationship with Aaron and the rest of the Stoltzfus family, though it began under the most horrible circumstance, had grown into a legitimate, normal relationship. They had forgiven me, and never, ever went back on that decision. And they backed it up with a real relationship. Consider this: five years after the accident, Michelle and I invited them to our wedding, and they came—for the ceremony and the reception, bearing gifts! Some may read this and think, "How insensitive! You invited them to your wedding? Isn't that a slap in the face?!?!" On the surface, it certainly looks like it. It does seem odd to me that we would invite the Stoltzfuses to share in our celebration when only five years earlier, I had totally shattered theirs. But that viewpoint fails to realize the depth of the relationship. The past has been forgiven, and we are actually friends. People invite their friends to their wedding. I particularly like the idea of trumpeting to the world their brand of forgiveness. To me, having the Stoltzfuses at my wedding was not to show off the fact that I had friends in the Amish community, it was to display to everyone who knew us the glory of God that results when people obey His commands! To accent this further, when we moved to Jamaica to be missionaries three years later, the Stoltzfus family supported us financially. Forgiveness, they taught me, is not always a one-time event. Perhaps this is one angle of what Jesus intended when He replied to Peter that we ought to forgive someone not just seven times, but seventy times seven. In other words, Jesus said, in order to follow its purpose of freedom, it requires follow-up, the rebuilding of a relationship or, as in my case, the creation of a new one.

God blessed the situation even further as Aaron eventually remarried Sarah's younger sister, Levina. To me it was as though God allowed the family to be whole again. They now have a beautiful family, full of children.

This past year when we visited Melvin and Barbara (Aaron and Levina live in a house on Aaron's family's property in Leola, so we don't see them as much) on their farm/bakery in Lititz, it was the first time we had seen them in a couple years. We missed one year when we lived in Jamaica, and the next year because we had just returned home, so it was good to see them after a 2- or 3-year gap. For the first time in 11 years we talked about the accident frankly, but very kindly. Again, they were never condemning, just admitting how hard it was. How they miss Sarah. I had the chance to express my gratitude and share with them how the freedom of forgiveness they gave me impacted so many people whenever I share the story. I cried then as I am now as I type this.

In this land of liberty, that kind of freedom I received often eludes us. We have so few pictures of what it actually looks like. God glorified Himself in my life, however, by blessing me with a wonderful picture of how people can handle terrible crimes against themselves. My uncle, Jim Ohlson, when commenting on an early manuscript of my story added, "What I have seen in you is that the forgiveness of the Amish gave you the confidence to live life to the full." Jesus said, "I have come that they might have life, and life to the full!" That full life is only possible through the freedom of forgiveness.

© 2003 Joel A. Kime, Lancaster, Pennsylvania*Joel Kime is Tom Figart's nephew*
Contact faithecvouth@juno.com

Joel A. Kline and The Center for Parent/Youth Understanding grant permission for this article to be copied in its entirety, provided the copies are distributed free of charge and the copies indicate the author as Joel A. Kime and the source as the Center for Parent/Youth Understanding.

For more information on resources to help you understand today's rapidly changing youth culture, contact the Center for Parent/Youth Understanding.

THIS HAPPENED ONE year and one month after Mervin was killed. I do not know if I can even put this into words, but it was so real. I was lying in bed at about 2:00 in the morning. I was kind of in a daze. The first thing I remember is struggling with Mervin to hold him. There was something pulling him from me, not Mervin pulling, but me just really struggling to hang on. A real bright light was shining down on him and I knew it was the light of God. This was so real I can hardly explain it. I guess it was not a long time that I was struggling with Mervin to hold on, but it seemed real long. The part I couldn't understand was that Mervin himself was not trying to get away, it was some other force pulling away. After what seemed like a long time, I let Mervin go and the "most peaceful" feeling I have ever had came over me. I watched as he just glided ever so slowly away. I got up out of bed and went outside, looking up into the sky with that "most peaceful" feeling I have ever known. I wish I could make this more real to you all, but to me it was so real, so real!

—Dad

Together in Heaven

I want to be with my Savior in heaven some day,
And meet daddy and mother up there.
I want to meet all our children and their children too.
Oh, Lord, I pray some happy day, that we will all be together in heaven.

Chorus—
Together, Lord, together, Lord, oh bring us all home together in heaven.

So many good-byes with love ties and we wonder why, Lord,
I'm leaving it all up to you. Then a voice softly whispers with love and assurance.

Each tear is drawing us nearer to mansions above,
And the pain is so hard to bear.
Oh, Lord, whatever it takes to fulfill Your will.
Amazing grace will win the race. Lord, bring us all safe together in heaven.

Chorus—
Together, Lord, together, Lord, oh bring us all home together in heaven.
So many good-byes with love ties and we wonder why, Lord,
I'm leaving it all up to you. Then a voice softly whispers with love and assurance.

By faith I see all the beauty awaiting us there,
As we stroll thru our beautiful home.
I know we can't comprehend it, my heart fills with joy.
Oh what a sight, eternal light, and love will bring us together in heaven.

Chorus—
Together, Lord, together, Lord, oh bring us all home together in heaven.
So many good-byes with love ties and we wonder why, Lord,
I'm leaving it all up to you. Then a voice softly whispers with love and assurance.

Our earthly sorrows, reminding, our earth view grows dim,
And we see things eternal and true.
For God is alive and He knows broken hearts turn to Him.

Chorus—
Together, Lord, together, Lord, oh bring us all home together in heaven.
So many good-byes with love ties and we wonder why, Lord,
I'm leaving it all up to you. Then a voice softly whispers with love and assurance.

P.S. "*I hear your cries with sad good-byes and love will bring you together in heaven.*"

July 6, 2006

OUR FAMILY TRIP to the "accident" site in Wyoming was a big, big, big step. It was to be at the exact spot that Mervin was killed. Some of you might think, well... what does that help? He's not there anyway. Well, let me tell you how this parting is really not the same for us all. We had the privilege to go, the whole family—five girls, our son-in-law and son Gideon. I will never be able to fully explain the feeling walking out over that vast wide-open land to the "accident" site. So I will just name a few things that happened. On our way and before we left, I kept thinking, if God would just show me a rainbow when we are out there in Wyoming, then everything would be alright with Mervin. I also really thought if God does not show me a rainbow, I do not want to be sad and not believe that God has all things in His hands and control. Well, folks, our God is an awesome God! He showed me the most beautiful, perfect rainbow I have ever seen in my life. If we believe like the little seed, we can find comfort in death. We do not know where Mervin is, but we do know that God said, "Revenge is mine." He will take care of us and has the final say. It will not matter what other people say at our end, it is what God says. Also, as we were all there at the "accident" site, we were singing, "All the good-byes with love ties and we wonder why, Lord, I'm leaving it all up to you"! Slowly, one by one, we started walking back to the van and I just could not make myself go just yet. After a while I was the only one left at the site, just looking at the ground where it happened. The sun was shining and it was the most beautiful day with white clouds floating in the sky. As I was standing there all alone a bright reflection came from the ground. It was the sun shining on a piece of glass from the "accident". It shone right into my eyes. I picked up the piece of glass and have really wondered since what was that supposed to mean? We'll understand it all by and by. After the reflection and me picking up the piece of glass, I felt like now I can go back to the van. Also, while we were out there a moose came out into the small pond and then disappeared again back into the woods. Just over on the woods side of the "accident" site, the moose vanished from our sight. Now we saw the moose and then he was gone, just like this short time here on earth. Like a flower, soon we fade away, and then we are just a memory. Praise God in everything. "Precious memories".

—Dad

He is sleeping, calmly sleeping, in a new-made grave today;
We are weeping, sadly weeping, for the darling gone away.
One by one the gentle Shepherd gathers lambs from every fold,
Folds them to His loving bosom, with tenderness untold.

He is singing, sweetly singing, in the paradise above,
Where celestial courts are ringing, with a melody of love.
One by one the Savior gathers earthly minstrels for His own,
And our brother has joined the chorus, of the angels round the throne.

He is blooming, brightly blooming, 'mid the fairest flowers of light
In the garden of sweet Eden, where the flowers never blight.
One by one the Father gathers choicest flowers rich and rare,
And transplants them in His garden; they will bloom forever there.

He is waiting, ever waiting, for the friends he loved the best,
And he'll gladly hail their coming to the mansions of the blest.
One by one the Lord will call us, as our labors here are done,
And then as we cross the river, we may meet him one by one.

"Then we which are alive and remain shall be caught up together with them in the clouds, to meet the Lord in the air: and so shall we ever be with the Lord" (I Thess. 4:17).

Where Is Mervin?

Come, let's look into the kitchen,
But we see an empty chair.
We glance into each corner,
But we do not find him there.

We open up the barn door
Where he once the horse prepared.
We look into the bedroom,
But we will not find him there.

We listen for his footsteps;
We call him by his name.
There really is no answer;
It seems it's all in vain.
We look out through the window
And we open up the door,
But Mervin will not answer;
He will not come anymore.

We wander to the graveyard,
His final resting place.
But it is not really easy,
For we cannot see his face.

So we look up towards the heaven;
Hark, now what's that we do hear...
Could it be the angels calling,
Come up here to Mervin dear.

Dear Brother Mervin

The moment that you died
My heart was split in two.
The one side filled with memory,
The other died with you....
I often lie awake at night
When all the world is fast asleep.
I'll take a walk down memory lane
With tears upon my cheeks.
Remembering you is easy,
I do it every day.
But missing you is a heartache
That never fades away.
I hold on tightly within my heart
And there you will remain.
Life will go on without you,
But will never be the same.....
I remember so well you always enjoyed
Looking at the beautiful rainbows
And sunsets..... You always told us to
Come up to your room (the porch),
We could see them better up there,
But I'm sure they can't compare to the
Beauty and joy you share up there......
People tell us to keep looking up!
Someday we hope to see you there.

A rose may lose its bloom
But still the fragrance lingers long
A bird may fly away
Yet we can still recall its song.

So when someone who is loved departs
To join the Lord above…
They'll live and laugh and be with us
In memories of love…

A Prayer of the Bereaved

Dear Lord, amid the thronging multitude
I stand, alone, aching, and burdened with sorrow.
Although You know that I trust in You,
And realize that this experience
Is according to Your Divine Will
For my eternal good,
Yet my heart is torn and bleeding;
Thoughts of my loss are never far away.
Lord, I feel so alone!
Does no one realize my need?
Does no one see how my heart aches?
Is there no one who cares,
Who will offer me a warm handclasp,
A few words of encouragement,
A nod, or a smile?
They seem to ignore me.
Or poke a hand toward me in a hasty greeting,
Then quickly turn away.
Gracious Lord, help me to see the other side of the coin,
For they do realize!
Many hearts are aching for me!
They long to clasp my hand,
To weep with me, and tell me of their love,
Concern, and prayers for me.
But they hesitate, not wanting to reopen my wound.
They pause, and turn away.
Not knowing what they could possibly say
*   that would help me bear my loss.*
They would like to share, but the crowds are everywhere,

And they do not wish to make a show of their feelings
and mine.
Lord, I thank You for those who pray for me,
Known and unknown,
Realizing that their prayers are strengthening me,
Lifting me up above the shadows, nearer to You.
Thank You, Lord, for all those who remain silent
Rather than risk deepening my wound by some
careless word of theirs,
But most of all, blessed Lord, thank You! O thank You!
For those who understand my longing enough to clasp my hand,
Even though they may have no words with which to express
their deep feeling for my sorrow,
For those who care so much that they whisper a message,
Or smile sincerely, or give an understanding nod,
For You know, Lord, that these manifestations of
Your love, Your care, Your compassion are what I need to
help me on the long, hard, lonely road to recovery,
For then I am certain that I am not alone!

Mervin Jay Beiler

"Son of Aaron F. and Mary Ann Beiler"
Born: September 30, 1981, Died: February 28, 2005
Age: 23 Years, 5 Months
Gone but not forgotten

Mervin was a young man who always had a smile
Everyone was his friend, he would go the extra mile
Relying on Jesus to guide him through life
Very loving and patient in this world with its strife
Imagine him now in his home up above
Never to leave God's presence and love.

Joining the loved ones who have gone on before
An angel in white on that beautiful shore
Young as he was, the Lord knew his soul.

Born again Christian, he has now reached his goal
Evening has now come on his life here below
In heaven at last where we all hope to go
Life is splendid here in Glory where we never grow old
Every gate is of pearl and the streets are of pure gold
Rejoice evermore, trust in God come what may.

May we all meet again in Heaven some sweet day.

In Loving Memory of a Dear Friend
Mervin Jay Beiler

Sleep on, precious one, and take your rest;
There now waits for you a great reward.
We love you, but Jesus loved you best.
Enter now in the joys of the Lord.

You fought the fight and won the victory,
An inspiration on the battleground.
You were a light for everyone to see,
And now it's time to lay your weapons down.

We'll keep our memory of you day by day,
And often we'll be calling out your name.
Lord, help us to remember on life's way,
That our loss down there is heaven's gain.

Perfect Peace

THERE ONCE WAS a king who offered a prize to the artist who would paint the best picture of peace. Many artists tried. The king looked at all the pictures, but there were only two he really liked, and he had to choose between them.

One picture was of a calm lake. The lake was a perfect mirror for the peaceful towering mountains all around it. Overhead was a blue sky with fluffy white clouds. All who saw this picture thought that it was a perfect picture of peace.

The other picture had mountains too. But these were rugged and bare. Above was an angry sky from which rain fell, in which lightning played. Down the side of the mountain tumbled a foaming waterfall. This did not look peaceful at all.

But when the king looked, he saw behind the waterfall a tiny bush growing in a crack in the rock. In the bush, a mother bird had built her nest. There, in the midst of the rush of angry water, sat the mother bird on her nest…perfect peace.

Which picture do you think won the prize?

The king chose the second picture. Do you know why?

"Because," explained the king, "peace does not mean to be in a place where there is no noise, trouble, or hard work. Peace means to be in the midst of all those things and still be calm in your heart. That is the real meaning of peace."

"I have told you all this so that you may have peace in me. Here on earth you will have many trials and sorrows. But take heart, because I have overcome the world" (John 16:33—NLT)

There's Peace and Calm in the 23rd Psalm

With THE LORD as "YOUR SHEPHERD"
    You have all that you need,
For, if you "FOLLOW IN HIS FOOTSTEPS"
    Wherever HE may lead,
HE will guard and guide and keep you
    in HIS loving, watchful care;
And, when traveling in "dark valleys,"
    "YOUR SHEPHERD" will be there…
HIS goodness is unfailing,
    HIS kindness knows no end,
For THE LORD is a "GOOD SHEPHERD"
    on whom you can depend…
So when your heart is troubled,
    You'll find quiet, peace, and calm
If you open up the Bible
    And just read this treasured Psalm.

Psalm 23

The Lord is my shepherd; I shall not want.

He maketh me to lie down in green pastures;

He leadeth me beside the still waters.

He restoreth my soul; he leadeth me in the paths

Of righteousness for his name's sake.

Yea, though I walk through the valley of

The shadow of death, I will fear no evil;

For thou art with me;

Thy rod and thy staff they comfort me.

Thou preparest a table before me in the presence of

Mine enemies; thou anointest my head with oil;

My cup runneth over.

Surely goodness and mercy shall follow me all the days

Of my life; and I will dwell in

The house of the Lord forever.

One Is a Big Number

The following is part of a letter received by a family after the death of their son. Its message is perhaps especially meaningful because it was written by one who had herself experienced the loss that death can bring—by a widow who wishes to remain anonymous.

AS YOU AND YOUR FAMILY are left alone, after we have all gone home, that empty space will seem so big. You will never feel like saying, nor will you want to hear someone else saying, "Only one is missing."

When the empty space is permanent, one is a big number.

One less plate at the table, one less appetite to cook for. One less coat on the hook, one less shirt in the wash, one less pair of shoes.

Only one?

Only? The word does not belong.

One less smile, one less voice to join in the conversation around the table. One is a lot. You have experienced it now, and no one can ever tell you differently.

Now you will begin to live with the painful reminders. There'll be a certain dish you'll not feel like cooking—your son liked it best. A certain song you'll not be able to sing— it was his favorite. Here will be a little reminder, and there another one. A scrap of paper he wrote on, or a job that was always his, or his empty chair...

Then in the quietness of the night you will weep and cry out, "Oh, God," and then again, "Oh, God." But what words can you say beyond that plea? Are there any words with enough meaning and feeling to fit to your prayer?

Wait. Wait and be still. It comes. The Comforter. God promised. He sees your distress and He feels your hurt. He bears your wordless praying. Why should you be surprised? He promised. God is near to supply this need, too. It is a miracle to feel the peace and comfort that can only come from God.

Another day, and again you feel squeezed and twisted tight, hurting with a fresh reminder of your loss and grief. And again you seek and find this miracle of comfort. How often? As often as you need it. As often as we knock, seek, and ask.

This deep sorrow can bring a great joy, a closeness to Christ that you didn't expect and can't understand, much less describe.

This heavenly combination of sorrow and comfort—may it be your experience in the days to come.

Understand your sorrow,

—A Sister

Mervin Jay Beiler

1981—2005

Gone to Bloom Above

—Daniel S. Warner, 1842—1895, D. Otis Teasley

A gentle hand unseen by us
Has plucked our tender bud;
By this alone our grief is blest—
It was the hand of God.

Refrain
O gentle one, we miss thee here,
Sweet form we love so well;
But in our Father's better care,
We know the child is well.

In all our hearts He planted deep
This precious little one;
As forth He takes His own, we weep,
But say, "Thy will be done."

Refrain
O gentle one, we miss thee here,
Sweet form we love so well;
But in our Father's better care,
We know the child is well.

No care was lavished here in vain

Upon this plant of love;
Tho' soon removed, 'twill bloom again
In sweeter form above.

Refrain
O gentle one, we miss thee here,
Sweet form we love so well;
But in our Father's better care,
We know the child is well.

Would not our grief forever flow
Upon thy silent tomb,
Did not our hearts this comfort know—
We soon to thee shall come.

Refrain
O gentle one, we miss thee here,
Sweet form we love so well;
But in our Father's better care,
We know the child is well.

Dear Jesus, Thou hast died for us,
And for our darling, too;
We trust Thee in each providence,
Thy love is ever true.

Refrain
O gentle one, we miss thee here,
Sweet form we love so well;
But in our Father's better care,
We know the child is well.

Mervin Jay Beiler

Mervin Jay Beiler, 23, of 840 Peters Rd., New Holland, died unexpectedly Monday, February 28, 2005, in an accident in Wyoming. Born in Lancaster, he was the son of Aaron F. and Mary Ann Esh Beiler of New Holland. Mr. Beiler worked as a laborer for Beiler Bros. Roofing & Siding, New Holland, and was a member of the Old Order Amish Church. He loved to hunt. Surviving in addition to his parents are: 5 sisters, Lydia J., wife of Daniel Esh of New Holland, Esther E., Suzanne Marie, Verna Mae, Rosanna Beiler, all at home; 1 brother, Gideon Ray Beiler, at home; paternal grandmother, Mary Beiler, of Gordonville; maternal grandparents, Samuel and Mary Esh, of Paradise. Services will be held at home on Friday at 9:00 A.M. Internment in Dry Hill Cemetery.

Friends may call at the home from Thursday afternoon until the time of service. Please omit flowers.

Furman Home for Funerals, Leola, PA.

New Holland Man Killed in Wyoming Snowmobile Crash

—by Brett Lovelace

Intelligencer Journal Staff

A 23-YEAR-OLD NEW Holland man was killed Monday in a snowmobile accident near a Wyoming resort.

Mervin Jay Beiler was snowmobiling with friends near Square Top Mountain in Sublette County, Wyo., shortly after 10 a.m. Monday, when his snowmobile collided with another snowmobile, Sublette County Coroner Don Schooley said Tuesday.

Beiler was following four friends, who also were on snowmobiles, when one of the machines stopped just past the crest of a hill. Beiler followed the group over the hill, and his machine struck the back of the stopped snowmobile, Schooley said.

"They were all headed in the same direction when one snowmobile suddenly stopped," Schooley said. "He didn't see it in time and had no place to go."

Northwest Wyoming has about 1,000 miles of snowmobile trails on mountains ranging from 7,200 to 10,000 feet above sea level, according to the Sublette County web site.

The accident happened about 40 miles north of Green River Guest Ranch in Cora, Wyo. The five friends were staying at the resort, said Heidi Schwab, a spokeswoman for Green River Guest Ranch.

"Our hearts are broken," Schwab said Tuesday night. "Mervin was a wonderful young man."

"Bottom line, this is a tragedy that is really hard for us to talk about."

Beiler, a laborer at a New Holland roofing and siding firm, was knocked unconscious during the collision.

A witness called the Sublette County sheriff at 10:38 a.m. Monday and reported cardiopulmonary resuscitation was being performed on Beiler. Medics, police and a search team located the accident site and transported Beiler 17 miles in a snowmobile to an ambulance. Beiler had suffered massive head trauma and severe internal injuries, Schooley said.

"A complete investigation was performed by the sheriff's office, and no signs of foul play were indicated," said Lt. Bardy Bardin, who works in the Sublette County sheriff's office.

A memorial service for Beiler is scheduled for 9 a.m. Friday at his home at 840 Peters Road, New Holland. He will be buried at Dry Hill Cemetery.

Our Daily Bread the Day Merv Died

Monday, February 28, 2005

Child's Play

Read: Matthew 18:1-11

"Unless you are converted and become as little children, you will by no means enter the kingdom of heaven."   —Matthew 18:3

AFTER A SURPRISE storm blanketed the Middle East with snow, a newspaper photo showed four armed men smiling as they built a snowman outside the battered walls of a military headquarters. The wintry weather also caused a protest to be canceled and delayed a debate over parliamentary matters of pressing importance. Men wearing long robes and women in traditional black dresses and headscarves were seen playing in the snow. There's something about snow that brings out the child in all of us.

And there's something about the gospel that beckons us to abandon our deep hostilities and feelings of self-importance in favor of a childlike humility and faith. When Jesus was asked, "Who then is greatest in the kingdom of heaven?" (Matthew 18:1), He called a little child to come to Him and said, "Unless you are converted and become as little children, you will by no means enter the kingdom of heaven" (v3).

It has been said that age diminishes our imagination, hopes, and possibilities. The older we get, the more easily we say, "That could never happen." But in a child's mind, God can do anything. A childlike faith filled with wonder and confidence in God unlocks the door to the kingdom of heaven.

—David McCasland

God, give me the faith of a little child!
A faith that will look at Thee—
That never will falter and never fail,
But follow Thee trustingly.

—*Showerman*

Faith shines brightest in a childlike heart.

310

Adjusting to Grief

The following selected article was sent to us by bereaved young parents who, after burying their baby, found the words to be very comforting and meaningful.

GRIEF IS THAT mental pain, that heartache that naturally comes over us when someone close to our hearts has been torn away. We feel that tear and the open wound it leaves. The pain that fills the breast is very real.

Times of sorrow are providentially sent to us, and can be a blessing in disguise. Our lives are so planned that periodically God sees best to bring some startling event into our lives to regain our full attention. Sometimes He takes away a loved one.

Our Lord was an example of how to respond to grief. He stood at the grave of Lazarus and wept. The observers said, "Behold how He loved him." It is our deep and intense love for our dear ones that causes us to weep at the time of their passing.

Christ was a "man of sorrows" and "acquainted with grief." That is, He felt the pressure of grief, but He was not mastered by it. So it is for us. We experience times of grief, but it ought not master us. We sorrow in a disciplined and Christ-mannered way. As such, our sorrow is consistent with our deep faith in Jesus Christ. We sorrow, but not as those who have no hope.

Grief is spiritual when it is prompted by God. There is a refinement of spirit that comes through spiritual sorrowing. As we respond properly to the saddening strokes of God, a spiritual softening takes place. Like Job, we say, "For God maketh my heart soft" (Job 23:16). With soft hearts we are clay in the Potter's hands. As such, He molds, shapes, and tempers us for His greater service.

Rest in the arms of God. It is the most secure and satisfying place to be. Just before Moses' death, he revealed this truth when he said, "The eternal God is thy refuge, and underneath are the everlasting arms" (Deut. 33:27). Those arms are very precious in times of grief! At each continuing surge let them press you deeper into His embrace. He is an understanding companion—the companion of all companions.

David knew His secret when he pled, "…when my heart is overwhelmed: lead me to the rock that is higher than I" (Psalm 61:2). Concentrate firmly on that Rock in times of sorrow.

Enjoy the calm repose of fellowship with Christ in prayer. Your prayer may be almost wordless; but the Lord knows the heart and He hears the faintest cry. He hears you when you say, "Lord, I do not understand it, but I know what Thou doest is right." Fellowship with the Lord enables you to see His gracious hand of providence. Then you marvel at His perfection. You know He makes no mistakes.

How great the name of Jesus sounds, In a believer's ear!

It soothes his sorrows, heals his wounds, And drives away his fear.

Let the word of Christ dwell in you richly.

It is a wonderful source of comfort. Review His promises—they are endless. Refresh yourself in the experience of Job, and of Joseph and others who found grace to face their tests.

Weep your tears. Jesus wept! A good cry, spiritually prompted, is good for the soul. Do not think that it is good discipline to steel yourself against the shedding of tears. Be yourself—but be under the Spirit's control. Then there is a time to put the handkerchief away, because life with Christ moves ahead and the Christian life is more joyful than sad.

There may be times when you are up and doing, deep in your work, when unexpectedly a surge of sorrow comes. Let it come. Enjoy the presence of Christ. Be glad that God has such ways to draw us nearer to Himself, and to cause our lives to be more fruitful for Him.

Editor's note: We would appreciate knowing the identity and address of the author of the above piece. Thank you.

Funeral of Mervin Jay Beiler

Prayer at home in Morning List . . . . Gärtlein, Page 177

At house . . . .Wilmer Riehl, Gebet, Page 138

Lied . . . . .Samuel Smoker, Page 442 #29

Main Sermon Anfang. . . . . Eli Stoltzfus

Main Sermon . . . .Jacob King

. . . . Mark 13:31 to end.

Lied . . . . John Riehl, Page 437 #24

At Graveyard . . . . Yonie King, Page 473 #2

At Grave . . . . Absheid David Esh, The Lord's Prayer

Prayers in Evening		*Prayers in Morning*
First Evening	Wilmer Beiler	
Second Evening	Yonie King	Eli Beiler
Third Evening	Wilmer Riehl	
Fourth Evening	Yonie King	

Helped Dig Grave

Samuel Beiler, David King, Elam King, Benuel King

Pallbearers

Samuel Beiler, Norman Stoltzfus, David Smucker, Jonathan King Jr.

Jake King, Johnny King

Main Helpers at House

Jacob Beilers, Jacob Zooks, Aaron Eshs, John Eshs,

The Lord taketh pleasure in them that fear him, in those that hope in
His mercy. Psalm 147:11

Mervin Jay Beiler

Died February 28, 2005

Age 23 Years, 5 Months

Gone But Not Forgotten

Some Things to Do When There Is Nothing to Be Done

Guidelines for Coping with Loss

1. Recognize the loss: It has happened; it is real.

2. Be with the pain: It is important to the healing process that you experience the desolation and feel the hurt.

3. You are not alone: Everyone experiences loss.

4. You will survive: Give yourself time to heal. Nature is on your side.

5. The healing process has its ups and downs. The process of healing is like a lightning bolt, with dramatic leaps and depressing backslidings. Be aware of this and let yourself heal fully.

6. Get lots of rest, eat nutritiously, try to exercise: Healing takes energy, physical as well as emotional.

7. Try to stick to a schedule: Not at first perhaps, but when the inner world is chaotic, schedule in the outer world gives a sense of order.

8. Keep decision making to a minimum: Expect your judgment to be clouded. Enough change has taken place.

9. It's okay to need comforting: Seek the support of others. Allow yourself to be taken care of for awhile.

10. Be gentle with yourself: Treat yourself with the same care and affection that you would offer a good friend in a similar situation.

11. Anticipate a positive outcome: That to which we give our attention grows stronger in our lives.

12. Having weathered the crisis, expect to discover: *A stronger you, a different you, a growing you......*

215-492-3688

Airlines: Delta   *Permits Enclosed*

	City	Day	Time	VIA
LV	Salt Lake City, UT	Wed. Mar. 2	4:45 PM	Delta, FL 1142
AR	Philadelphia, PA	Wed. Mar. 2	10:50 PM	Delta, FL 1142
LV				
AR				
LV				
AR				

Name of Descendant: Mervin Jay Beiler

Sending Funeral Home	*Receiving Funeral Home*
Hudson's Funeral Home	Furman Funeral Home
164 N. Bridger Ave	59 W. Main St.
Pinedale, WY 82941	Leola, PA 17540
(307) 367-2321	(717) 656-6833

Mervin Beiler

Mervin Jay Beiler

Son of Aaron F. and Mary Ann Beiler
Born September 30, 1981, Died February 28, 2005
Age: 23 years, 5 months
Gone but not forgotten

Our dear loving brother was called Home on high
It was the eleventh of February, he wished us all good-bye
His place was all ready, in Heaven far above
He will be remembered, in Christ's everlasting love.

Out to the beautiful West, where he loved to go
Nature and hunting he always loved so
Full of life was this precious young man
God needed another angel way up in Gloryland.

Four of his friends got to share his last day
So much fun, good memories, in so many ways
His smile and kind ways we will never forget
He left special memories, so why would we fret?

In the pure white snow he took his last breath
An unseen angel must have helped him rest
Oh, how we wished he could have talked again
So peaceful and beautiful he still looked then.

For Dad and Mom, oh how love grew
Precious memories as a child, raised for God you knew
A hi, bye, good morning and night
Always shining and wanting to do what was right.

Light in the Shadow of Death

His sisters he loved, always took special time
A game, a joke, extra special moments he would find
He would say be good, and do what's right
So in Heaven we will meet in that everlasting light.

Dear brother, you knew there was always love there
Little words were spoken, with the great bond we would share
I tried to guide you in a loving way
So you would say, with Jesus I'll stay.

He did things for others, never told anyone
Many a friend, he always won
A pat on the shoulder, a better next time
Always looking ahead, the first one in line.

But interest in things on earth looked more dim
As his days were numbered, his goal he would win
He was one of a kind, the things that he did
We will never really know, to all, his friendship he bid.

He seemed so young, so much yet to do
But his work was over, his suffering too
There were a few times, we thought close calls
His head, his arm, ankle and falls.

Baptized with church, in the summer 2004
He wanted God's ways, forevermore
He trusted in Him, never a doubt he could find
The road he was on would bring peace of mind.

Follow Jesus every day, He will always guide the way
Good night to grandparents, grandmother, and friends
Uncles, aunts, cousins, nephews, to you I send

Live on for Jesus, I'll meet you in the end.
Thank you, Dad and Mom, for praying for me
Your guidance through life to Jesus did lead
I have gone to a land where joys have no end
In Heaven someday we want to meet again.

God's ways are best, His timing is right
He makes no mistakes, we must all take flight
He piloted him to that beautiful shore
Resting in Jesus where tears are no more.

Oh, how we miss you!
—written by a sister

"Where were you on September 11, 2001?

WORDS FAIL TO describe the unbelievable tragedy—the devastation—of that fateful day. At 8:45 a.m., a plane hijacked by terrorists crashed into the north tower of the World Trade Center in New York City. Minutes later, another plane hurtled into the south tower. Massive explosions ripped through multiple floors of both office buildings. As terrified employees on the lower floor scrambled to evacuate, miles away a third plane slammed into the Pentagon building in Washington, D.C. Before it could reach its intended target, a fourth plane nosedived into a field in Pennsylvania, killing everyone aboard. Back in New York, onlookers watched in horror as one after another, the 110-story Twin Towers collapsed on the heads of rescue workers, firemen, and police officers.

In just a matter of moments—before anyone really understood what was going on—thousands of lives were lost.

America was stunned. Nothing like this had ever happened in the history of the country, or even of the world. Politicians and pundits struggled to put the disaster in perspective, comparing it to such catastrophic events as the assassination of President John F. Kennedy, the Cuban Missile Crisis, and the Oklahoma City Bombing. Others insisted that this was "the Pearl Harbor of the 21st century," a "new Day of Infamy." President Bush called the terrorist attacks "acts of war." An entire generation would now be asking each other, "Where were you on September 11?"

For thousands of people at the World Trade Center and in the Pentagon, the answer would have been simple: "At work." It had begun like any other ordinary day. Men and women, parents and grandparents, office workers, visitors, and tourists—they were simply going about their everyday lives. Riding in the elevators, sitting at their desks, chatting across the hallway to a coworker, or talking on the phone. Never in their wildest dreams could they have imagined that a commercial jet would come crashing through their office windows, obliterating everything in its path. They had no idea that their very next breath would be their last, that in an instant they would be ushered into eternity.

Few of us do. Somehow, in spite of the reality of death, we all feel invincible. We think that the things we see in the news couldn't possibly happen to us. We get caught up in the dailiness of living—work to do, bills to pay, errands to run—scarcely giving eternity to thought. Few—if any of us—wake up in the morning thinking, *Today may be my last day on this earth.*

But sooner or later, one way or another, it happens to all of us. The Bible says we're all "destined to die once, and after that to face judgment" (Hebrews 9:27). The truth is that every one of us will one day die. None of us knows for sure just how and when our time will come. For most of us, it will be a complete surprise. And then we will face judgment. We will be called to account for every one of our sins and failures. We will have to pay the penalty—unless we have put our faith in Jesus Christ. "For the wages of sin is death, but the gift of God is eternal life" (Romans 6:23).

Jesus died on the cross to pay the penalty for us. If we believe in Him and receive His forgiveness, then our sins have already been paid for and we can face the judgment without fear. Jesus explained, "I am the resurrection and the life. He who believes in me will live, even though he dies; and whoever lives and believes in me will never die" (John 11:25, 26).

If we put our faith in Christ, we don't have to live in fear of death. We can rejoice, knowing that God has prepared a heavenly home for us and that one day we will live there with Him forever. We can rest in the assurance that we are ready for whatever comes our way.

On September 11, 2001, thousands of people entered eternity in a heartbeat. Some of them were ready; some of them were not. What about you? Are you ready today?

Nickel Mines School Shooting

THIS IS THE day the Lord has made, let us rejoice and be glad in it. I feel the need to put on paper what I was honored to have a part of on this day, October 9, 2006. As we all know, one week ago was the shooting of innocent little girls in Nickel Mines School. It is most likely one of the saddest but yet uplifting experiences I have ever been through. I will try and write, with the Lord's help, of my experience this very day.

Monday morning, bright and clear, the sun coming up, a fresh new day, but I was thinking of the parents of these children so much. Sometimes we are so burdened down I really think we should put some action into it, and maybe try hard to put some sunshine or cheer into someone's life. Last week, the day after the shooting I just could not get started with anything; work or other things just would not go. So I decided to go around to these parents. With a heavy heart we started making our rounds. As we went from one place to the other my burden started lifting. "What is going on?" I thought. Here just a few hours ago my heart was so heavy. I hope I can put this into words so that you all will understand. My heavy, heavy burden was lifted and I knew it was by the grace of God helping me and I could also feel it in the air. Those of you who have been where we were with death in your family or another tragedy will know what I'm talking about. God's presence is so real at times, but this time I could almost touch it. There was lots of crying and a lot of sadness, but on the other hand there was peace. God promised He will not give us more than we can handle and that day He really came through.

Light in the Shadow of Death

Well, I want to get to this day, October 9, 2006. At the market last week so many people were crying and bringing flowers and donations. I went to Naomi Rose's parents and tried in my weakness to encourage them but felt like I really didn't know how. So after spending some time with them I went over past Nickel Mines School to Ernies, just to see if I could be of any help. Well, Ernie said they were looking for another van and driver and I thought, "Well, we have a van and driver, but me?" They were expecting all the school children and their parents, and those who had buried their children. Quite a few of the parents were still in hospitals with their children. What they were planning was to go to school and take everything out—books, papers, school desks, etc.

I kept thinking, "Am I strong enough and why me?" But I felt so unworthy to actually have a part in something so sacred. God works if we let Him, in ways beyond our understanding. I was thinking of all the other people in our community and thinking, "Why me?" I can hardly put into words how I felt. So unworthy of this! Well, we waited for about one-half hour and people started to gather at Ernies.

Lots of tears and faces that showed that forlorn look, but also that "so real" peace. Thank the Lord in everything! Once all the children and parents were there, we started loading the vans. Yes, the school, was just a little ways down the road, but they wanted to get there together. I still was not sure if I could handle this, but that peace was in the air. We followed the van down the road and as we got closer to the school, the State Police had to open the gate. The State Police had been guarding the school day and night since the shooting. No one could get near the school except local Amish and police. As we were going in the driveway, I saw the bishop of the church district standing there. I still had this "what am I here for" feeling but not for very long. I was kind of staying back and then the bishop said, "Aaron, come. Go with us." The gesture lifted a big burden from me. Thank you.

Well, now there was plywood on all the windows and plywood over the doors. We started taking plywood off the side door. The front doors had glass broken and plywood on, so they decided to go in the side. The school boys were right there and could hardly wait to go in. They showed me so much courage. Oh, to be like the Bible says, "a little child." I guess what touched me the most at that time was as soon as those boys were inside, they knew right where to look. The bullet holes were there and they knew. Some of them put their fingers into the bullet holes. All of us were just choked up, but that "so real" peace was there too. Each one of the boys went straight to his desk. The parents went to their little girls' desks. Oh, how sad! Their little girls had put such an effort into their art and had their little desks so neat and orderly. How can this be? My heart was almost torn in two, but yes, I still felt that "peace".

Now one of the parents asked the bishop to do a little speech and prayer. His words rang out in that little schoolhouse. I wish I could remember every word. He wished us all God's richest blessings and talked about thanking Him in everything. Tears were flowing, but again, these peaceful tears. He also talked to the little school boys of how they showed such great courage coming in here and going to their desks. He ended with prayer: "Our Father which art in Heaven, Hallowed by thy name. Thy Kingdom come. Thy will be done on earth, as it is in Heaven. Give us this day our daily bread. And forgive us our debts, as we forgive our debtors. And lead us not into temptation, but deliver us from evil: For Thine is the Kingdom and the power and the glory forever. Amen" (Matthew 6:9-13).

Well, now came the time to start taking art off the walls and cleaning out their school desks. Everyone went at their own with effort. I couldn't help but see the forlorn, blank look the Miller family had standing there and getting their girls' things. Two of their girls had been shot and killed, and now all of a sudden they have no children going to school. Pray for them so they can feel the peace that I felt. It seems to me that I cannot even come close to knowing how they feel, but do so much want to offer a shoulder to lean on, if needed. The courage that was shown to me helped me more than I could put into words. I feel so much since Mervin's death, our oldest, our firstborn, that I really, truthfully want to put it all in the Lord's hand completely. This experience has most likely helped me more than any other thing has in the year and a half since Mervin died. Thanks again to you parents for letting me have this very small part in your deaths. Thank you from the bottom of my heart. Praise God!

Now, back to cleaning out the school desks and the bookshelves. Tearing down the blackboard with the arithmetic numbers on it. Telling signs of the start of a new school day. Box after box and bag after bag was carried out and loaded into the van. The temporary school was moving just up the road into Ernie's shop. When we would take loads of school supplies up, the women were there cleaning and getting ready for the new school. Just exactly what happens with the old school is not sure, but they do plan on tearing it down and building a new one.

Now things are going along quite smoothly, and as we were working, the Chaplain Grover G. Devault from the State Police Chaplaincy Program came to offer support. With him was a State Police Trooper. The State Police Trooper did not make any words, but just stood there on the schoolhouse porch. To me it is just unbelievable how the State Police and firemen and all who were involved came together to help. How can we ever repay? Ernie then asked the State Trooper for the time because at exactly 10:45 the whole community was asked to have a moment of silence. It was getting close to that time. Also, the churches everywhere in Lancaster City and all surrounding areas were asked to ring their bells. This would have been the time or very close to the time the shooter, Roberts, had come into the schoolhouse, one week ago. The trooper was watching his watch and the schoolchildren, the boys, and the one and only girl were asked if they wanted to ring the school bell. Here again the courage and effort of these little children shone brightly. I was standing on the porch beside the bell rope and there were many little hands on that bell rope. I really think all the remaining children had their hands on the rope waiting for the Police Officer to say when. The Police Officer gave a little nod and they pulled the rope, but there was just too much strength in those little hands. The bell rang one time and then it tilted. Some of the boys knew how to get on the roof and they were there before we really knew what was going on. They got ahold of the bell and rang it from up there on the roof. What a great effort they made. After that, all was so very, very quiet for quite a while. Our minds could just roll, and yes, there was that peace again.

Now back to taking boxes, bags, school desks and chairs outside. Each desk was marked with the child's name on it and given to the parents to take home. Just an old school desk, but a part of their children's lives, a part to keep and to hold dear. Those things mean so very much to grieving families. There will be new school desks for the new school, hopefully a new beginning, but also a real nice thought to know that the Lord prepared a new beginning for us all if we only let him into our lives. How beautiful heaven must be! Sweet home for the pure and the free. Our loss is His gain with these innocent little children. Praise God in everything.

So many things happened on this day, and it is my wish to give the accounts as accurately as possible. While we were working, taking more books and things out, I noticed the boys seemed to be in a conversation and world of their own, gathering very close to each other. I felt like I should walk out over the school yard to talk to them, but what should I say? It looked so private. Well, being me and asking the Lord as I went to put some words into my mouth, I walked out over the ball field toward them. To break the tension, I asked, "Who's the homerun hitter here?" That's all it took. They got all excited and one said he is! The other said he is! Then one boy said he is and he has the same name as you do, Aaron. I really wondered how they knew who I was. So we talked a little and what I gathered was they were already planning where they could play at this new temporary school. Also, they were wondering about the different teams. There are ten missing! Ten little girls will not be there to help them play. How can this be? Five of their little classmates were now gone and five remained in the hospital. I guess this will by far not be the last time they all of a sudden realize life as they knew it had changed.

Now back to the finishing of taking out desks and so forth. I was asked to take the desks to different parents' homes. As we were doing that, some of the men were again putting the plywood back up over the doors and windows and closing up the school. I couldn't help but think how it was inside that schoolhouse. I really think God's hand and His angels were there helping these little girls all the way. Also, I can't help but think of how we can read in the Bible we are not to plan ahead or think ahead of what we will say in situations like this. God promised He will put the words in our mouth. What a comfort! Praise God!

Also, we want to remember these parents, not just this week and next week, but if we can for a very long time. Your prayers have made a difference. A difference that I could "see". It was real. We, as Christian parents, should put in every effort we have to let our light shine, if we want to come up to what I feel the "English" think that we are. Help me, Lord! I feel so unworthy, and starting now let's all bond together and try just a little bit harder.

Once again, I would like to thank these grieving families from the bottom of my heart for what you let me have a part of. My wish for all of you is that God will provide the comfort only He can give to you; no, not too comfortable, but keeping on the straight and narrow road that is pleasing to Him.

Thank the Lord in everything. Written to you all with heartfelt sympathy.

—Aaron Beiler

A sign on a church bulletin:

"Preach the Gospel and if necessary use words."

Personal

Dear Mom and Dad,

I know I'm overweight; but you don't have to keep reminding me of this. Okay, maybe you haven't said so in so many words, but I've seen those disapproving looks and I've heard what you say when you think I'm out of earshot.

I know you wish I were more like Ellen, but I'm not, I'm not. I'm not pretty like my sister and I'm not as smart; but it doesn't help any when you make comparisons. Thanks to you, I can't stand the sight of "Miss Perfect."

You think I'm rebellious and hard, but I cry myself to sleep a lot more than you think. Nothing I do seems to please you anymore. If I stay home and study you worry about my social life; if I go out with friends and have fun, you're suspicious about what we did.

My friends are very important to me, even though you consider them a few degrees below normal. Sure, maybe they're kind of loud some of the time and don't get dressed up for parties like kids did in your day. That doesn't mean they're bad or have low morals, however.

Yes, I've smoked a couple times and even tasted beer. I didn't want to, but I did it anyways because I want my friends to like me. Since you can't or won't accept me the way I am, I have to find acceptance somewhere else.

If you could trust me a little more, that would help. I'm old enough to know what's right from wrong and resent it when you give me the third degree. At the same time, I do want some sort of rules, but they should be realistic for someone my age, and flexible. If we could talk about things like curfew instead of you just announcing when I had to be in, it would make me feel like you respected me more.

About my complexion. Okay, it's not great. I hate my zits as much as you, and probably a whole lot more. But that doesn't mean I want to hear about it all the time. I really wish you wouldn't say anything at all, not even about how I'll outgrow it, or that I'm just going through a stage.

Telling me I'm eating wrongly doesn't help either. I've taken enough health classes at school to know I shouldn't eat greasy, starchy foods or drink sugar-

laden colas, but sometimes I just crave that junk. And
more I eat, even if that doesn't make sense.

I wish you wouldn't talk about me in front of you
I'm right there. It makes me feel less than a person. I c
to answer for me when they ask questions. You may
I have a mind of my own, and my opinions and ideas may not be the same
as yours. That doesn't automatically make yours right and mine wrong, you
know.

When I was getting something out of my dresser the other night, it was
very obvious that someone had gone through my things. This isn't the first
time either. Don't get me wrong. I have nothing to hide, but I just don't like
the idea of your snooping in my room. I'm entitled to a certain measure of
privacy, after all.

You aren't going to like this, but I really get mad when you try to preach
to me. I've been going to church all my life and I read the same Bible you
do. I don't necessarily agree with everything you say, but I can't discuss it
with you because I know exactly what would happen if I did. You'd cry,
Mom, and say you've failed as a parent. You might not say much, Dad, not
verbally anyway, but there would be those all-knowing disappointing looks.
So I just keep my thoughts to myself.

There's something else you need to know. When I was growing up, I wasn't
really sure that you loved me. I knew you loved Ellen, but who didn't? Sure,
you gave me a place to live, fed me, and kept me supplied with clothes, but I
always felt that your love depended on whether I was good enough to please
you. I forget when I gave up and stopped trying, but I guess it was when
Ellen won a first place blue ribbon at the school science fair and I only got
an honorable mention. You didn't even ask to see my ribbon.

I don't think we'll ever be close, even though I'm sure now that you really
do love me, in your own way. To be honest, I've thought a lot about leaving.
Not right away, of course. Running off wouldn't solve anything; see, I'm not
as dumb as you think. But when I get older maybe I'll get a place of my
own, or maybe with a couple of girlfriends. I figure you won't really mind
too much.

o thank you for raising me in a home and for caring for my physical needs, if not my emotional. I'm sorry I'm not the kind of daughter you wanted, but you always have Ellen.

If it sounds like I'm blaming you, I'm sorry. I really don't anymore. You did the best you knew. You just didn't know enough. Like one of my teachers said, "Most people have the ridiculous notion that bringing a child into the world qualifies them to be parents."

In spite of everything, though, I do love you.

—your daughter

Light in the Shadow of Death

Teenage Death Since 1923

NAME	PARENTS	DATE DIED	AGE	REASON
John	Isaac & Malinda Stoltzfus	10/15/1923	12	
Andy	Amos & ? Stoltzfus	8/19/1924	21	
Amos	Sam & Annie Zook	2/25/1925	16	
Elias	Jake & Arie Fisher	6/6/1925	18	
Dannie	Jonathan & ? Stoltzfus	6/8/1925	11	
John	Joseph & Hannah Lapp	12/24/1925	15	
Jacob	Levi & Barbara Smoker	8/25/1926	19	
Elmer	Menno & Sarah Fisher	2/16/1928	17	
John	Jonas & Fannie Beiler	10/14/1929	20	
Stephen	Widow Lydia Lapp	9/25/1930	20	Fell
Mary	Widow Mary Stoltzfus	12/16/1930	16	
Samuel	Elias & Barbara Smoker	2/1/1931	21	Pneumonia
Stephen	Ben & Sadie Yoder	10/15/1932	15	
Aaron	John & Malinda Zook	11/16/1932	23	Appendicitis
Henry	Henry & Lydia Beiler	3/3/1934	16	
Aaron	Jonathan & Katie Smucker	4/16/1934	20	Pneumonia
Katie	Christ & Sarah King	11/24/1934	24	Accident
Earl	Elam & Rachel Stoltzfus	9/8/1936	18	Accident
Noah	Isaac & Lydia Zook	11/13/1936	18	Accident
Mary	Christ & Mollie King	3/1/1937	26	Sick
Sadie	Eli & Rachel Beiler	7/22/1937	17	
Dora	Christ & Sarah King	11/17/1938	21	
Lydia	David & Rachel Glick	4/22/1939	17	Sick
Elizabeth	Amos & Rachel Zook	6/29/1940	23	
Amos	Sam & Sue Lapp	12/24/1941	16	
Leroy	Amos & Katie Zook	3/13/1942	23	Accident
Elias	Aaron & Mary Fisher	5/10/1942	23	Leukemia
Ivan	John & Emma Stoltzfus	3/9/1943	25	Diabetes
Joel	David & Fannie Zook	12/8/1943	16	
Samuel	Samuel & Saloma Stoltzfus	4/7/1944	22	Invalid
Levi	Levi & Lizzie Fisher	9/11/1944	17	Grass Mower
Urie	Stephen & Lydia Stoltzfus	3/24/1945	21	
Simeon	Daniel & Emma Esh	7/25/1945	19	Kicked by Mule
Rachel	John & Anna Stoltzfus	8/18/1946	18	Hit by Car
Christ	Abram & Lizzie Stoltzfus	3/15/1947	18	

Benuel	Aaron & Fannie Stoltzfus	6/4/1947	21	Fell
Anna	Elam & Mattie Zook	5/16/1948	16	Measles
Noah	Noah & Rebecca Stoltzfus	11/25/1949	17	Diabetes
Amos	Christ & Mary Beiler	5/24/1950	21	Fell
Gideon	Jacob & Annie Zook	6/3/1950	17	Accident
Samuel	David & Lizzie Blank	7/12/1953	18	Drowned
Daniel	Sam & Annie Stoltzfus	11/21/1953	22	Invalid
Rebecca	Samuel & Elizabeth Fisher	5/27/1956	19	Diabetes
Aaron	John & Leah Lapp	10/20/1957	17	Sudden Death
Samuel	Samuel & Rachel King	2/3/1958	19	Accident
David	Samuel & Mary Fisher	12/1/1958	25	Polio
Leah	Daniel & Lydia Lapp	6/5/1959	20	Accident
Daniel	Daniel & Sarah Zook	10/25/1959	21	Car Accident
Samuel	Christ & Lydia King	10/25/1959	19	Car Accident
Lydia	Stephen & Malinda Stoltzfus	4/22/1960	19	Sore Throat
Ephraim	David & Sarah King	4/17/1961	19	Accident
Daniel	Ben & Fannie Petersheim	7/2/1961	16	Drowned
Amos	Amos & Rachel Fisher	10/4/1961	19	Heart Attack
Henry	Christ & Susie Stoltzfus	3/1/1963	25	Car Accident
Amos	Samuel & Mary Esh	12/18/1964	17	Fell from Silo
Levi	Samuel & Mattie King	6/22/1965	26	Invalid
Stephen	Christ & Salina Stoltzfus	7/20/1965	20	Drowned
Katie	David & Lydia Stoltzfus	6/1/1966	16	Brain Tumor
Melvin	Aaron & Ruth Fisher	6/16/1966	26	Accident
George	Jacob & Annie Stoltzfus	10/14/1966	18	Accident
Samuel	Samuel & Susie Lapp	10/24/1966	19	Sawmill
David	Abner & Annie King	11/12/1966	18	Accident
Sally	Aaron & Mary Glick	1/24/1967	18	Leukemia
Leon	Leon & Hannah Beiler	8/7/1967	24	Accident
Levi	David & Rebecca Glick	4/16/1968	21	Leukemia
Mary	Amos & Susie Fisher	7/26/1968	17	Bright's Disease
Aaron	Ephraim & Rebecca Riehl	7/28/1968	23	Drowned
Chester	Henry & Mary Stoltzfus	1/2/1969	17	Sawmill
Amos	John & Lydia King	8/20/1969	29	Drowned
Fannie	Emanuel & Sarah Stoltzfus	10/29/1969	19	Accident
David	Jacob & Saloma Stoltzfus	12/16/1969	24	Accident

John Henry	David & Susie Stoltzfus	5/11/1970	14	Farm Accident
Joseph	Benj & Rebecca Stoltzfus	7/27/1970	18	Tractor Accident
Annie	David & Emma King	1/27/1971	18	Diabetes
Amos	Levi & Mary Fisher	6/11/1971	15	Runaway Team
Mervin	Phares & Katie Fisher	6/12/1971	13	Bicycle Accident
John	Jacob & Mary Hershberger	7/14/1971	24	Accident
John	John & Barbara Fisher	8/2/1971	24	Diabetes
Jacob	David & Bena Glick	10/15/1971	29	Kicked by Mule
David	John & Annie Lapp	5/16/1972	18	Accident
Elmer	Christ & Mary Riehl	5/16/1972	17	Accident
Samuel	Benj & Lizzie Kauffman	6/22/1972	23	Drowned
Benuel	John & Barbara Lapp	7/11/1972	17	Leukemia
John	Joseph & Annie Lapp	1/7/1973	20	
Leroy	Alvin & Priscilla Ebersol	7/18/1973	13	Drowned
Samuel	Henry & Malinda Esh	3/13/1974	14	Farm Accident
Leroy	Dan & Katie Stoltzfus	5/26/1974	14	Aneurysm
Priscilla	Samuel & Mary Stoltzfus	7/31/1975	19	Sick
Jacob	Levi & Rachel Beiler	11/5/1975	19	Riding a Horse
Amos	Jonathan & Lizzie Kauffman	2/16/1976	16	
Rachel	Ephraim & Sarah Lapp	3/9/1976	15	Sick
Malinda	John & Miriam King	1/12/1977	22	Sick
Levi	Levi & Rachel Beiler	2/7/1977	17	Kicked by Horse
Emma	Jacob & Rebecca Miller	7/24/1977	17	Express Wagon
Aaron	Jonathan & Mary Smucker	7/29/1977	20	
Mervin	Christ & Susie King	8/9/1977	18	Car Accident
John	Amos & Anna Beiler	1/8/1978	20	Car Accident
Emanuel	Eli & Lydia Ebersol	10/7/1978	13	Fell
John	Aaron & Mary Miller	11/13/1978	32	In Wheelchair
Daniel	Joel & Susie King	10/11/1979	20	Hit by Car
Steve	Jonas & Naomi Esh	12/17/1979	18	Fell
Emma	Ben & Susie Fisher	3/16/1980	17	Accident
Susan	Isaac & Barbara Dienner	5/4/1980	16	Car Accident
Levi	Mose & Lydia Stoltzfus	6/18/1980	23	Kicked by Horse
David	Levi & Naomi Esh	8/10/1980	16	Buggy Accident
Mervin	Henry & Nancy King	8/10/1980	16	Buggy Accident
Lizzie	Ben & Emma Lantz	8/8/1981	21	Leukemia

Amos	Amos & Sarah King	11/14/1981	22	Car Accident
Amos	Christ & Lydia Beiler	12/14/1981	20	Car Accident
Mervin	Samuel & Mary Riehl	5/16/1982	18	Car Accident
Fannie	Israel & Suvilla Stoltzfus	6/18/1982	17	Runaway Team
Samuel	Benj & Sadie Stoltzfus	3/11/1983	23	Cirrhosis of Liver
Mattie	Jesse & Barbara Lapp	6/19/1983	17	Drowned
Ephraim	Abner & Mary Allgyer	8/3/1983	21	Buggy Accident
Samuel	Chester & Mary Stoltzfus	9/14/1983	15	Silage Cutter
John David	Aaron & Susie Ebersol	9/28/1983	18	Fell from Silo
Mervin	Samuel & Malinda Stoltzfus	9/28/1983	20	Fell from Silo
Jacob	John & Mary Esh	1/9/1985	20	Power Takeoff
Samuel	Amos & Annie Stoltzfus	3/5/1985	15	Farm Accident
Reuben	Dan & Priscilla Bawell	7/4/1985	25	Drowned in Alaska
Samuel	Amos & Annie Stoltzfus	9/19/1985	17	Hit by Truck
John	Amos & Malinda King	8/9/1987	15	Drowned
Samuel	Levi & Mary King	10/18/1987	18	Hit by Car
Joseph	Daniel & Ruth Zook	11/16/1987	25	Fell at Work
Mary	John & Arie King	1/24/1988	19	Buggy Accident
Jesse	Aaron & Susie Ebersol	4/15/1990	19	Car Accident
Mervin	Elmer & Verna King	1/10/1993	17	Car Accident
Elizabeth	Stephen & Sarah Fisher	2/3/1993	18	Brain Tumor
Isaac	Isaac & Mattie Zook	6/16/1993	32	Silo Accident
Jacob	Daniel & Rachel Stoltzfus	6/29/1993	36	Fell at Work
Samuel	Ammon & Mattie King	8/27/1993	17	Drowned
Steven	David & Lena King	6/21/1994	17	Drowned
Michael	John & Emma Fisher	2/18/1995	18	
Abram	Levi & Rachel Lapp	7/25/1995	17	Fell 60 ft.
Emanuel	Levi & Rachel Kinsinger	8/1/1995	21	Farm Accident
Emanuel	Samuel & Emma King	8/19/1995	14	Drowned
Mary	John & Leah Fisher	10/25/1995	17	Heart Failure
Leah	Paul & Katie Stoltzfus	1/5/1996	13	Heart Failure
Daniel	Dan & Dorothy Stoltzfus	1/18/1996	20	Smowmobile Acc.
Reuben	Joseph & Fannie Zook	6/4/1996	19	Invalid
Susie	Emanuel & Nancy Stoltzfus	10/3/1996	14	Farm Accident
Isaac	Isaac & Rebecca Fisher	10/10/1996	14	Hit by Car
Elam	Daniel & Malinda Stoltzfus	3/13/1997	21	Invalid

Jacob	Benj & Saloma Stoltzfus	7/14/1997	15	Kicked by Horse
Amos	Joseph & Annie Miller	7/26/1997	19	Hit by Car
John	Eli & Malinda Stoltzfus	8/21/1997	29	Was in Wheelchair
Mattie	Samuel & Effie Kinsinger	11/22/1997	18	
Martha	Samuel & Nancy Kinsinger	12/28/1997	16	Invalid
Arie	Benuel & Hannah Fisher	7/22/1998	14	
John	Samuel & Priscilla Fisher	11/22/1998	20	Fell from Silo
Simeon	Abram & Mary Ebersol	5/1/1999	16	Drowned
Amos	Eli & Sylvia King	5/31/1999	21	Car Accident
Lydia	Jake & Esther King	5/31/1999	20	Car Accident
Susie	Jake & Esther King	5/31/1999	16	Car Accident
Martha	Samuel & Rachel Stoltzfus	5/31/1999	17	Car Accident
Stephen	Benuel & Naomi Smoker	9/8/1999	22	Leukemia
Amos	Benj & Susie Glick	4/7/2000	25	Invalid
Annie	Ezra & Mattie Beiler	5/6/2000	19	Cancer
David	John & Barbara Kauffman	5/13/2000	18	Cancer
Daniel	Mose & Elizabeth Lapp	12/31/2001	20	Car Accident
Michael	David & Ruth King	8/2/2003	21	Drowned
Amos	Ben & Katie Stoltzfus	10/10/2003	18	Silo Gas
Henry	Enos & Rebecca Miller	12/14/2003	20	Car Accident
Omar	Jonas & Sarah King	12/14/2003	19	Car Accident
Mervin	Elam & Verna Esh	12/14/2003	19	Car Accident
Abner	Christ & Ruth King	12/14/2003	17	Car Accident
Christ	John & Salina Stoltzfus	12/14/2003	18	Car Accident
Rebecca	Amos & Rachel Stoltzfus	4/8/2004	22	Cancer
Christ	Daniel & Sarah King	5/26/2004	13	Trampled by Horse
Samuel	John & Lydia Allgyer	12/2/2004	15	Shooting Accident
Emanuel	Samuel & Nancy Zook	1/19/2005	16	Turnpike Accident
Jacob	Elam & Annie Smoker	1/20/2005	20	Hit and Run
Mervin	Aaron & Mary Ann Beiler	2/28/2005	23	Snowmobile Acc.
Aaron	Aaron & Rachel Esh	3/20/2005	16	4-Wheeler Acc.
Benuel	Daniel & Sadie Esh	4/28/2005	16	Invalid
Stephen	Enos & Rachel King	7/7/2005	17	Roller Blade Acc.
Anna	Samuel & Katie King	7/20/2005	10	Aneurysm
Jonathan	Bennie & Barbara Stoltzfus	7/27/2005	13	Farm Accident
Samuel Jr.	Samuel & Nancy Kinsinger	7/31/2005	18	Heart Failure
Jonathan	Jonathan & Sue King	8/14/2005	23	Drowned

Sarah Ann	John & Sadie Stoltzfus	9/23/2005	20	Fell off Horse
Annie Rose	David & Sadie Mae Esh	9/30/2005	19	Cancer
Christ	Elam & Emma Beiler	12/15/2005	17	Sawmill Accident
Elmer	Sam & Susie Stoltzfus	8/12/2006	22	Accident
Emanuel	Amos & Sadie King	9/24/2006	12	Scooter Acc.
Nickel Mines School Shooting				
Anna Mae	Christ & Lizzie Stoltzfus	10/2/2006	12	Shooting
Marian	John & Linda Fisher	10/2/2006	13	Shooting
Mary Liz	Christ & Rachel Miller	10/2/2006	8	Shooting
Lena	Christ & Rachel Miller	10/2/2006	7	Shooting
Naomi Rose	Amos & Katie Ebersol	10/2/2006	7	Shooting
Leah	John & Fannie King	2/ /2007		Car Accident
Katie Mae	John & Barbie Fisher	6/16/2007	12	Leukemia
Amos	John & Lydia Stoltzfus	7/2/2007	24	Pit Gas
Sarah	Levi & Annie Fisher	8/14/2007	19	
Indiana Sudden Deaths				
NAME	**PARENTS**	**DATE DIED**	**AGE**	**REASON**
Andy	Willie Miller	4/3/1956	19	Walking, Hit by Car
Josie	Rudy Hershberger	5/19/1956	17	Car Accident
Viola	Sam Bontrager	12/7/1961	15	Car & Buggy
Harry	Samuel Bontrager	11/21/1962	24	Eve. before Wedding
Irene	Levi Mast	1/28/1964	18	Cancer
Paul	Levi Jones	5/7/1965	19,	Bulldozer & Tree Acc.
Leon	Harold Riegsecker	7/4/1966	19	Car Accident
Melvin	Ura Gingerich	7/4/1966	18	Car Accident
Magdalena	Jacob Yoder	10/26/1966	16	Cancer
Daniel	Vernas Herschberger	8/18/1967	18	
Richard	Calvin Lambright	8/31/1968	18	Cancer
Mervin	Dan Lehman	3/22/1969	17, Stone Thrown into Buggy	
Daniel	Amos Miller	6/15/1969	25	Car Accident
Glen	Levi Raber	9/14/1969	18	Car & Buggy
Ivan	Emanuel Chupp	1/1/1970	19	Car Accident
Freeman	Ervin Miller	3/10/1972	20	Airplane Crash
Katie	Crist Troyer	7/9/1972	25	Shot
Wilbur	Harley Miller	10/22/1972	18	Car Accident
Wilma	Nathaniel Miller	1/6/1973	19	Car & Buggy

Katherine	Nathaniel Miller	1/8/1973	18	Car & Buggy
Andrew	Willie Fry	5/11/1975	19	Car & Train
William	Willie Fry	5/11/1975	18	Car & Train
William	Amzie Miller	9/9/1976	18	Car & Buggy
Christ	Harold Miller	5/19/1977	18	Car & Bicycle
David Alan	Ervin Hostetler	5/19/1977	20	Car Accident
Eli	Henry Yoder	5/28/1978	19	Tractor Accident
Ervin	Lester Hochstetler	6/23/1980	18	Car Accident
John	Monroe Bontrager	3/18/1981	16	Hit by Tree Branch
Perry	Daniel Lambright	6/6/1981	17	Van & Buggy
Willard	Dan Fry	3/24/1983	26	Fell from Silo
Jay Dee	Will Yoder	7/7/1984	19	Car & Moped
Brian	Robert Schmucker	7/14/1985	17	Car Accident
Gary	Richard Slabaugh	7/14/1985	17	Car Accident
Harley	Alvin Lambright	4/20/1987	24	Diabetic
Thomas	Owen Yoder	6/28/1987	17	Drowned
Alan	Perry Hochstetler	3/3/1990	29	Blood Clot
Eli	Perry Raber	6/19/1991	17	Invalid
Vernon	Orva Bontrager	7/26/1991	17	Car & Moped
Samuel	Harley Lehman	5/15/1992	19	Car Accident
Kenneth	Elmer Miller	6/27/1993	20	Drowned
Katie Marie	Andy Miller	1/15/1994	28	Car Accident
David	Monroe Borkholder	7/29/1995	21	Drowned
Danny	Mervin Miller	11/25/1995	15	Shooting Accident
Lynn	Glen Miller	8/4/1996	19	Car Accident
Alan	Glen Miller	8/4/1996	17	Car Accident
Martha	Vernon Weaver	8/15/1996	20	Car Accident
Benjamin	Mose Miller	12/18/1996	18	Car Accident
Junior	Levi Schwartz	3/29/1997	17	Electrocuted
Benjamin	Leo Miller	4/25/1997	16	Moped & Buggy
Linda	Daniel Miller	6/13/1997	16	Walking, hit by car
Marvin	Ira Fry	11/17/1997	17	Car & Buggy
Norman	Sam Miller	2/24/1999	21	Cancer
Daryle	Ernest Lambright	6/25/1999	26	Gunshot
Larry	Wyman Yoder	2/6/2001	18	Car Accident
Cynthia	John Burkholder	6/8/2001	19	Diabetic

Wilma	Atlee Miller	6/20/2001	17	Van & Bicycle
Floyd	Lee Miller	10/25/2001	41	Heart Attack
Steve	Noah Miller	10/26/2001	32	Burned
Paul	Willie Miller	11/18/2001	17	Car Accident
Ralph	Lamar Schmucker	6/26/2002	16	Car Accident
Brian	Gary Schmucker	12/13/2002	16	Tumor
Jane	Lloyd Miller	2/2/2003	17	Car Accident
Joe Dean	Howard Chupp	5/2/2004	23	Brain Aneurysm
Willis	David Lehman	5/5/2004	16	Car & Moped
Kenneth	Howard Schmucker	6/1/2004	20	Car Accident
Irvin	William Troyer	6/6/2004	17	Drowned
Joas	Vernon Miller	3/5/2005	21	Snowboarding
Kristina	Larry Hostetler	10/7/2005	17	Van & Bicycle
Leon	Jerry Wingard	6/25/2006	15	Van & Pony Cart
John Henry	Orla Yoder	8/14/2006	19	Car Accident
Samuel Ray	Sam & Barbara Miller	12/29/2006	17	Enlarged Heart
Anthony	Samuel Yoder	5/26/2007	17	Toll Road Accident
Kenneth	Ronnie Molley	5/7/2007	21	Car & Bicycle
Perry	John Burkholder	5/14/2007	26	Diabetic

Dry Hill Cemetery

	Fisher BI	Name	Relations
1	3711	Lydia Jane J. Lapp	Amos & Lavina (King)
2	5978	Seth Fisher	David B. & Tarie (Lapp)
3	7835	Jonas Ebersol	Eli & Sadie (Stoltzfus)
4	6931	John S. Beiler	Christian R. & Levina (Stoltzfus)
5	2877	Aaron S. Esh	Samuel Jr. & Naomi (Stoltzfus)
6	10789	Anna Mary (Esh) Fisher	Jacob Z. & Susan (Beiler)
7	4301	Ivan Smucker	Amos F. & Fannie (Stoltzfus)
8	6937	Sarah B. (Zook) Beiler	David K. & Hannah (Blank)
9	4223	Daniel L. Riehl	Omer & Barbara Lapp
10	8702	Daniel E. King	Abraham & Malinda (Esh)
11	6937	Gideon B. Beiler	Elias R. & Fannie (Fisher)
12	4027	Jacob Z. Riehl	Joseph B. & Lydia (Zook)
13	9140	Rachel Ann Stoltzfus	Samuel K. & Rachel (King)
14	1627	Joshua Fisher	Elmer & Rachel (Riehl)
15	1898	Enos Petersheim Jr.	Enos S. & Sadie (Riehl)
16	1514	Aaron B. Lantz	Isaac S. & Rachel Beiler
17	6084	Stephen Stoltzfus	Stephen & Rachel (Esh)
18	9142	Rebecca S. Stoltzfus	Amos K. & Rachel (Stoltzfus)
19	1190	John Arlan Esh	Jason & Martha (Stoltzfus)
20	6633	Mervin Jay Beiler	Aaron F. & Mary Ann (Esh)
21	972	Aaron P. Esh	Aaron P. & Rachel (Zook)
22	4301	Emma Smucker	Amos F. & Fannie (Stoltzfus)
23	6609	Elam E. Fisher	Amos M. & Rebecca (Esh)
24		John Eldron Blank	Jesse L. & Miriam (Fisher)
25	10786	Michael Fisher	Levi & Mary (Stoltzfus)
26	2629	Abram S. King	Jacob & Rebecca (Stoltzfus)
27	417	Jacob S. Beiler	Elam & Susie (Stoltzfus)
28		Joshua W. Ebersol	Elmer M. & Barbie (Fisher)
29	6926	Jacob H. Peachey	Ezra F. & Ella (Swarey)
30	2804	Fannie King	Daniel B. & Susie (Fisher)
31	9140	Samuel K. Stoltzfus Jr.	Samuel K. & Rachel (King)
32	5692	Alvin K. Lapp	Gideon & Elizabeth (King)
33	4373	Jacob E. Glick	Amos U. & Anna (Esch)

This was the family burial plot on the farm of Joseph Rutter Sr. (1682 - 1775) and his wife Barbara Glenn. He was the son of pioneer Conrad Rutter (1651-1737) whose stone and bronze memorial is located on Colonial Road just to the south. This 187-acre part of Conrad's 588 acres passed on to Joseph Jr. in 1775, and then to several of his offspring in 1812. Only the remains of a stone

	Spouse	Born	Died	Age	Row	Plot	No.
1	Stillborn	8/16/1996	8/16/1996	0	1	H	2
2	Annie (Riehl)	12/30/1923	12/13/1998	74	1	B	1
3	Sarah (Riehl)	6/3/1932	5/31/1998	65	4	B	1
4	Leah (Flatie)	7/2/1926	7/18/1998	71	4	C	1
5	Lena (King)	4/25/1939	5/14/1999	60	4	F	1
6	David S.	11/15/1948	5/10/2000	51	4	D	2
7		4/2/2001	4/16/2001	14D	0	G	2
8	Gideon	3/6/1926	6/25/2001	75	4	E	1
9	Stillborn	7/26/2001	7/26/2001	0	3	H	1
10	Mary (Lapp)	10/31/1918	1/4/2002	83	4	G	1
11	Sarah B.	11/8/1921	3/9/2002	80	5	E	2
12	Lizzie	10/21/1927	6/10/2002	74	5	H	1
13		4/14/1990	6/20/2002	12	5	G	1
14	Stillborn	8/13/2002	8/13/2002	0	1	E	2
15	Sadie (Stoltzfus)	6/17/1941	12/6/2002	61	8	H	1
16	Lizzie	2/4/1942	6/17/2003	61	1	C	1
17		4/ /2003	8/24/2003	5M	1	F	2
18		5/13/1981	4/8/2004	22	5	F	1
19		5/4/2003	4/18/2004	11M	7	F	2
20		9/30/1981	2/28/2005	23	9	H	1
21		9/2/1988	3/20/2005	16	9	G	1
22		3/8/2005	3/22/2005	2W	1	G	2
23	Barbara	10/16/1943	4/1/2005	61	1	D	1
24		6/1/2005	6/1/2005	0	1	E	1
25	Ruth (Beiler)	12/22/1940	7/17/2005	64	3	D	1
26		3/3/1928	12/16/2005	77	2	B	1
27	Salome (Stoltzfus)	2/23/1945	5/3/2006	61	0	H	2
28	Stillborn	7/14/2006	7/14/2006	0	3	C	2
29	Emma	7/27/1920	8/17/2006	86	3	B	1
30	Stillborn	10/14/2006	10/14/2006	0	9	D	1
31		8/8/1979	12/15/2006	27	5	G	2
32	Sallie (Beiler)	1/24/1950	12/19/2006	56	7	H	1
33	Emma (Stoltzfus)	2/16/1924	8/21/2007	83	9	F	1

wall, funded in the will of Natie R. Rutter (1879-1936), defined the graveyard through the last half of the 20th century. Then in 1997, Rutter descendants surveyed the plot, unearthed sunken fieldstone markers and restored the burial ground, with the kind help of Amish friends who created the surrounding cemetery.

Death Record from Ohio				
NAME	**PARENTS**	**DATE DIED**	**AGE**	**REASON**
Susanna	Nicholas Weaver	3/25/1860	14	
Barbara	Nicholas Weaver	1/12/1861	19	
Nicholas	Sam Weaver	12/22/1872	6	
Abraham	Yost Weaver	3/5/1876	8	
Andy	Christ C. Yoder	2/7/1939	20	
Mike	Eli Gingerich	10/12/1904	14	
Albert	Menno N. Troyer	2/26/1935	12	
Ura D. Yoder		5/20/1932	18	
Dan	Mose Beachy	5/9/1905	19	
Sarah	John Kurtz	9/21/1906	16	
David	Jacob Coblentz	11/1/1901	20	was accidently shot while coon hunting
Lydia	John P. Nisley	4/3/1908	22	measles
Mose	Christ Wengerd	7/22/1903	21	
Elmer	Stephen Wengerd	3/1/1906	23	
Sarah	Jonas Keim	1/17/1906	15	
Emma	Dan J. Raber	2/16/1920		flu-5 family members died in 5 days
Dan	Steven Y. Miller	5/2/1906	21	
Andy	Jacob A. Miller	11/3/1905	16	
Andrew	Benjamin Beachy	2/22/1882	19	Broiler explosion
Elias	Benjamin Beachy	2/22/1882	16	Broiler explosion
Leonard	J. Hershberger	2/22/1882	17 or 18	Broiler explosion
	Son of Mose C. Yoder	2/24/1921	10	
Isaac	Jacob Hershberger	6/19/1926	21	drowned
Emma	Sam J. Miller	4/14/1913	17	accidently shot
John J. Farmwald	these two were published to be married and died before their wedding	12/3/1918	22	flu
Verna L. Yoder		12/5/1918	20	flu
Reuben	Benj A. Miller	9/15/1932	20	accidently shot
John	Emanuel J. Yoder	7/15/1956	15	riding horse - car accident

John Ed	Noah Beachy	11/25/1952	16	suffocated in corn crib
Mattie	Christ C. Miller	3/9/1954	11	
Peter Jr. Miller		8/28/1948	18	electrocuted
Menno Jr. Coblentz		7/25/1949	18	killed by truck
John J. Yoder		7/?/1950	18	playing ball
Katie	Mose Miller	9/30/1950	25	auto accident
Harold	Mart Wengerd	11/16/1950	24	truck accident
Jr. Crilow		5/21/1946	18	accidently shot
Norman	Eli Mullet	3/12/1946	17	carbon monoxide fumes from the motor of a stalled car in a mud hole
Levi	Jacob J. Beachy	3/10/1946	16	
Aden	Eli J. C. Miller	3/12/1946		
Joe	Menno Gingerich	6/2/1948	21	strip mine
Melvin	C. O. Schlabach	11/18/1944	17	accidently shot
Henry	Eli Mullet	9/7/1940	18	killed from blasting stone
Vernon	Abe Raber	11/22/1957	18	
Albert	Amos Miller	5/11/1959	17	tractor accident
Elsie	John Mullet	3/25/1959	13	
Harvey	Atlee Byler	9/22/1959		fire
Clyde	Pepper Andy Miller	12/17/1959	29	
Albert	Ammon Troyer	11/2/1960	18	car accident
Sarah R. Weaver		4/23/1962	21	tuberculosis
Fannie	Andrew Miller	11/20/1962	20	
Christ D. Hershberger		5/26/1963	19	motorcycle accident
Levi	Henry Miller	6/29/1963	15	Drowned
Ada	Valentine Hershberger	12/27/1963	12	invalid
Henry	Eli S. Miller	5/19/1964	6	wagon accident
Peter	? N. Miller	5/17/1964	16	Sudden death in IN.
Sovilla	William Burkholder	5/29/1964	15	car accident
Aden	Dan Miller	11/5/1965	8	leukemia
Ivan	Jacob Schlabach	9/5/1966	14	
Paul	Dan Troyer	1/5/1967	21	truck accident
Levi	Jacob Miller	1/8/1967	30	37 lbs.
Robert	Orris Troyer	5/14/1967	21	car accident
Roman	Pepper Amos Miller	11/12/1967	19	fell from silo

Mahlon Jr. Schrock		6/23/1968	7	hit by car in IN.
Noah	Andy Miller	8/22/1968	24	
Roman	Henry Yoder	8/15/1968	24	car crashed in house
Henry	Demas Mast	1/30/1969	20	auto accident
Aden	Joe Beachy	6/1/1969	21	accident
Laura	Eli Miller	7/14/1969	20	
Henry	John Miller	12/8/1969	22	fell off horse
Fannie	Joe Hershberger	12/19/1969	15	hit by car
Dennis	Dan Miller	4/23/1970	10	cancer
Levi J.Weaver		5/18/1970	18	drowned
Daniel	Ezra Wengerd	6/26/1970	16	killed by lightening
Edward	Mel A. Miller	7/24/1970	16	
Merle	Emanuel H. Beachy	8/2/1970	18	drowned
Joe	Hershberger	9/16/1970	15	shot accidently
Andy	Ben Yoder	3/27/1971	17	
John	Dan B. Kaufman	6/20/1971	19	car accident
Ada	Emanuel N. Yoder	10/4/1971	9	
Leroy	David Miller	11/25/1971	22	suicide
Ruth	M. Miller	2/22/1972	7	ran over by bus
Mary	Ura E. Miller	3/31/1973	16	
Bruce	Raber	10/10/1973	16	
Sam	E. Yoder	11/7/1973	19	hit by semi on their way home from taking blood tests to get married
Fannie	D. Miller	11/7/1973	20	
Noah	Mahlon A. Troyer	3/28/1974	17	high lift hit him
Laura	Mose Erb	9/4/1974	16	cancer
Regina	Beachy	1/25/1975	13	
Adrian	Levi Beachy	3/15/1975	12	
Allen	Nelson A. Kauffman	5/22/1975	21	fell from silo
John Mark	Perry Miller	5/23/1975	14	
Paul	D. Mast	6/18/1975	23	
David	Jerry Kiline	12/23/1975	21	tractor accident
Allen	Henry Beachy	5/9/1976	10	leukemia

Monroe	John Hershberger	10/1/1976	14	silo filler accident
John	Mose L. Troyer	3/5/1977	19	car/truck accident
Mark	Troyer	5/15/1977	20	auto accident
Mark	John Yoder	8/17/1977	20	drowned
Adrian	Levi A.C. Troyer	4/29/1978	21	buggy accident
Roy	Eli Yoder	7/15/1978	20	died in Mexico
Abe	Alvin Keim	12/22/1979	20	
Edward	Schlabach	3/8/1980	23	auto accident
Neal	E. Miller	7/5/1980	12	
Larry Ray	Jacob Kurtz	2/14/1981	13	bike/car accident
David	Albert Hershberger	12/9/1981	17	Pedestrian/car accident
Iva	Levi Yoder	4/30/1982	10	
Edwin	Miller	5/31/1982	15	drowned
Betty	Paul Kline	6/6/1983	13	cystic fibrosis
Rebecca	Perry Miller	6/14/1983	18	cystic fibrosis
Dan	Enos Shetler	7/28/1983	18	electrocuted
Wayne	Aden J. Hershberger	8/11/1984	15	riding horse accident
Henry	Jacob E. Miller	3/12/1984	26	kidney patient
Micheal	John A. Miller	11/21/1984	21	car accident
Jason	Mahlon Schucker	9/24/1985	18	bike/car accident
David	Joe Schlabach	1/19/1986	17	buggy semi accident
Johnny	Sam Hostetler	8/26/1986	14	drowned
Albert	Ervin Keim	6/21/1987	16	drowned
David	Henry Troyer	8/17/1987	18	traffic accident
Robert	Jonas D. Yoder	12/11/1987	21	cancer
Olen	Nelson Miller	1/16/1988	20	car accident
Norman	Albert A. Miller	2/11/1988	18	auto accident
Marie	Emanuel H. Yoder	5/15/88	19	leukemia
Allen	Emanuel L. Troyer	8/20/88	20	auto accident
Nora	Joe D. Yoder	12/15/88	14	sudden heart failure
Brent	Wallace Detweiler	3/13/89	17	cancer
Elsie	John Raber	3/24/89	14	
Iva	Abe D. Yoder	1/2/90	25	got caught in lineshaft
Alma	Melvin A. Miller	3/25/90	25	
Vernon	Wayne R. Miller	8/13/90	13	cancer

Wesley	Abe R. Yoder	2/14/91	19	auto accident
Paul	Roy E. H. Miller	6/16/91	17	drowned
Susan	Joe Beachy	2/8/92	18	auto accident
Aden	Yoder	8/6/91	27	car-buggy accident
Esther	Yoder	8/6/91	25	car-buggy accident
Eli	Aden Yoder	8/6/91	6	car-buggy accident
Clara	Yoder	8/6/91	16	car-buggy accident
Noah	Yoder	8/6/91	14	car-buggy accident
Joseph	Paul A. Beachy	6/8/92	17	car accident
John	David D. Miller	6/9/92	12	drowned
Daniel	Jonas R. Troyer	11/24/92	16	buggy accident
Clara	Marty Kuhns	2/5/93	11	
Wilma	Roy J. Weaver	5/13/93	11	hit by car
Freida	Roy J. Weaver	5/13/93	8	hit by car
Ivan	Roy J. Weaver	5/13/93	2	hit by car
Ruby	Melvin E. Troyer	5/13/93	10	hit by car
Neva	David D. Kurtz	5/13/93	14	hit by car
Daniel	Roman J. Yoder	7/4/93	19	lightning
Merle Ray	Marvin Hershberger	3/14/94	14	
Ida Mae	Mose J. Miller	3/16/94	6	house fire
Marlin	Ben L. Miller	9/11/94	17	auto accident
Malva	Owen M. Hershberger	10/4/94	15	hit by grind-stone
Henry	Hershberger	5/15/94	12	
Barbara	Albert Raber	3/8/95	22	cancer
Reuben	Amos Yoder	6/13/94	10	hit by car
Betty	Joe D. Hostetler	4/28/95	23	heart failure
Noah	Albert N. Yoder	5/4/95	32	auto accident
Joshua	John C. Miller	8/2/95	25	farming accident
Norman	Jonas L. Schlabach	11/6/95	19	auto accident
Allen Ray	Wayne J. Troyer	19/9/95	14	cancer

Noah	Eli Barkman	1/22/96	18	logging accident
Mary	Atlee Y. Miller	4/29/96	16	
Andrew	Leroy Stutzman	7/20/96	13	drowned
Atlee	Jonas J. D. Yoder	2/22/97	17	cancer
Emery	Reuben S. Bowman	4/6/97	15	house fire
Joseph	Eli Weaver	6/11/97	16	baler accident
Joseph	Marlin C. Yoder	1/1/98	12	cancer
Naomi	Dan J. Yoder	7/3/98	17	car accident
Merlin	Levi E. L. Hershberger	7/15/98	12	farming accident
Joe	Dan J. J. Schlabch	11/24/98	26	car accident
Mark	Abe M. Yoder	1/26/99	21	car accident
Myron James	Ivan L. Yoder	5/3/99	13	tractor accident
Nelson	Sam J. Miller	9/7/99	10	auto accident
Andy	Emanuel E. Miller	11/18/99	22	car-buggy accident
Allen	Roy J. Yoder	12/15/99	16	tree hit van
Robert	David R. Yoder	12/30/99	26	suicide
Vernon	Atlee J. Yoder	4/8/00	21	auto accident
Elmina	Marty E. Kuhns	1/11/01	20	
Rosanna	Atlee Y. Miller	5/26/01	23	
Henry	Eli E. Wengerd	9/4/01	21	traffic accident
Titus	Ivan L. Yoder	10/11/01	19	suicide
Daniel	Ezra Petersheim	11/1/01	24	logging accident
Steven	Marvin M. Erb	6/9/02	19	drowned
Lewis	John E. Weaver	8/6/02	18	heart failure
Andrew Jay	Wes A. Yoder	9/25/02	19	car accident
Allen	Mose M. Yoder	1/26/03	11	seizure
Martha	Jonas Hershberger	7/23/05	15	
Megan	Hershberger	8/8/03	20	atv accident
Steven	Reuben Keim	9/1/03	23	was shot
Rebecca	Joe Hostetler	9/11/03	11	
Ryan A.	Gingerich	9/11/03	11	auto accident
Susan	Melvin E. Troyer	9/5/04	19	atv accident
Edward	Sam Heshberger	9/5/04	18	atv accident
Adrian	Eli Miller	9/26/04	26	found in bed
Allen	Schlabach	1/6/05	14	

Elizabeth Ann	Sam J. Yoder	2/12/05	28	cancer
Stevie	Nevin A. Hershberger	5/8/05	14	hunting accident
Levi	Mose Nisley	6/11/05	16	cancer
Micaela	Lester D. Wengerd	7/21/05	11	tractor accident
Brenda Sue	Henry L. Chupp	9/12/05	19	car accident
Jacob	Eli Miller	10/9/05	19	
Kari Beth	Firman Miller	10/30/05	12	pony cart-car accident
Joe D.	Hershberger	3/15/06	19	car accident
David	Levi H. Mast	4/8/06	25	auto accident
Mervin A.	Miller	5/22/06	19	
Dean Allen	Levi G. Weaver	7/4/06	16	cut neck while playing ball
Milan	Mose V. Hershbeger	1/15/07	24	hunting accident
Jenalee	Robert A. Yoder	2/21/07	16	car accident
Robert Jr.	Weaver	6/5/07	25	moter bike accident
Melvin	Eli D. Troyer	7/8/07	16	drowned
Robert	Levi Miller	8/4/07	15	bike-car accident
Amanda	David Wengerd	9/17/07	20	cancer
Andy	Perry Miller	5/30/08	15	cancer
Marcus	Eli E. Shetler	8/5/08	15	bike-car accident
Andrew	Vernon Stutzman	9/18/08	313	bike accident
Brenda	Christ A. Miller	12/17/08	12	

Conclusion

February 7, 2008

There are two things I know and one I believe. The first thing I know is that my son, Mervin, died on February 28, 2005, at the age of twenty-three. Like all bereaved parents, life as I knew it ended and a new life began. I now live in a different world, forever changed by that event. Like a newborn child, my new life grows slowly, one breath at a time. The second thing I know is that Mervin lived. For me, that's important! That life, my child living through my memories is where I now focus my attention. This healing journey is difficult and slow. It has taken a long time for me to reconnect with my son's life, but smile has returned and here is how it happened.

My smile began to return when I was able to let go of Mervin's physical death. When I was able to say and completely believe *"Mervin is never coming back in that form and I will never hold him again."* For a long time I denied his death and thought somehow, someway I could change that fact. I wanted and needed to turn back the hands of time and bring my son back. As my suffering continued, so did my belief that I had control over his death.

Our greatest suffering comes from the loss of the physical presence of our children. We so much want one more hug, one more kiss, *one more anything*. It hurts knowing we can't have them back in the physical form, and we try to fight for it, but if we fight too long, it can hold back our healing. When our children were alive, their physical and spiritual being was together. When they died, those two separated, their bodies going one way and their spirits another. We don't have to think of them as spiritual beings, so we don't know how to search for that part of their lives. When they were alive, all we had to do is find them, talk to them and look at them for us to be satisfied. Once their bodies died, we thought they'd left us forever. The more we struggled over their physical deaths, the further away their spiritual life became.

At some point in my journey, I believed the fact that my son's physical body wasn't coming back ever. I will not hold him in my arms again. That was a painful truth to believe, but a very necessary one for me to believe, so I could move forward in my healing. When I accepted the fact that Mervin's body wasn't coming back, I said to death, "Okay death, you won. You won the battle for Mervin's body; I can no longer fight you for that. "Mervin's body is gone.

But I also said to death, "Death, you may have won the battle for his body, but that's all you won. You will never, ever win the war for his life. My child living through my memories is mine forever. You cannot and will not have that part of him."

It was then that I was able to let go of Mervin's physical death. When that happened, his spiritual life flooded back into mine. Letting go of Mervin lifted a huge burden from me because for a long time I tried to make his life more powerful than his death, and it never happened until I let go. Mervin then became the child that I know when I put my head on my pillow at night. His life returned to mine and my memories became good, comforting memories. I now know that Mervin is so much more than just his body.

Now the pain I once had for him has become more bearable because I now know that I didn't loose all of him when his body died. Mervin still lives through my memories. Memories can cut like a knife. In the beginning those memories are so hard because we think of our child as dead, and those memories are of a dead child, never to return. As we heal and are able to let go of their physical death and feel the return of their lives, those memories can comfort us, knowing that they are a spiritual child who has returned to our lives. The past can be comforting if we use our memories to once again feel the lives of our children. Once again, we can say "I love you " and not "I loved you," they can be an "is" and no longer a "was" if we allow it.

We all have our beliefs. The one thing I believe about Mervin is that he now lives a life that is much more rewarding, satisfying and beautiful then I will ever understand or know here on earth. He lives free of fear, pain or suffering. He lives free of stress, sadness and loneliness; I believe Mervin is one full time, all the time happy, happy guy. Believing that makes me feel good and helps me find happiness in my life. My smile has returned because Mervin lives in that smile and in the goodness I've found in my life. One thing his death has taught me is that if I pay attention I have much to be grateful and thankful for. The important thing is to pay attention and live more in the moment. We don't get any of those moments back and if we miss the opportunities in them we can miss a lot.

I now stop and recognize my happy moments because each one helps me heal a little bit more. They're out there waiting for me. Sure there's lots of bad in the world, but if I concentrate on that, I will miss the good and the opportunity to do more good. I now appreciate the simple act of getting out of bed each morning. What a blessing it is to be able to take more opportunities to be happy and to reach out to others. When I hold my grandkids hands, I'm happy and feel the moment. It's like Mervin is saying to me, "Dad, I'm living a happy life. It's okay for you to be happy too." Thank you, Mervin.

Even though our lives have been forever changed, and we will forever grieve the deaths of our children, it doesn't mean we need to live grief-stricken lives. Through our healing work, we can bring the lives of our children back into our lives. Our smiles can return. We can take the happiness of their lives and make it our happiness too. A big thing happened to us, but it's our choice as to how we let that build our new lives. We can either let their deaths become our deaths too, or we can let their lives continue to enrich and inspire us.

This is a slow journey of patience and kindness to ourselves, one that we can never stop working on because building a new life takes time. We can find our happiness and smiles again because it is those feelings that we find where our kids live.

Dad Aaron Beiler

June 12, 2008

The pain of losing a child is not make believe, it is real pain. Does time heal all wounds? If you're a griever, you have no doubt heard this more than one time. On February 28, 2009 it will be four years since the death of our first born son, Mervin. As a parent I will never forget the shock, the empty feeling the....................that moment will be forever fresh in my mind and just in a flash I can go back to the exact moment we received the news. Mervin was killed.

Grief hurts, pain, real pain cannot be hidden. It hurts. We remember every detail as if it happened yesterday. Lots of times when we are talking about something we say, "Was that before Mervin was killed or after he was killed"? Holidays, birthdays, dreams and special family events all were changed by this death. We now have a new date on the calendar, the date of Mervin's death.

It's easy to become stuck in our grief. We are human. We want others to know we hurt and are determined not to "let go". Such negative energy takes its toll and weakens us mentally and spiritually. Friends and family somewhat drift away because they are confused with us. They might even think we are out of reach and they may hope that "time" might heal those wounds that have left those awful scars. During our intense grief we exist in a world that seems unreal.

I really do not believe that time will heal all wounds. Time just goes by. It becomes one year, two years, three years, etc. Our lives go on day after day whether we want it to or not. Time does give us that choice to start to heal and think things over. If we really look in the mirror we realize that grieving doesn't just go away. We see others' living life around us and we so much want to be like them. We want to get out of this emptiness and become halfway normal again.

What I can tell you to be very true is that intense grief does change if we allow ourselves to live again. Although this grieving process is complicated, there are a few simple signs that say it's time to let go and move forward. We may tell stories of Mervin and even might do so with a chuckle or smile. We connected with God in a new ways that are personal and fulfilling. We search for new meanings. What is the purpose of my life? What is your plan for my life? Is God' still watching over me? We look for signs to believe in ourselves and yes to live again. We appreciate the little miracles every day.

The one most positive sign that life is moving forward in the best direction is when we are willing to share our journey positively or do anything to help others to enrich their lives. We become more compassionate. We can understand the "pain" that people feel in their life in a new way. Even though we are all different, our life's changes become new paths so different than we can ever imagine.

Depending on what we do with our lives is what heals the wounds. We see others who have "overcome". We compare our loss to theirs, we may say, "I can't imagine how they did it"? What is their secret?

What heals the wounds, is finding the courage to step over the pain and reach out for something we can appreciate. It's called "Hope". Grab it and hang on to it. Know that life goes on and so can you.

Who am I now? Changed! Change is a must in our real lives. Things change! When we quit accepting change we are stuck. I feel blessed to have gotten through the intense times and to learn to live with the results. I feel blessed to be able to look back and remember, as awful as it was, and recognize that the flashbacks to that pain are temporary. I can return to the present world of the living. I will never forget Mervin, who was such a wonderful part in our lives.

There is no doubt that I am not the same person I was three years ago. On the outside I got older but on the inside I'm really different. I have tried to put my regrets (I wish I would have, could have) behind and focus only on the happy memories. Loving family and friends have shared my sorrow, listened to my story, and helped me to move forward.

On the inside I understand the word "friend" and I have been blessed with many new ones. I'm still Mervin's Dad, and realize he is gone. I still feel sad dreaming dreams that will never come true but I move on. Time has healed the deepest wounds, but a shadow of the scars will always remain. They are battle scars. It's a mighty battle that can be won with "hope". I consider it a privilege to have fought this battle. It reminds me of the song "When the battles over, we shall wear a Crown...," I chose to heal the pain and replace the suffering with hope. To do this I need prayers of those we love and our Almighty God forever by my side. Behold the eye of the Lord is upon them that fear him, upon them that hope in his mercy. (Psalm 33:18-19) My prayer for you is that you would choose to live life as best as you can (Deuteronomy 30:20) Choose to love the Lord your God and to obey Him and to cling to Him, for He is your life). All of the great people in the Bible were possibility thinkers. On yes, they were real people who knew what it was like to be discouraged, depressed or on the verge of defeat. But, they were great because even in the middle of their troubles, they chose to turn their attention to God's beautiful possibilities for today.

Even Jeremiah, the weeping prophet, in the depths of great depression finally chose to focus on God's great love. When he did, his depression left him (Lamentations 3:1-24). He chose to look at God's possibilities rather then pay attention to the negative forces surrounding him.

Are you troubled today? Do you feel that life is closing in on you and there is no way to escape? Don't let your mind dwell on negative thoughts. Choose life! Believe in Gods' ability to overcome the troubles and give you a great and exciting today and tomorrow. God's message to you is, "I know the plans I have for you...plans for good and not for evil, to give you a future and a "Hope" (Jeremiah 29:11).

God bless you,
Dad Aaron Beiler

July 4, 2008

Dear Friends, Greetings in Jesus's name. I know through the death of our loved ones we have so many questions. At first, scripture just does not make sense. But, I truly believe God's word stands to be the truth and if we really want to listen by and by we will understand it better. (Hebrews 12) has for me been a big question. "For whom the Lord loveth he chasteneth, and scourgeth every son whom he receiveth. If ye endure chastening. God dealeth with you as with sons, for what son is he whom the Father chaseneth not"? (Hebrews 12: 6-7) What does this word chastening really mean? The first time after Mervin's death that we had these scriptures the preacher put it as that means correcting. Oh my, correcting what...Oh yes, I have so much to be corrected but...............? The next time we had these scriptures a year later the preacher said he thinks it would mean get with it, or get it together, straighten out! What? Then a year later this young preacher again had Hebrews scripture and he said he thinks it would mean to get or have something that we would rather not get or have. Something that we would think we could very well do without.

Chastening is always painful, but we know that it is for our own good. It corrects things in us that are wrong and brings out things in us that could never happen without death ETC. The writer of Hebrews reminds us that we are Gods's sons. My hope for you is that you will heed the chastening of the Lord and not faint when he reproves you.

We must understand that as fathers we may not always chasten wisely or lovingly, but our heavenly Father always chastens us right with no mistakes for our own good.

We go on to read (Hebrews 12:11) "Now no chastening for the present seemeth to be joyous, but grievous; nevertheless afterward it yielded the peaceable fruit of righteousness unto them which are exercised thereby". Hummmm! Pretty clear there, not? Even though chastening is painful, we know that it is good for us. Many of the richest blessings that have come down to us from the past are the fruits of sorrow or pain. My wish for you is that your tears roll and as we go on the journey through this pain of losing our loved ones that you will harvest with Joy. We should never forget that redemption, the world's greatest blessing, is the fruit of the world's greatest sorrow. I'm hoping to write here that you can receive a blessing in due time. Mervin's death has been so painful and so...but in trying as hard as we can to deal with such a shock and putting our all into it by God's grace we must say we want to go on. This is just what I have gathered from "Hebrews 12" and I am open for other opinions.

Are we following? All chastening by our Father is for our profit and if we receive it gratefully and take it patiently, it will yield the fruit of righteousness in our lives.

Jesus says in (John 15: 1-2) "I am the true vine and my Father is the husbandman. Every branch in me that beareth no fruit he taketh away: and every branch that beareth fruit, he purgeth it that it may bring forth more fruit". This has much comfort for us during our painful grief work.

We realize here that our Father is the husbandman. We know that our Father loves us and would never do anything unloving or harmful to us. He has a plan way ahead of our plans. He also has the best plan, not just for us now, but for the future. When we really need sharp pruning it is great comfort to read "My Father is the husbandman". Notice that it is the fruitful branch that the Father prunes. We all sometimes think surely God does not love me, or he would not do something like this? Read this "Every branch that beareth fruit he purgeth" (Trims). We must realize that we are not being punished, but pruned and that we are being pruned because we are fruitful. Yes, if you're like me that takes awhile to sink in! Its' not like we were just a big nothing here on earth. Not that we might not have been fruitful, but "that we may bring forth more fruit". The reason for God's pruning says here is to bring forth more fruit. In taking Mervin from our circle was one of the most traumatic ways to get our attention and isn't this what God wants...our full attention, not just some of it, but all of it.

Sometimes when we see someone pruning vines or trees it seems like nothing is left and looks like there isn't a chance for that tree or vine to grow again. But look at the big picture, in the future that tree or vine will bring forth more fruit. That's what God's plan is for you! A man told of a place where big clusters of grapes were hanging from vines on all sides. The owner told him, when my new gardener came, he said he would have nothing to do with these vines unless we could cut them clean down to the stalk. And, so he did. We had no grapes for two years, but look at the result. Grapes much bigger and better than before. Here it seems to us that the pruning was destroying the vine, but the gardener was looking into the future, just like God does with us, and knowing that the vine will be much richer and bear more fruit because they were trimmed. Can we believe that every trouble that comes into our lives brings some gift from God? Some blessing can only be had through pain and loss. There are songs we will never learn to sing while we are enjoying the so called pleasures of this life. Do we realize and believe that there are some blessings we can never have unless we are ready to pay the price of pain? There is no other way to reach them.

How many times did I cry out to God to take this pain away, this suffering, this sorrow? We want relief! This is so hard to bear Lord! We forget that our trial is a message of good from God to us. We cry for a season and have this ongoing battle with our loss but I try to think of the rich gifts that came along. How then should we pray? I do not think there is any harm in asking that this suffering may pass, but we should also say "Thy will be done". Maybe we should pray that if He does not take away the pain, He would strengthen us to handle it, so that we do not fail to see its blessings. If there is a blessing coming would it not be sad if God took it away before we receive it! To be free from it would be to miss the benefit that is in it for us. We grow best with loads on our shoulders!

Do we understand the word comfort? When we want comfort in sorrow we think we should be given it, or at least make its bitterness easier to bear. But the word comfort comes from a root that means "to strengthen". After Jesus prayed for the Father to remove the cup from him there appeared an angel unto Him from Heaven strengthen Him". (Luke 22:43) To receive comfort is not a promise to make our burden lighter, or our grief less. God comforts us by giving us strength to endure our trial.

We realize when we turn to Him after the death of one we love, He does not bring them back to life for us. He does not make the loss seem less but could do so by making us love our loved ones less. We realized that love and grief grow on the same page.

Jesus in the Garden is an example of how comfort can work. Jesus dreaded the trial he was facing just as we dread the trials we face. He prayed to be delivered, but also prayed "Thy will be done". God did not answer his prayer in the way we would expect. Instead of relieving Him of his suffering, God gave him strength to bear it. So he received comfort and went through his trial on the cross without one cry of rebellion, His heart filled with perfect peace. I so much hope you will find the perfect peace, not by removing the weight of your sorrow or pain but by strengthening them to endure it in victory. God's comfort can protect your heart in sorrow and trials and bring you through the darkest hours in a shining changed you. People talk of getting over a great sorrow, passing it by, putting it behind us. Not so! Nobody ever does that. The only way is to pass through it slowly and yes we carry it with us wherever we go. This is not something we will forget, but do realize that when the trumpets shall sound there waits a renewing of bodies and through our suffering, trials hardships and all, everything will be made new if we lived for the Lord. Faith will see you through! We also realize that when these great and mighty waves that we are passing through calm down at the end it will be worth it all. My prayer for you is that you would land safely on the other shore. We can also get comfort in God's promise that "all things work together to them that love God, to them who are called according to his purpose (Romans 8:28)

My compassion to you.

Aaron Beiler

Light in the Shadow of Death